RED DIRT BASEBALL-
THE FIRST DECADES:

SMALL TOWN PROFESSIONAL BASEBALL IN OKLAHOMA 1904-1919

RED DIRT BASEBALL–
The First Decades:

SMALL TOWN PROFESSIONAL BASEBALL
IN OKLAHOMA 1904–1919

By **Peter G. Pierce**

ISBN: 978-1-938923-05-0

Library of Congress Control Number: 2013930364

Oklahoma Heritage Association
1400 Classen Drive
Oklahoma City, Oklahoma 73106
405.235.4458
www.oklahomaheritage.com

OKLAHOMA HERITAGE | Association

CONTENTS

INTRODUCTION

Oklahoma has a remarkably rich baseball history. Baseball has been part of the State's DNA since the first game was played in the Indian Territory in a battle of mining towns with Krebs vanquishing Savanna on July 4, 1882. In the Oklahoma Country —the name given the Unassigned Lands opened for settlement on April 22, 1889 before the Oklahoma Territory was organized— on June 30, 1889 in the Land Office camp of Guthrie under the watchful eyes of patrolling United States cavalry troopers locals and bluecoats defeated a team from Oklahoma City, recently known as the Oklahoma Station.

I have undertaken the ambitious project of chronicling the history of professional baseball in Oklahoma from 1904 until the date the Ardmore Rosebuds of the Texas League gave up the ghost in September, 1961. Oklahoma City and Tulsa have been intentionally excluded except insofar as ball clubs representing those cities were members of leagues that included the towns covered in the several volumes written and to be written. Others, Bob Burke for Oklahoma City, Wayne McCombs for Tulsa, have treated those histories earlier and well. We are indebted to Royse "Crash" Parr for chronicling the story of sandlot and semi-pro baseball in books and articles. *Glory Days of Summer,* the 1999 comprehensive history of Oklahoma baseball devotes limited space to minor league baseball in the small towns of Oklahoma. Its authors Burke, Parr, and Kenny Franks did not have access to digitized research including newspaper archives containing *The Sporting News* and *The Daily Oklahoman* not to mention the minor league database of the Society for American Baseball Research. Their work is even more remarkable for that reason. What would have taken years of toil in scattered libraries today can be done in a matter of months largely from a home office connected to the internet. This book is built on their efforts.

Red Dirt Baseball: The First Decades, is actually the third of a series that is called "Red Dirt Baseball." The name refers to the baseball played in small towns and the low minor leagues, the "bushes," that operated in Oklahoma. Oklahoma's baseball history antedates the first recorded use of the term "bush league" in 1906. The first two books

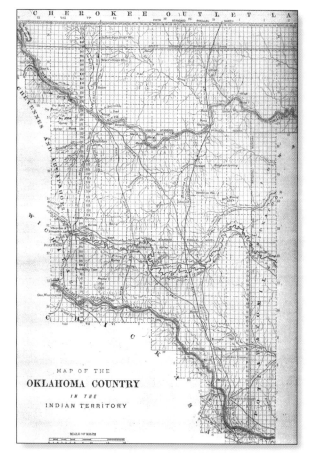

LEFT: Oklahoma Country of the "Unassigned Lands" before The Run of April 22, 1889.

in the Red Dirt series, *Territorians to Boomers* and *Indians, Cardinals and Rosebuds*, tell the story of the professional game in Ardmore beginning with the arrival of the Texas League in 1904 and ending with the departure of the Texas League in 1961. Those are the models for telling the stories of individual cities or groups of cities that own histories too large to include in a work such as this. The plan is to do separate books for Ada (*Eight Seasons of the Herefords: Red Dirt Baseball in Ada*), Muskogee, Okmulgee, Bartlesville, Enid and McAlester. Lawton and Duncan with the Southwest Oklahoma communities in this volume will have their stories told in *Big Pasture Ball: Red Dirt Baseball in Southwest Oklahoma*. Chickasha and Pauls Valley will appear in *Washita Valley Ball: Red Dirt Baseball in the Chickasaw Nation*. Ponca City and Blackwell will share a book as will Shawnee and Seminole (with Maud). Places such as the towns treated here that continued to have teams from between the World Wars as well as Miami, Bristow, Drumright, Cushing, and Clinton will find coverage in *Red Dirt Baseball: Oklahoma's Bush Leagues 1920-1940*.

In baseball, this was the "Deadball Era." The two decades treated here fell squarely within the Progressive Era and ended with America's loss of innocence: joining France and the forces of the British Commonwealth on the Western Front against the Central Powers. Over one million doughboys from farms and small towns as well as the big league cities went to France, Italy, and civil war Russia and Siberia; over 100,000 never returned with over half of those combat deaths. Another 320,000 were gravely wounded. To add to the misery, millions died world wide —including 25,000 American troops—of the Spanish Influenza. The World had come to small town America. The popular lyrics captured the times

> *How 'ya gonna keep 'em, down on the farm,*
> *After they've seen Pa-ree?*
> *How 'ya gonna keep 'em away from Broad-way;*
> *Jazzin' a-'round',*
> *And paintin' the town?*
> *How 'ya gonna keep 'em away from harm?*
> *That's a mistery;*
> *They'll never want to see a rake or plow,*
> *And who the deuce can parleyvous a cow?*
> *How 'ya gonna keep 'em down on the farm,*
> *After they've seen Paree?*

Sheet music of a popular vaudeville number from tin pan alley.

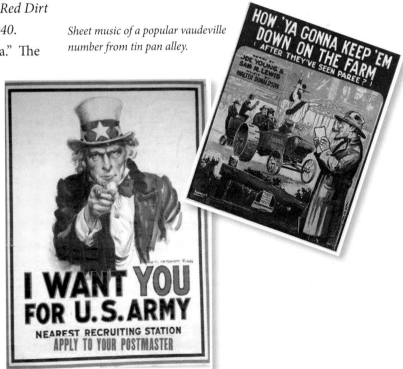

James Montgomery Flagg's 1917 recruiting poster. Military conscription began in July, 1917. The "Work or Fight" order stripped the supply of minor league players. The National Association of Professional Baseball Leagues lost eleven of its twenty-one members between institution of the draft and the beginning of the 1918 season. Only the International League completed a "normal" 1918 season.

The United States had been changed forever.

Baseball in the first half of the last century was divided between sandlot —church, town, and civic pick up clubs— and "high" semi-pro teams —those whose players were paid to play by an employer such as the Halliburton Oil Cementers— on the one hand and "league" baseball on the other. Every place with a sidewalk, crossroads store, and usually two or three churches had one of the former, amateur teams who came together on weekends and after work against all comers. A league team played a fixed schedule under regular rules against from three to seven other members; the players' only job was to play baseball.

The 1908 edition of the *Spalding's Official Base Ball Guide* contained, in addition to statistics and photos of dozens of teams, the following promotion of the game:

BASE BALL TEAMS ADVERTISE A TOWN
The experience of the new century annals of professional Base Ball, as regards the beneficial effects of advertising a town or small city, on account of its having a professional Base Ball club located in its midst, or of a town or city being connected with a Base Ball League or association, has practically taught a lesson to business people of small cities and towns, which the progressive and intelligent class of hotel and storekeepers of a country town have not been slow of late years to avail themselves, for such business men have realized the advantage above referred to.

* * * *

We know of many small country towns which would never have been known or heard of outside their own immediate vicinity, but for its Base Ball club and team. The fact is, if the business people of a town, not previously benefited by having a Base Ball club and a good enclosed ground, were to get their best men together for organization purposes, they would soon realize what an advertising medium a well-managed professional club is to the hotels, boarding houses and stores.

The mercantile firm Westheimer & Daube took a full page advertisement in *The Daily Ardmoreite* urging the community to turn out for the season opener and by "Boost[ing] Baseball Put Ardmore on the Map."

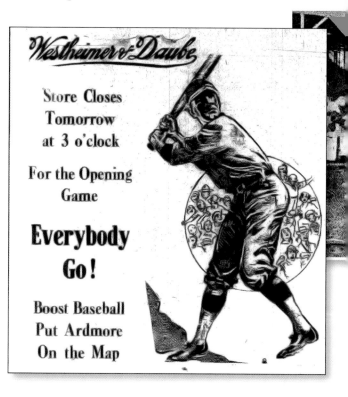

Typical booster advertisement. Westheimer & Daube was a pioneering general mercantile store begun in Ardmore, I. T. in 1888

Without exception, for a season opener the small towns and cities that had snared a coveted "league" membership declared a "half-holiday" when the stores and schools closed early so that young and old could process behind the parade of some local band, dignitaries in automobiles, and the two uniformed teams. Usually all marched first around the square and then to the baseball grounds where they were awaited by a wooden covered grandstand, bleachers, and a high outfield fence covered with advertising by the local who's who.

It is hard today to recall that all baseball was once played only in the sunshine. Games typically were "called" (as in "Play Ball!") around 2:00-3:00 p.m. Standard Time and finished by supper time.

A good depiction of a pre-War minor league baseball crowd. Those not admitted to the grandstand or who could not find a bleachers seat lined one side of the field. Viewers with automobiles lined the other. "Drive-in" space disappeared from ball parks until Albuquerque Sports Stadium (1969-2000) opened an area in right field for car loads of fans.

Not infrequently, games ended early because one or both of the teams had to catch a train. For all practical purposes, there was no vehicular transportation between cities. The first paved road— brick later covered with asphalt— ran from the Territorial capital in Guthrie to Oklahoma City. Old cattle trails, military roads, and convenience tracks

that some town council or entrepreneurial county commissioner cut out were the "highway" system. Oklahoma has seventy-seven counties because the county seat had to be no further away than a horse-drawn wagon could carry a family round-trip in a single day. It was not until 1918 that Oklahoma had a federally-sponsored road project, the Newcastle bridge across South Canadian River. Even by 1925, Oklahoma still had less than 1,000 miles of roads, only 374 of which were paved. The 1918 *Classon's Guide to Oklahoma* shows the Jefferson Highway and King of Trails paralleling today's U.S. 69 with Denison, Durant, McAlester, Muskogee, Vinita, Miami on the way to Joplin; the Meridian Road roughly along the old Chisholm Trail from Wichita to Ft. Worth via Enid, El Reno, Anadarko, Lawton, and Wichita Falls; the Postal Highway from Oklahoma City to Amarillo with El Reno and Chickasha *en route*; the Ozark Highway as the track between Oklahoma City and Tulsa; the Oklahoma, Texas and Gulf Highway, a precursor to U.S. 77, south to Oklahoma City from Arkansas City via Ponca City and Guthrie then further south to Pauls Valley and U.S. 177 from Sulphur through Mill Creek, Tishomingo and Durant to the "Gate City," Denison; and the Albert Pike Highway west from Ft. Smith to Tulsa and then through Drumright, Cushing, Guthrie, and Enid to Alva. All of these were dirt and gravel, and frequently mud, without shoulders or bar ditches. There would be no interstate bus service in the United States until 1924. The first motor coach travel would not come to Oklahoma until the late 1920s when a subsidiary of the Atchison, Topeka & Santa Fe began connecting unserved towns and villages to its rail depots.

Rail was the connection between cities. There were twenty-nine railroads operating in 1918 Oklahoma as well as eight electric traction or interurban systems. An excerpt from the *Classon* map gives an idea of what confronted these ball clubs in getting around. Oklahoma was indeed "The Bushes."

Bush league baseball was decidedly less genteel than the game played in the dozen large cities on or east of the Mississippi River comprising the American and National Leagues. As it would be for the

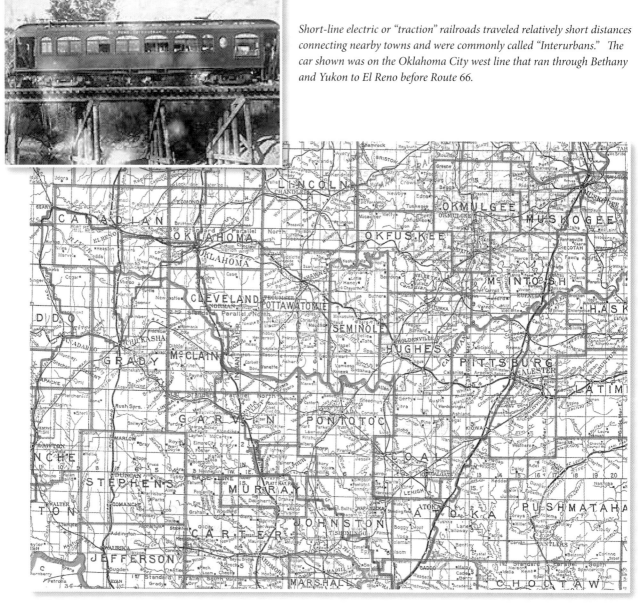

Short-line electric or "traction" railroads traveled relatively short distances connecting nearby towns and were commonly called "Interurbans." The car shown was on the Oklahoma City west line that ran through Bethany and Yukon to El Reno before Route 66.

Classon's 1918 road map of south central Oklahoma showing railroads and vehicle roads. Only 374 miles of those were paved. Virtually every town had a "good roads" committee.

next half century, there were only 400 places on big league rosters. Farm systems were non-existent before 1924. Every minor league franchise had to make or break based on ticket sales, concessions and advertising, sales of player contracts, and more often than not the largesse of members of the business community and fraternal organizations.

Organization came to the minors in 1901 with the formation of the National Association of Professional Baseball Leagues (now Minor League Baseball, Inc.). It established classifications (A, B, C, D and, after 1912, AA) based on league population. The Association established roster and salary limits for those, required teams to post with the league or association "guarantee" or "forfeiture" money, i.e. two-week's salary in case a club failed, enforced the reserve clause in player contracts, granted free agency, and provided a system for the major leagues and higher minor classifications to draft players. It also created a National Board of Arbitration that settled disputes regarding rights to players, territorial rights, rules disputes (with the power to over-rule a league president), and discipline including suspending players, managers, and owners. J. H. Farrell, president of the New York League, served as secretary of the National Association for a number of years and was the real power in minor league baseball through the early 1930s. Any circuit that was not a member of the National Association or a major league signatory to the National Agreement was an "outlaw league." That characterization included not only Oklahoma's 1903 attempt at a professional league but the Federal League of 1914 and 1915.

Until Oklahoma City briefly entered the Class A Western League on June 8, 1918, every professional team in Oklahoma was a member of a Class C

John H. Farrell ran the National Association of Professional Baseball Leagues as secretary-treasurer from his office in Auburn, New York from its founding in 1901 until his passing in 1931. He also served as president of the New York League.

or Class D league. D Leagues had aggregate member populations of under 200,000. C Leagues were between 200,000 and 399,000. Rosters generally were thirteen or fourteen players including a manager who usually played. During the Deadball Era, there was a salary cap of $1,000-$1,200 per month in Class D. Class C was as high as $1,400. Roster numbers and salary caps were set annually by the league owners. One way of skirting the compensation rule was to take players on "optional assignment." A player who had been optioned to a lower classification was still compensated at the rate provided in his contract with the higher club. Another was a "sell-back" agreement by which a higher club would sell a player to a lower team who would pay the player at the lower level then give him a piece of his sales price when sold up. Of course, some teams just cheated. Denison in both the Texas-Oklahoma League and Western Association was notorious for ignoring both the roster limit (although never suiting up more than league rules allowed) and having a payroll of nearly double the league limit. The Denison club also won four consecutive pennants in two leagues.

The economics of a minor league team depended on high attendance, low salaries, and as little travel as possible. The home team had to pay a "guarantee" to the visitors for every game. This was a minimum figure or a percentage of the gate. Often the gate receipts from a weekday contest were not enough even to pay the guaranteed amount. One innovation that came from Oklahoma was ending the custom of paying the transportation of prospects trying out during spring training. A number of clubs had dug themselves financial holes by this practice. Any farm boy with a mitt and a bat could receive a free vacation simply by someone recommending him. After Western Association president Bell ended the practice, only a hopeful with confidence in his ability to take away a position from a veteran or the other rookies would lay out the cash to tryout.

Playing for an Oklahoma franchise was tough duty. As pay was typically under $100 per month April through August or September, every player had a regular off-season job. While some clubs provided board in the home town, players were on their own for most everything else beyond train fare, minimal meal money, and hotels while on the road. Players routinely played injured. There was no disabled list. With many pulling double duty as both position players and pitchers, a ball club could not afford the luxury of carrying an injured player. A broken bone or wrenched knee easily could be a season-ender or even end a career. So could a sore arm. Unlike contemporary prima doñas who may throw ninety pitches every four days, in the first two decades of the twentieth century pitchers frequently worked with a day or two of rest. It was not unusual for a hurler to toss both ends of a double header.

Playing fields were rough. Crowds were rougher. Fights were frequent between players, umpires, and fans. The spit ball was legal. The fewer balls used in a game the better; four or less was the norm. Pitchers could and did throw at batters. Batters could and did throw bats at pitchers. Homeruns were usually inside the park. Players not infrequently received in change (including silver and gold dollars) from the fans through the screen or over the dugout as much in a month as their salary. Only one umpire called a game and those were often inept or corrupt. If the umpire didn't show up, the teams would each appoint a player to serve alternate sides of innings. There was an active Sabbatarian movement that pressured clubs and players to refrain from playing baseball on Sunday. Oklahoma had a statute on the point. Many towns had Blue Law ordinances. Those were the main reason many ball parks were located beyond the city limits.

While the Indian Territory was a "no alcohol" zone and would remain so until at least 1928 under the Statehood Act, liquor flowed freely in the Oklahoma Territory. With the passage of the Prohibition Ordinance along with the Oklahoma Constitution on federal Constitution Day in 1907, all of the new State became "bone dry." Even near beer (3.2% alcohol by volume) was illegal until 1933. The County Attorney in El Reno went so far as to obtain injunctions against all landlords in El Reno's business district prohibiting them from renting to anyone who sold or distributed alcohol of any kind. Still, players and fans patronized local bootleggers and moonshiners. In Krebs, an Italian-majority town in Pittsburg County, there were dozens of micro-breweries where Choc beer was made and illegally sold. There was always a way to wet a whistle. Before the Eighteenth Amendment and the Volstead Act became effective on January 17, 1920, trips to out-of-state league venues were something to look forward to. Baseball players were not an abstemious lot.

Pietistic Protestant denominations that dominated the Midwest, the old Confederacy and border states provided the impetus behind the movement that led to Prohibition. The era of the Ku Klux Klan's dominance coincided with the zenith of Prohibition. The Klan took it on itself to be the champion of the values Prohibition encompassed.

A minor league player in Oklahoma could look for a playing career of from a few days to a few years. The guiding philosophy was "catch and release." Many prospects would receive mid-season tryouts. Most were Rubes who found their way back to the sandlot. Those worth signing would replace a player who received a release. If he panned out, he was either "reserved" for the next season or sold upstream to a higher league —usually the Texas League, Western League, or American Association— or occasionally to a big league club. It was not unusual for a league player to sit out a season or two with a semi-pro outfit. Frequently the working conditions and money were better. Most ball clubs played exhibitions with town teams during the championship season on off-days or between season halves. It was a form of salary enhancement as the players shared in the gate.

To keep interest in the pennant contest, some, but not all, leagues would split the season either at the outset or after one team was far ahead of the pack. A playoff system was followed with the winner of each half squaring off following the regular season. The championship series sometimes didn't work out or worked too long. Ardmore lost one series because its team failed to show up for the last game. Cleburne won the first Texas-Oklahoma crown when Wichita Falls refused to finish the playoff, claiming that the Irish Lads' guarantee money (larger of $40 or a piece of the gate) had been shorted in Train Town. Corsicana and Ft. Worth played nineteen games for the 1904 Texas League crown.

To transform a game into a sport, three elements must be present: publicity, statistics, and wagering. Gamblers want certainty and something more than instinct to make odds. Baseball became a sport by 1870. Wagering was endemic in baseball and Oklahoma was no exception. After off-track betting was outlawed it was surmised that more was bet on baseball games in a single week in Oklahoma City than the governor's annual salary. Try as the leagues might —the president of the Texas-Oklahoma League sent an anti-gambling epistle general to his teams— money was put on every professional game played in Oklahoma.

Red Dirt Baseball: The First Decades is an excursion into a time and place long gone. It is divided into two halves. The first tells the stories of the several professional leagues that had members from Oklahoma. The second is about the cities that fielded teams —if only for a few days.

It was rough sledding for the early leagues. Between 1904 and 1910 five leagues rose and fell with a life of but a single season. One went through

continued on page 16

SABBATARIANS AND PROHIBITIONISTS

Professional baseball collided with two social movements that were ascendant during the early twentieth century. One was the ban on desecrating the Sabbath. The other was Prohibition.

The Sabbatarian movement that took on the force of law in a number of American jurisdictions as early as the late eighteenth century sought to not only prohibit commerce on Sundays but play as well. The 1794 Pennsylvania General Assembly law stated that it was to an "Act for the prevention of vice and immorality, and of unlawful gaming, and to restrain disorderly sports and dissipation." That was the core of the so-called "Blue Laws." At the turn of the nineteenth century, Sunday baseball was legal only in Chicago, St. Louis and Cincinnati. In 1917, Hall of Famers John McGraw and "the Christian Gentleman" Christy Mathewson were arrested for Sabbath-breaking following a game at the Polo Grounds against the Reds. As late as 1927, the Pennsylvania Supreme Court threw out the appeal of Connie Mack and his Philadelphia Athletics ruling that Sunday baseball was "unholy" and forbidden "worldly employment." An early Oklahoma publisher, Santford Hardy in the weekly *Comanche* [I.T.] *Reflex* of August 5, 1904 summarized the reasoning "Sunday baseball is not a Sabbath breaker, but a detriment to the Sunday School of our country, and I believe that if there is not a law against it, there should be one established, and the church going people, especially the parents, should see that it is enforced."

Since the Indian Territory lacked a legislature, the legal "gap filler" was the civil law code of the State of Arkansas which contained a Blue Law forbidding conducting business —including professional baseball—on Sundays. The June 25, 1903 *Sentinal of Christian Liberty*, a Seventh-Day Adventist journal, reported the federal prosecution of Sabbath-breakers in Wilburton and Okmulgee. During late April of 1905, sitting at Vinita U.S. District Judge for the Northern District of Indian Territory, Joseph A. Gill —a McKinley appointee and hard shell Southern Baptist— had enforced the Arkansas Blue Law and ordered the U.S. Marshals to arrest players taking the field on the Sabbath. At the close of the 1904 season, District Attorney Wilkens in South McAlester had promised the ministers that he would enforce the Blue Law against playing baseball. With a dateline of May 18, 1905 from South McAlester, I.T., *The Daily Oklahoman's* correspondent relates an instance of law enforcement intimidation of ball players in Vinita, the pastors of all Muskogee churches petitioning the district attorney to prosecute Sunday violators, and league games being played in South McAlester with great apprehension. While no steps were taken to halt a Sunday game there before 1,500 viewers, the correspondent opines that the Indian Territory clubs will have to disband if the Blue Law is enforced. The reason advanced was that no team could survive only on weekday revenue. This was Connie Mack's argument and behind his threat to build a new stadium in Camden, New Jersey for his A's unless the ban on Sunday baseball was repealed.

Like so many laws attempting to legislate a particular kind of morality, insofar as baseball was

concerned in Vinita, Tulsa, Muskogee and South McAlester the summer of 1905 saw the Blue Law honored in the breach. While Oklahoma Attorney General West ruled in 1913 that "gaming" in the Blue Law did not apply to baseball without more, it would not be until 1921 that the statewide battle in Oklahoma was settled when the legislature killed a bill that would criminalize Sabbath-breaking. Blue Laws became a matter of local option. In Garvin County, where the sale of liquor except in retail stores was forbidden until November, 2010, the Pauls Valley Raiders of the Sooner State League as late as 1954 could not play Sunday games at home because of the thrall the ministerial alliance had over the city council.

The entire public was not behind the Temperance bandwagon.

The Southern Club in Oklahoma City was one of the most up-scale saloons in the Territory.

Carry Nation was an icon of the Temperance Movement at the turn of the nineteenth and first decade of the twentieth century. Initially alone and then with dozens then hundreds then thousands of followers in the Women's Christian Temperance Union, Nation was a tornado of saloon destruction first in her native Kansas then in the Oklahoma Territory. She published The Hatchet *from her home in Guthrie and then, after her husband divorced her, moved to Seiling, O.T. where she wrote her autobiography,* The Use and Need of the Life of Carry A. Nation.

While the Indian Territory was dry, beer, wine and liquor flowed freely in the Oklahoma Territory. The 1906 Enabling Act that gave the Twin Territories Statehood banned alcohol from the old Indian Territory until 1928. During the Constitutional Convention, the Anti-Saloon League lobbied for prohibition to operate statewide. By a majority of 18,000 votes, Oklahoma adopted the Prohibition Ordinance in tandem with the 1907 Constitution. The Anti-Saloon League under the name "United Drys" remained a power in Oklahoma until repeal of prohibition in 1959. Before 1959, the wealthy could retire to the comfort of their country clubs for a drink and a few pulls on the slot machines. For the rest, illegal alcohol was widely available to working people through bootleggers and fraternal organizations, explaining in some part the popularity of Masons, Odd Fellows, Knights of Pythias, Elks, Moose Clubs and the like.

two iterations. The second ten years was dominated by three leagues that would all appear again in the early 1920s.

Most of the cities fielding teams became county seats with Statehood. Sapulpa had a brisk fight with Bristow for the honor of hosting Creek County's government. Holdenville had a similar battle with Wetumka. Guthrie had to settle for being a county seat after Oklahoma City won the 1910 election for State Capital. Formerly the Senators, Guthrie's teams sported no names after 1910 other than "ex-Senators" in the Oklahoma City press. The college town and rail center of Shawnee lost out on county seat status in 1907 and the contest for State Capital in 1910. It did not become the seat of Pottawatomie County until 1930.

All of the people named or who participated in our early baseball have died. Teams and leagues have been forgotten or are remembered, if at all, by nonagenarian grandchildren. The ball parks have long since been demolished, destroyed, and built over without a trace. The cities have changed. Booms and busts have happened. Small town Oklahoma, even with its cultural and social conservatism, is a very different place than during the years 1904 through 1919.

If immortality is being remembered beyond one's own generation, then I hope this book will extend to the twenty-first century the memories of the players, owners, and fans who created this unique time in Oklahoma's history.

One final word about terminology. In the late nineteenth and early twentieth centuries, "league" baseball —i.e. full time players, a regular schedule, membership in a recognized league— is what today is called "Organized Baseball." The team "manager" was either the owner or worked for the owner primarily as the business manager although it was not unusual for the manager to also serve as "captain." The captain was the one today called the "manager."

The index is extensiver and deserves perusal. More than a few players appeared over a dozen seasons in different towns. Dad Bennett, for example, was 53 when he first apppears in 1904 Guthrie and is still playing in 1911 at Lawton. Deacon White, born in 1847, had a playing career from 1871 through his final campaign at Tulsa in 1908. These are great personal stories. Enjoy!

Peter G. Pierce
New Orleans, Louisiana
January 12, 2013

PART ONE

LEAGUES

SOUTHWESTERN LEAGUE   1904

Kansan Frank Quigg had bounced around the old Western Association from his debut at age twenty with Topeka in 1893 through stints in an early incarnation of the Texas League, then in the New York-Pennsylvania League and finally with Little Rock in 1899.   The 1900 season found him in territorial Oklahoma City where he joined the semi-pro team as a pitcher and outfielder.   When that group disbanded —that was the nature of non-league clubs— he found himself with Enid in the Cherokee Strip for 1901.   That fall and over the winter, Quigg promoted a local team to be called the "Statehoods" in a league to be formed with Shawnee (that also took the name "Statehoods"), El Reno, Enid, Chickasha, and Lawton.   The City

Frank Quigg shown with the Des Moines ball club in 1905. Scion of a wealthy family from Atchison, Kansas —his brother George was one of Roosevelt's Roughriders— Quigg spent three partial seasons playing in the Texas League and three full seasons umpiring there. It was said that he had umpired in Japan in 1906. He later fell in with bad companions. Having learned of a December 31, 1909 plot to rob the Post Office and bank in Harrah, Oklahoma, a posse led by "Wolf-Killer" U. S. Marshal Jack Abernathy awaited the would-be thieves and opened fire. Quigg was killed instantly in the fusillade.

squad —including several from the 1900 nine—
played before its largest crowd, 5,000, at Colcord
Park on May 27, 1902 where Shawnee humiliated
the newly christened Metropolitans by a score of
eleven to two. Quigg soon headed south where it
was reported that he had turned to umpiring in
Texas. No league was ever formed. Quigg was back
in 1903 promoting the Southwestern Association
with Enid, Arkansas City- Winfield, and Shawnee
joining Oklahoma City. It was not a member of the
new National Association of Professional Baseball
Leagues ("National Association") so not considered
part of Organized Baseball; its members' reserve
clauses would not be honored.

A season was begun and games played. The
last reported league standings had the Shawnee
Blues in first. The "league" spontaneously dissolved
around May 18 following a feud between Quigg
and the Shawnee manager. Quigg again jumped
ship to return to the ranks of arbiters, reportedly to
call balls and strikes in Japan. Strong drink and a
pugnacious nature were his down fall. He was shot
by lawmen as he fled from an attempted bank robbery in Harrah on New Year's Eve 1909.

The headless and unpaid 1903 Mets soon
disbanded. In early June, the Shawnee club with
Emmett Rogers and Pat Flaherty in its infield, relocated to Oklahoma City assuming the unused name
"Mets." Rogers and Flaherty were archetypal of the
aging baseball alumni of the 1890s: brief stints in a
major league, a dozen or so seasons in the minors
and semi-pros, jumping contracts, generally impe-
cunious, but, with good fortune, finally landing a
job as a manager or even owning a ball club in the
bushes. These two players wintered over in Oklahoma City in 1903-1904 in hope of achieving the
goal of their kind.

*Emmett Rogers played professionally begin-
ning with Hot Springs in 1887 and ending
with Guthrie in 1904. His career included
1890 with Toledo of the then major league
American Association. Rogers owned and
managed the 1911 Ardmore Blues. He died
in 1941 at his hometown of Hot Springs,
Arkansas.*

*Pat Flaherty (1866-1946) first played
for Denver in 1887. Like Rogers,
his playing days ended with Guthrie
in1904. He spent part of the 1894
season with the Louisville Colonels of
the National League.*

Rogers and Flaherty proposed in December,
1903 the formation of a professional baseball league
with members located along the main rail routes in
Kansas and the Twin Territories. Appropriating
the name of Quigg's 1903 failure, "Southwestern
League," the two actively promoted baseball people
and civic boosters from Oklahoma City, Shawnee,
and Guthrie, O.T. and received unsolicited applica-
tions from as far away as Newton, Kansas on the
A.T.& S.F. line north from Guthrie.

*A native of County Clare, Ireland, Ted
Sullivan (1851-1929) made his profes-
sional debut at age thirty-three in
three games with the 1884 Kansas City
Cowboys of the American Association.
He managed the St. Louis Maroons,
St. Louis Browns, and, in 1888, the
Washington Nationals. He had a keen
eye for talent and discovered Charles
Comiskey, future owner of the Chicago
White Sox. He credited himself with
inventing the word "fan" to refer to a
follower of baseball.*

Kansan Ted Sullivan, whose major league baseball career as manager of the St. Louis Browns and Washington Nationals overlapped with Rogers' and Flaherty's playing days, formed a troika in February, 1904. Meeting in the Territorial Capital, Guthrie, Oklahoma City, Wichita, and Hutchinson were admitted with Shawnee waiting in the wings; Enid would be a suitable sixth. If either of those failed, Sullivan could add his hometown Winfield, Kansas club.

A six-team circuit was beginning to take shape on March 15. Management had been identified: Rogers and Flaherty in Oklahoma City, Ernest Jones and former major leaguer William "Billy" Hughes for Guthrie, Ted Sullivan in Wichita, Ed Moore and Park Smith with the Hutchinson franchise, and Harry Plagman for Winfield. For the sixth, Walter Frantz, young pitching star of the Kansas City Blues, would sit out a season to lead Enid's first professional ball club. A target date of May 1 was selected for the season openers. Five days later, it was announced that Shawnee would replace Winfield.

Three weeks before the planned first pitch, the Southwestern League had shrunk to four: Enid, Wichita, Guthrie and Oklahoma City. Then an interloper in the person of banker and ardent amateur first baseman for the Chickasha, I.T. town team, W. M. Hazlett, appeared. After watching the St. Louis Browns dismember the Oklahoma City Mets, he challenged the new professional Mets to a game with his team. The object was gaining a league franchise for himself. The other Oklahoma clubs were impressed with his brass and braggadocio and he soon succeeded to the Wichita slot and the Southwestern League's fourth franchise.

As opening day approached the Guthrie Blues, Enid Evangelists — co-owner and field general Frantz was a strict Sabbatarian and would not permit play on Sundays— and Oklahoma City Mets were set.

While it had been taken for granted that Hazlett's team would represent Chickasha, he let it be known that the home base for his "Indians" had not yet been decided. Rail centers El Reno and Shawnee seemed to offer better prospects.

1904 Enid Evangelists (who became the "Backsliders" when they began playing on Sunday). Upper L-R: Gene Price, Tom Anderson, Brown Miller, Mel Cooley, Claude Fetz. Lower L-R: Howard Price, Hunt, Anson Mott, Findley, Walter Frantz.

Charles F. Colcord (1859-1934) had run cattle in the Cherokee Outlet in the 1870s and staked the claim to Lot 1 in Block 1 of Oklahoma City on April 22, 1889. He served as police chief and became wealthy in ranching, banking, and oil. Delmar Gardens was located on part of his property southwest of downtown. There was a racetrack (shown) adjacent and to the north of which was a ball park.

When Sunday May 1, 1904 came, the Shawnee Indians sat idly by as the Mets and Blues squared off at civic leader Charles Colcord's ball park.

Hazlett's nine would have to wait until Monday, May 2 to meet the Evangelists at the new facility in Enid's Waverly addition. After completing the initial four-game league series, Oklahoma City and Enid stood atop the standings at three wins against one loss while Shawnee was playing .500 ball and Guthrie had yet to take a scalp.

Outfitted in green flannels with maroon trim, the Hazlett ball club became Chickasha's on May 6, before making even a single appearance at Shawnee. Beginning with the Chickasha home opener being rained out, the franchise that would be the Southwestern League's biggest problem would prove to be ill-starred.

Rapidly Hazlett's financial situation became a cause for concern. The club needed $200 per month to operate. On June 3, a local committee of C.M. Fechheimer, R. Stephens, James Pettyjohn, Hugo Roos, and W. F. Grandee was formed to solicit the Chickasha merchants and businessmen for support. Yet even with a troubled franchise, one month into the season there was talk of Wichita and Shawnee expanding the league to six.

Chickasha was not alone, however. At Guthrie, Jones and Hughes were ousted from ownership and replaced by the Guthrie Base Ball Association headed by D. Fatima Smith who claimed to have been —with no substantiation the author could find— the past sheriff of No Man's Land. Popular Billy Hughes was retained as field manager until June 18. Jones went on to Perry, O.T. to become a journalist and Republican operative.

John Sinopoulo and Joseph Marre had trained at Delmar Gardens in St. Louis and upon moving to Oklahoma City in 1902 opened a park with the same name on forty acres of a quarter section belonging to Colcord. It was bounded by Western on the east, Reno on the north, and by the meandering North Canadian River on the south and west. With the exception of Abner Davis' 1912 field on South Robinson, all Oklahoma City ball parks from 1900 until Holland Field in 1924 were located in or near the site. For eight years it was the premier entertainment venue of the young city. Mosquitoes, annual flooding, and Prohibition led to its demise. Delmar Gardens closed in 1910 and was demolished the next year.

Oklahoma City lost its ball park and saw its franchise change hands on the same day. Delmar Gardens was the City's best and favorite recreation venue with a beer garden, vaudeville and horse racing. A mile west of downtown, it was located on the then-undammed North Canadian River. Colcord Park was inundated by a June flood. A new facility, known as Sportsmen's Park, was quickly built on higher ground north of the Colcord Park race track.

At the same time, it was learned that Messrs. Rogers and Flaherty had not remitted the mandatory guarantee money to the National Association and that the Southwestern League was not recognized as a part of Organized Baseball until a month into the season. As no player contracts had been registered, none of the Mets were under binding contract; they were all free agents. The two fathers of the league were banished, later to emerge with an independent team in Coffeyville. The Mets became the operation of the Oklahoma City Base Ball Association.

On June 21, Chickasha failed to appear in Oklahoma City for a series there. Unpaid, the team returned home. League president Will Kimmel of Wichita called a special meeting attended by Hazlett, Gene Barnes for the Mets, Howard Price for Enid, and Frank Overby on the Senators' behalf. The Chickasha franchise was moved to Shawnee on June 24 with the first game there called for July 1.

Another threat to the new league was the Corsicana club of the Texas League relocating to Oklahoma City. Both that club and the Paris franchise were in trouble; the latter would land in Ardmore, I.T. in August with Guthrie's Billy Hughes at the helm. J. H. Farrell of the National Association halted the Corsicana move, ruling that the South-western League had exclusive rights to the Oklahoma Territory's largest city.

A third dispute ended up with league play being delayed for ten days. A new schedule had been agreed to on June 24 that called for Sunday games. Meanwhile, Walter Frantz had agreed to sale of his Enid club to Howard Price and league president Kimmel.

W. J. Kimmel owned and operated professional franchises in Wichita, Kansas and Enid. He succeeded Sullivan as president of the Southwestern League. The president of the Guthrie Base Ball Association, D. Fatima Smith, followed him.

Frantz suddenly backed away from his approval of the schedule. He proclaimed that he would first burn all the bats and equipment before breaking the Sabbath. Kimmel resigned his presidency. Enid was suspended from the league. Within the fortnight the issue was resolved. Kimmel becoming the sole owner of the Enid franchise that now played baseball on Sundays. The Evangelists became the Backsliders. The post of president remained vacant as Gene Barnes, the Mets manager, as secretary-treasurer, succeeded Kimmel as acting league president.

Renamed the Orioles, Hazlitt's club played for a few days after July 17 when he threw up his hands and ostensibly repaired to the bedside of his ailing wife. From July 23 through July 31, Shawnee suspended play or, as the league reported "Shawnee is temporarily out of business awaiting new management." The Hazlett era formally came to an end on July 29. Idle players free-lanced with semi-pro outfits.

The "new management" came in the form of the El Reno semi-pros headed by Tom Reid and managed by Charles Palmer, neither with prior experience in Organized Baseball. El Reno made its debut on August 1 at Enid dropping a four to two decision.

At the August 4 meeting where Guthrie's D. F. Smith was elected president and his protégé Corb M. Sarchet secretary-treasurer, El Reno was awarded a franchise and a new schedule was adopted effective August 5 that ran to October 2. The pennant race was started anew with games from July 17 to August 4 wiped out to give the new franchise, which had signed a number of former Shawnee players, an even shot at the league pennant.

Corb M. Sarchet was a pioneer Oklahoma journalist who ran The Daily Oklahoman's *Guthrie bureau in the first decade of the last century. A protégé of Col. D. F. Smith, Sarchett followed him to the front office of the Southwestern League. He authored the article about the league in the 1905 edition of* Spalding's Official Baseball Guide.

When the east-bound train arrived in Guthrie on August 6, the only ones disembarking were players Ury, Cousins and Bennett each of whom had signed with El Reno. Their news was that the club had disbanded. El Reno was a pipe dream. The Guthrie Base Ball Association seized the laboring oar and frantically sought a replacement city. Perry was the best opportunity but it was too late in the season to raise interest there. Plan B was to form a new league with the three remaining clubs in the Oklahoma Territory and South McAlester, Vinita, Muskogee or Tulsa in the Indian Territory. A feeler to the South McAlester semi-pros —licking their wounds after Ardmore took the Indian Territory crown from

them— about joining the Southwestern League was extended but no agreement could be reached.

On August 13, the league re-organized. L. A. Lackey as manager brought to the table a new Shawnee team named the "Browns." Another new schedule running through October 2 was adopted that erased all games played before August 12. A number of the Hazlett-era players were picked up as well as Oklahoma City players who enjoyed free agency. Shawnee fielded a competitive team. Elderly first baseman James "Deacon" White took over field duties on August 25.

A round robin among the four members was played until September 5 when the Browns disbanded. Enid soon ceased to regularly appear in line scores. Guthrie and Oklahoma City played home and home series six days each week. To fill the scheduling gaps, exhibitions were played against semi-pros and road clubs such as Coffeyville, Rogers' and Flaherty's latest venture. When their proposal to substitute their Kansans for the vacant Shawnee dates fell on deaf ears, the two sent their players to their off-season homes and themselves joined the Guthrie Blues. The last game of the regular season was played for a $100 purse. Having already clinched the pennant on September 28, Guthrie lost the challenge leaving the Mets with a cash consolation prize. The final standings:

Guthrie Blues	56	44
Enid Evangelists/Backsliders	46	37
Oklahoma City Mets	45	49
Shawnee Indians/		
Chickasha Indians/		
Shawnee Orioles/		
Shawnee Browns	21	43*

*Records for Shawnee and Chickasha appear separately under their respective headings at page 86. *The Encyclopedia of Minor League Baseball* (3d. ed) shows the overall record to be 25 wins against 42 losses.

Oklahoma City's first "league" team. Upper L-R: Andrew Warner (Captain), Clarence Sullenberger, R.B. Swartzell, Clarence Nelson, Red Werner, Lewis Woods. Lower L-R: William Beeker, Eugene Barnes (Owner), Everett Sheffield. Seated: Fred Tullar, Alf Page.

The three survivors finished the season as hosts to the Kansas City Blues of the American Association, the highest level of the minors. Gene Barnes represented the league at the October 25 annual meeting of National Association members. Shawnee would sit out 1905 then return to Organized Baseball in 1906 as a member of the South Central League, a successor to the second Missouri Valley League. Enid would not have professional baseball until 1908 when the city would field the Western Association Railroaders who finished fifty games off the pace with a .277 winning percentage. Guthrie and Oklahoma City received invitations to join the Missouri Valley League for 1905 but by the time they accepted the circuit had changed its name to the Western Association, a league in Class C most seasons that would survive through the 1954 campaign and include a number of Oklahoma cities and towns. Barnes purchased the 1904 Missouri Valley champion Iola, Kansas and moved the club lock, stock and barrel to Oklahoma City. Guthrie had bought the Ft. Scott Giants operation as well as having reserved most of its 1904 players and entered the Western Association. A "flattering situation" had emerged.

TEXAS LEAGUE 1904

The Texas League, founded in 1888, revived in 1902 as a Class D circuit, was centered in north central and east Texas. The southern tier of Texas cities —Beaumont, Galveston, Houston, and San Antonio— formed a separate South Texas League in 1903. This division held until reunification in the 1907 season.

The 1904 Texas League, promoted to Class C, had only four members: Dallas Giants, Ft. Worth Panthers, Corsicana Oil Citys, and Paris Red Ravens but universally called the "Parasites."

Corsicana tried to move to Oklahoma City in June but was thwarted by a ruling of the National Association. Before the season began, the owners of what became the Paris franchise had tried to set up shop in the growing Indian Territory cotton and rail center, Ardmore, but were rebuffed. Deficient in capital, talent, and support, the Parasites were also the league's doormat.

Meanwhile, Ardmore had assembled a top semi-pro team, the Territorians, that by August 3 had taken the Indian Territory League crown away from the tough South McAlester Miners. With the

*1904
Dallas Giants.*

*1904 Ft. Worth
Panthers.*

*1904 Corsicana
Oil Citys.*

semi-pro league's season finished, the Paris club disbanded and many of the players took the train up the road to Ardmore where the remaining Parasites were incorporated into the Territorians. With that, Ardmore became the first town in either Oklahoma Territory or Indian Territory to be a member of Organized Baseball in a classification higher than the bottom rung, Class D.

The league was ailing. The owners decided to end the season on August 15. While Ft. Worth and Corsicana engaged in a nineteen game playoff, the Territorians reverted to semi-pro status. The results for the 1904 season:

Ft. Worth Panthers	71	30
Dallas Giants	58	45
Corsicana Oil Citys	48	53
Paris / Ardmore Territorians	26	75

The Texas League continues today. Along the way Oklahoma City, Tulsa, and, for the short 1961 season, Ardmore have been members.

WESTERN ASSOCIATION 1905-1911

A very tightly drawn league of small towns in the mining districts of eastern Kansas and western Missouri emerged in 1902 under the inspiration of Joseph B. Roe of Sedalia and direction of Dr. D. M. Shively, sports editor of the *Kansas City Star* newspaper. Jefferson City, Joplin, Nevada, Sedalia and Webb City in Missouri and Chanute, Coffeyville, Ft. Scott, Iola, Leavenworth and Topeka in Kansas fielded teams in the Missouri Valley League during its first three seasons.

D. M. "Doc" Shively, sports editor of the Kansas City Star, served as president of the Missouri Valley League from its inception in 1902 through its transformation into the Western Association in 1905. He was deposed in 1910 in a coup engineered by John Shaw, owner of the Enid franchise. He was criticized for lax enforcement of league rules, particularly the team salary cap. Shively also served as president of the 1908 Oklahoma-Kansas League.

1905

At its annual meeting in the fall of 1904, the five largest members of the Missouri Valley League —Springfield, Joplin, Sedalia, Leavenworth, and Topeka— voted to expand geographically west into Wichita and Guthrie and Oklahoma City under the new name "Western Association." The Oklahoma clubs were wholesale transfers of two 1904 rosters. The Oklahoma City Mets were the 1904 champion Iola Gasbags and the Guthrie Senators were the remnants of the last place Ft. Scott Giants.

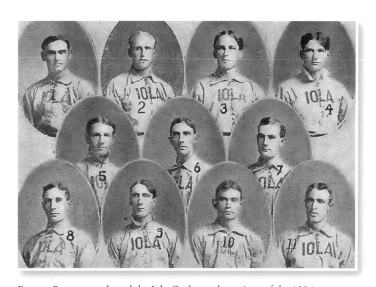

Eugene Barnes purchased the Iola Gasbags, champions of the 1904 Missouri Valley race, gaining entry into the 1905 Western Association. Renamed the "Mets," the club finished second, one and one-half games behind W. J. Kimmel's champion Wichita Jobbers.

The Association began the season in Class D but with a league population approaching 200,000 was promoted to Class C later in the campaign. Two 1904 umpires, Clarence Owens of Chicago and James Regan of Kansas City, an alumnus of the Pacific Coast League, joined A. H. Dempsey of Los Angeles, and veteran Matt Lewiston of St. Joseph to arbitrate. In the Association as in most other minor leagues below the top level, a single umpire called each game.

The league was extraordinarily well-balanced with only 170-180 basis points separating first from eighth. Until the last ten days of the season, Wichita, Sedalia, Leavenworth, and Oklahoma City were in and out of the lead. The largest members all showed a profit with only Guthrie and Sedalia finishing in the red.

Oklahoma City's George Hurlburt led the regulars of the league in batting with a .349 average and tied with Guthrie's George Dalrymple for

second in home run production. Pitching was the weak spot for both Territory teams. When the dust settled, the standings were:

Wichita Jobbers	79	56
Oklahoma City Mets	77	58
Leavenworth Orioles	75	59
Sedalia Goldbugs	70	64
Guthrie Senators	66	70
Joplin Miners	65	73
Topeka White Sox	54	80
Springfield Highlanders	54	80

Guthrie lost its franchise at the January, 1906 league meeting, the Senators relocating to St. Joseph, Missouri.

John Halla (1884-1947) saw action with the Cleveland Naps after a 15-11 1905 season with Oklahoma City. His career spanned from 1902 through 1917.

Frank "Frenchy" Genins (1866-1922), in baseball since 1888 at age thirty-eight hit .282 as the 1905 Mets' second sacker. Genins spent 1892 and 1895 in the National League and part of 1901 with the Cleveland Blues of the upstart American League. He finished his playing days in 1909 with Racine in the Wisconsin-Illinois League.

1906-1907

For the next two seasons, Oklahoma City was in Class C with the highest quality of baseball in the Territory and its only representative in the Association.

While a fifth place finish in 1906 looked poor, in fact J. H. Chinn's Mets had a winning season with seventy wins and sixty-nine losses.

The Association's next season was the worst so far both in terms of financial results and talent balance. Wichita took first place on the first day of

George "Speck" Hurlburt (1872-1945) played eleven professional seasons as an outfielder between 1898 and 1908. His best season was 1905 with Oklahoma City when he led the Western Association in batting with a .349 average.

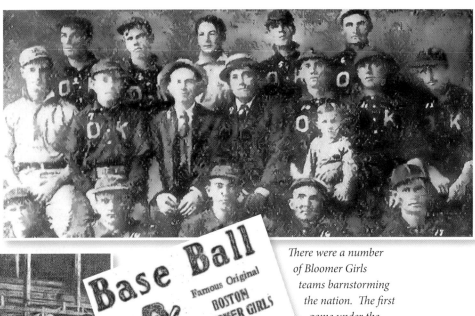

1906 Oklahoma City Mets finished fifth in the Western Association. Upper L-R: Charles Bemis, Arlo Scoggins, Frank Lofton, John Root, Roy Arnold. Middle L-R: Unidentified George Siegle, J. H. Chinn (Owner and Manager), Snodgrass, secretary-treasurer, Dudley Risley (Captain), Carl Lewis, R. Wilson. Seated L-R: Gus Wisser, John Green, Emery Olson, Lewis Woods, Clarence Nelson.

1907 Oklahoma City Mets finished second in the Western Association race.

There were a number of Bloomer Girls teams barnstorming the nation. The first game under the lights was played over the July 4, 1903 holiday in Geary, O. T. when the Bloomer Girls, who brought their own gas arc lights, defeated the local town team. Ned Pettigrew, who was with the 1904 Guthrie Blues, wore bloomers for the girls' team.

Base Ball

Famous Original
BOSTON
BLOOMER GIRLS
vs.
INDIAHOMA
BALL CLUB
Sunday, August 12
3:30 P. M.
SPORTSMAN'S
PARK
Admission 25 Cts.

the season and went on to win ninety-seven more. Jack Halla of Topeka threw a four nil gem at his former team mates on August 1.

Jack Pendry led the Association with ninety-one runs. Oklahoma City's Chappie McFarland batted .314 and won twenty-two games to propel the Mets into second place.

Chappie McFarland spent 1902-1905 with the St. Louis Cardinals before splitting 1906 with the Redbirds, Pittsburgh, and Brooklyn. 1907 with the Mets was his first as a manager. He was back in 1909 where he finished his playing career with the Texas League Oklahoma City Indians.

After leading the 1906 Austin Senators to the South Texas League pennant, Warren Gill (1878-1952) hit .289 as the 1907 Mets' first baseman. He played the last month of 1908 with the Pittsburgh Pirates, losing his job in 1909 to Bill Abstein. He played for Minneapolis in the American Association 1909-1912 and finished in 1913 with Los Angeles of the Pacific Coast League.

Bill Hoffer (1870-1959) threw the first no-hitter for an Oklahoma City club when he blanked Hutchinson by a score of eight to zero on August 17. He led the National League in winning percentage in his rookie and sophomore seasons with the Baltimore Orioles. He spent 1895, 1896, 1897, 1898, 1899, and 1901 in the majors. He was 19-9 in two seasons at Oklahoma City before completing a nineteen year career in 1909 at Cedar Rapids.

1908

The new State of Oklahoma boasted two Western Association teams in 1908. Enid became the new home of the last place Leavenworth franchise.

Magnates of the 1908 Western Association.

The move did not improve the team's performance beyond bettering the winning percentage, .277 versus .212 in 1907. Orville Selby, who finished the season with Topeka, accounted for most of the Railroaders' thirty-eight wins. Under

Jack McConnell's leadership, Oklahoma City fielded another first division club behind strong pitching. The Mets were not unlike the 1906 Chicago White Sox: hitless wonders. The 1908 results were:

Topeka Jayhawkers	89	50
Wichita Jobbers	87	53
Oklahoma City Mets	81	58
Joplin Miners	71	65
Hutchinson Salt Packers	69	70
Webb City Webbfeet	66	69
Springfield Midgets	48	85
Enid Railroaders	38	99

1909

The 1909 campaign began with four Oklahoma members. The Class A Western League had taken away the top two 1908 Western Association finishers while Oklahoma City moved laterally to the Texas League. Smaller cities in the new 46th State, Muskogee, Bartlesville and Guthrie, joined Enid. Within ten weeks, the collapse of the lead and zinc market took out two of the franchises in the Tri-State mining district, Joplin and Webb City. On Independence Day, Joplin fled to El Reno. Two weeks later, the Joplin suburb of Webb City moved to Sapulpa. The center of the Western Association was now in Oklahoma. Enid was the turnaround story. From thirty-eight victories and a finish in the cellar in 1908, the Railroaders took the 1909 pennant under the ownership of John H. Shaw and the field leadership of Ted Price. Mid-season in 1909, Shaw became league vice-president when the incumbent, A. J. Baker of Joplin, resigned after he lost his city's club to El Reno.

Third place Guthrie boasted the Association's top batter, Clare Patterson— .349 average and 180 hits— and pitchers, Floyd Willis with twenty-two

Following a dismal 1908 season, the Enid Railroaders bounced back to win the 1909 Western Association crown.

J. H. "Honest John" Shaw became Western Association vice-president in 1909 and the next season led the revolt against Doc Shively who had served as league president since its founding. He was responsible for dropping a very good El Reno team from the league in 1910 to place his Enid club into second place. He moved his club to Tulsa in January, 1911.

wins and a .818 percentage and Clyde Geist with 247 strike outs. Sapulpa's Frank Lofton crossed the plate 108 times and Enid's Tex Jones was the long ball king with eleven. The Oklahoma clubs that began the season formed the first division.

Enid Railroaders	82	44
Muskogee Navigators	74	51
Guthrie Senators	70	55
Bartlesville Boosters	66	59
Webb City Webbfeet/		
Sapulpa Oilers	64	59
Springfield Midgets	56	70
Pittsburg Pirates	52	73
Joplin Miners/		
El Reno Packers	36	89

Springfield led for the first six weeks until overtaken by Bartlesville. In mid-June Enid took the lead never to relinquish it. Guthrie and Muskogee charged from the second division in July. Despite a fifth place finish, Sapulpa was able to end with a winning record. El Reno began the season in the cellar and stayed there throughout the campaign. With the exception of the three mining towns, Joplin, Webb City, and Pittsburg, all league members turned a profit.

1910

For 1910, Joplin was back succeeding to Pittsburg's place. Tulsa joined the ranks of class C when Springfield moved its operation to the Oil Capital. "Honest John" engineered the ouster of long time president, Doc Shively, in July, 1910 after the Tulsa club disbanded and the former Muskogee franchise that had taken shelter in Okmulgee was dropped on July 22. Shaw managed the affairs of the Western Association under difficult circumstances.

Bartlesville disbanded on July 31 when its players walked away and refused to play El Reno after Booster management missed the payday. Shaw forced then-second place El Reno out of the league, the "double cross" leapfrogging Shaw's Enid club into the runner-up position in a new four-team league. Joplin, twenty-two and one-half games in front of the pack, Enid, Sapulpa, and Guthrie, the only remaining club with a losing record, stumbled to the end of the season on August 16. Enid's

manager Robert "Snapper" Kennedy won the batting crown with a .326 average. Henry Goodrich of Sapulpa had league bests with 139 hits and eleven home runs. Oklahoma teams produced three no-hitters with Guthrie involved in each. Central State Normal star Louis Listen hurled Guthrie past El Reno on June 7. Lou Shakespeare of Muskogee allowed two unearned runs in his four to two gem over Guthrie on June 22. Rube Robinson exacted a measure of revenge when the Packers whipped Guthrie a dozen to none on July 8.

Joplin Miners	90	34
Enid Railroaders	64	53
Sapulpa Oilers	65	61
Guthrie Senators	47	73
El Reno Packers	65	43
Bartlesville Boosters	51	51
Muskogee /Okmulgee Navigators	36	63
Tulsa Oilers	28	68

1911

The Western Association was reorganized for 1911, dropping to Class D.

Tom C. Hayden, former Webb City owner, having permanently squeezed Enid and John Shaw from the league, reigned as president, secretary and treasurer over a circuit with teams in Oklahoma (Muskogee, Sapulpa, and Tulsa), Arkansas (Ft. Smith-Van Buren), Kansas (Coffeyville and Independence), and Missouri (Joplin and Springfield). As *The Sporting News* noted in early 1912, 1911 had been a disastrous year for minor leagues. The Western Association would accompany the

Tom C. Hayden of Webb City, Missouri had owned and managed ball clubs since 1902 when he was a founding member of the Missouri Valley League. As president of the Joplin club that folded after five games and moved to Tulsa, he ousted Shaw both as owner of the Tulsa turf and president of the league. He flipped the Tulsa operation soon after arriving there. He was thoroughly disliked and accused of trying to steal the Muskogee and Ft. Smith franchises. The league failed on his watch. As insurance, he bought the Burlington, Iowa franchise of the Central Association in February, 1911 and focused his efforts there after the Western Association folded.

Wisconsin-Minnesota, Southern Michigan, Central California, Kansas State, Missouri State, Northeast Arkansas, Northern State of Indiana, San Joaquin Valley, Southwest Texas, and Twin States leagues into oblivion. Thirteen more leagues would not survive 1912.

The two Missouri franchises would fold just five games into the season. The Kansas clubs followed on June 14. Five days later, Tulsa and Ft. Smith gave up the ghost. With only Muskogee and Sapulpa left standing, they disbanded and the Western Association would be dormant until revived under Joplin's A. B. Baker for the 1914 season. No player records exist for the season.

Ft. Smith Scouts	29	14
Muskogee Redskins	23	21
Sapulpa Oilers	32	21
Tulsa Railroaders	20	25
Independence Packers	15	22
Coffeyville White Sox	15	24
Joplin Miners	3	2
Springfield Jobbers	2	3

MISSOURI VALLEY LEAGUE 1905

Former members of the newly named Western Association invited towns from the adjacent Indian Territory to Parsons, Kansas where, on February 1, 1905 a new baseball organization with a discarded name was formed. Jilted by the new league, Webb City, Missouri and Ft. Scott, Coffeyville and Parsons, Kansas joined hands with Muskogee, Tulsa and Vinita, I.T., each a newcomer to Organized Baseball. The Missouri Valley League was placed in Class C. Richard Robertson, Jr., protégé of

Western Association president D. M. Shively, was elected league president and secretary, publisher A. Garland Marrs of Vinita vice-president and Jesse Frankenberger, Webb City's justice of the peace, treasurer. They hired Maurice F. Dunihy of Rochester, N. Y., Eddie Oswald (who later joined the South McAlester club as a player) and Charles S. Boahne both of Kansas City, and Steve Collins of Seamonon, Kansas to call balls and strikes. The league's first and only season opened on May 14 and was scheduled to run through September 17. By the time the new season opened, Pittsburg, Kansas —which, like Iola, had seen its 1904 ball club purchased and moved to the Western Association— had replaced Coffeyville. South McAlester, I.T. became the eighth.

The opening series scheduled to be played at Tulsa was moved to Vinita because Creek Nation District Attorney Mellate had banned Sunday games. Pittsburg took the lead from the first day and never looked back, topping the loop with six wins against one loss in the first week. Muskogee faced problems early on and South McAlester was slow in getting up to speed.

Charles Shafft, Tulsa manager, tried to reduce travel costs when he sought to take over the league outlier, South McAlester, by a vote of the other Missouri Valley League owners. J. B. Roe, the South McAlester owner, fought back and forced the league to reverse itself. Despite references to the contrary, South McAlester never moved to Ft. Smith as Shafft planned. He began the 1906 season as owner of the Tulsa club but left to take his mitt to St. Joseph in the Western Association just to be released when Monroe from the Vinita, I. T. club was signed.

Motivated by a new schedule that shrank the league, the other owners conspired with Charles E. Shafft, Tulsa's manager, to invoke the "for the good of the league" clause in the league constitution and on July 9 had president Robertson wire Giants' owner and manager, Joseph B. Roe, that his franchise had been pulled and awarded to Shafft who would move it to Ft. Smith. Roe was not much of a business man; he would run the Shawnee franchise of the South Central League into insolvency the following season. Still, his club was paid up and in good standing. Inundated with letters and telegrams and threatened with litigation in the Southern District of Indian Territory, Robertson capitulated and telephoned on July 13 to assure Roe that there had been no transfer. The Giants finished the season in South McAlester forty games behind champion Pittsburg.

O. H. Baldwin managed the Pittsburg "Irish Brigade" for owner W. M. Schiefelbein to the 1905 Missouri Valley League Championship. He played for the 1904 Pittsburg club.

About the time of the attempted putsch, Pittsburg began agitating for a Kansas State League that would drop the Indian Territory members. Nothing came of that in 1905 but a fault line was exposed that would assure the Missouri Valley League would not continue in 1906. At that same meeting, Tom C. Hayden of Webb City succeeded Judge Frankenberger and J. F. Darby replaced Garland Marrs while a new schedule with less frequent trips

was drawn to begin on July 6 and end September 26. But even that did not cure all the ills. For example, Vinita moved a home series to Muskogee because the gate and guarantee there, some $230, would net more than a home stand plus the cost of a round trip was saved. By the third week of August, Pittsburg had an insurmountable lead in the standings and, after Muskogee disbanded on September 1, to stanch the financial bleeding, the owners agreed to end the season on September 5. When the dust settled, the Missouri Valley League final results showed Pittsburg on top.

Pittsburg Irish Brigade	75	26
Parsons Preachers	61	40
Muskogee Reds	52	46
Ft. Scott Hay Diggers	49	52
Webb City Gold Bugs	47	54
Tulsa Oilers	44	58
Vinita Cherokees	41	63
South McAlester Giants	33	63

As noted, the biggest threat to the Missouri Valley League was the internal division created by geography. The northern teams in Missouri and Kansas were in close proximity and traveling costs were minimal. Trips into the Indian Territory, especially to South McAlester, were costly and consumed a visitor's guarantee payment. The Indian Territory teams actually outdrew the northern clubs but the profits all went to the railroads. A poorly drafted first half schedule had dramatically increased travel expenses. While ameliorated with the new schedule, there was bad blood created between the Territorians and Staters that extended to the playing field. Contests between clubs from the north and south were fraught with fines, ejections and suspensions for fighting and umpire-baiting.

MISSOURI VALLEY IN THE MAJORS

For a league that lasted but a single season, the Missouri Valley League produced five players who appeared in the major leagues. In addition to Chick Brandom [page 147], Babe Adams, Raleigh Aitchison, Charlie Rhodes, and Joe Crisp saw action

Babe Adams (1882-1968) of Parsons spent 1906 with the St. Louis Cardinals and was 194-139 for the Pittsburgh Pirates between 1907 and 1926.

Raleigh Aitchison (1887-1958) of 1905 Vinita and Tulsa threw for the Brooklyn Robins in 1911, 1914 and 1915.

Charlie Rhodes (1885-1918) was 7-11 in four seasons for the Cardinals and Cincinnati.

Tulsa's Joe Crisp (1885-1939) ended the 1910 and began the 1911 seasons for the St. Louis Browns getting a single in his two major league at bats.

The two factions divorced at the league's first and only annual meeting. Webb City joined the Western Association. The three Kansas teams joined a newly formed Kansas State League. The "old guard" met in January, 1906 to form the South Central League, a six-member circuit centered in the Indian Territory and the east portion of Oklahoma Territory. As league president Robertson, who would be the first president of the South Central League, penned in the 1906 *Spalding's Official Base Ball Guide*:

> Thus, as an experiment, the Missouri Valley League was a success: it led to a better and stronger league.

SOUTH CENTRAL LEAGUE 1906

The South Central League grew out of the differing requirements of the northern and southern cities of the 1905 Missouri Valley League. After agreeing to go their own ways, the southern tier of the Missouri Valley comprised of Muskogee, Tulsa, and South McAlester in the Indian Territory recruited Oklahoma Territory's Guthrie, recently dropped from the Western Association, and Shawnee, out of Organized Baseball since the Southwestern League Browns folded, to form the core of a league. El Reno had been selected as a seventh team and the last slot would go to Arkansas City, Pawnee, Cleveland, Enid, Ft. Smith or Bartlesville. When the cities met ten days later, Enid and El Reno failed to send representatives and a six team league was decided on with Ft. Smith replacing Arkansas City.

The owners tried to draft Orville Frantz, brother and private secretary to Territorial Governor Frank Frantz and one of Harvard's greatest athletes, as figurehead president. He refused but consented to being named a hands-off vice-pres-

Orville Frantz served as private secretary to his brother, Frank Frantz, Oklahoma's last Territorial Governor. He was one of Harvard University's greatest athletes and coached the 1904 Crimson nine.

J. B. "Bun" McAlester played for the 1905 South McAlester Giants. His father was J. J. McAlester, founder of McAlester, and an early Oklahoma lieutenant governor. He relinquished his post as South Central League president to save the Shawnee franchise.

ident. Son of the founder of McAlester and a ball player, J. B. "Bun" McAlester, was elected president.

The field managers were seasoned. Ben "Dad" Bennett had led Guthrie in the Western Association. J. B. Roe managed Sedalia in 1902 and South McAlester in the Missouri Valley League the year before. Jimmie Callahan, manager of the Chicago White Sox in 1903 and 1904, continued his trade at Muskogee. Charles Shafft, the interloper who conspired to steal the 1905 South McAlester club, opened the season for Tulsa but soon returned to playing the outfield with St. Joseph in the Western

Jimmy Callahan (1874-1934) between 1894 and 1917 played for or managed the Chicago White Sox, Chicago Cubs, and Pittsburgh Pirates. He began 1906 with Muskogee but, seeing how much money White Sox owner Charles Comiskey was making, bought the Chicago Logan Square semi-pros whom he operated as an "outlaw" through 1910. He organized the successful 1913 Cubs-Giants barnstorming tour. He later was a successful construction executive.

Association. F. H. "Cap" Smith, a pitcher, took over command of the Oilers. Jimmy Fernandez, a hurler from the 1892 Texas League, led Ft. Smith. South McAlester was under the tutelage of sexagenarian Deacon White whose career spanned back to 1871.

South McAlester and Ft. Smith began the season a week early with the Miners sweeping the series. While those two clubs "loafed" around South McAlester, the rest of the league began play solidly if uneventfully.

Not long into the season one of the franchises got into a financial bind by failing to construct a grandstand, paying high salaries, and the manager's profligacy. Shawnee Blues owner and manager Roe twice ran out of funds while on the road. Home attendance was negligible because he failed to follow through on erection of a grandstand promised before the season began.

On May 26, league president McAlester resigned to take over management of the Blues on and off the field, ousting Roe in the interim. Orville Frantz reluctantly stepped into the top spot until June 14 when he walked away and left the mess with P. D. Harper whose only appearance in baseball —or apparently anywhere else— was in the front office of the South Central.

McAlester had temporarily saved the Shawnee franchise along with much local support in the form of a new ownership group led by C. F. Barrett, who ran a dry goods store, in the office and Roy Congdon, the laundry owner who had managed the Shawnee Statehoods in 1902, on the field. On June 7, the Shawnee Baseball Association directed Congdon to cancel the series with Ft. Smith that was to begin the following day due to the imminent insolvency of the club. As the local association had not assumed Roe's debts, it was problematic whether it would continue with the franchise. Somehow Shawnee remained on the field. Norman Nelson —another person unknown in baseball— turned around the ball club and added seven new position players. The fans were placated.

Because the league's records were in a state of disarray with not even the standings discernable, the owners decided to begin a new season on July 6 and erase the results since May 1. During the hiatus between seasons, there was speculation from players who had come to visit Oklahoma City, Leo Hite of Shawnee and Harry Womack of Guthrie, that the Capital City's team would be removed to Enid. It turned out to be just speculation. The next rumor would not be.

Coming from Guthrie though Oklahoma City on the way to South McAlester, on July 22 the Ft. Smith players reported that the Guthrie team had disbanded the day before and that Shawnee would be dropped, leaving a new four-member league. That was exactly what happened. President Harper telephoned Congdon to break the news that the Blues were out. The fans were livid and threatened litigation as well as a protest to the National Association.

For the next couple of weeks, the remaining teams played a round robin until on August 7, Tulsa gave up. Shawnee announced that the Oilers, under the new ownership of J. B. Roe, would be moving there to finish the season. Muskogee was scheduled to arrive in Shawnee on August 9.

At Ft. Smith, Muskogee learned what had happened. After consulting with Harper and explaining the financial strain that the extra travel to and from Shawnee would cause, the decision was made to disband. Before the scheduled league game in Ft. Smith, the two managers agreed to play an exhibi-

tion game for the benefit of the players. It ended in tens: ten innings, ten runs each. The game was called so Muskogee could catch the train home. No player records were kept. The finish:

South McAlester Miners	59	32
Muskogee Indians	50	38
Ft. Smith Razorbacks	47	39
Tulsa Oilers	45	42
Shawnee Blues	29	24
Guthrie Senators	18	55

Once again, a new league would emerge for 1907, this time from the remains of the South Central and the Kansas State leagues under the name Oklahoma-Arkansas-Kansas League.

KANSAS STATE LEAGUE 1906

Organized in 1905 by towns too small to be included in a Class C loop like the Missouri Valley League, for 1906 a new slate of ball clubs appeared including its only Territorial town, Bartlesville with a Statehood population of 4,215. A member of Class D, the league disbanded following the 1906 season, re-organized for 1909-1911 and after a two-season hiatus finished its life in 1914.

Competing against Missouri Valley League alumni Iola, Cherryvale, Parsons, Chanute, Ft. Scott, Coffeyville, and Pittsburg, the Bartlesville Indians, the town's first professional representative, managed to finish the season in fifth place among six survivors.

On June 6, Pittsburg with a winning 16-15 record but empty treasury removed to Vinita, I.T. When the Vinita club became insolvent and disbanded under just one month later on July 5, the

Gus Alberts (1860-1912) managed Bartlesville in 1906 and 1908. He spent part of 1884 with the Pittsburgh Alleghanys and Washington Nationals, 1888 as the Cleveland Blues' regular shortstop, and 1891 briefly with the Milwaukee Brewers.

Larry Cheney (1886-1969) spent 1906, 1907, and 1908 with Bartlesville before leading the National League with twenty-six wins in 1912. He played for the Cubs, Brooklyn Robins, Philadelphia Phillies, and Boston Braves between 1911 and 1919 compiling a 116-100 career record.

Bartlesville's first professional team, the 1906 Bartlesville Indians of the Kansas State League.

record revealed that fourteen wins had been added against ten losses. Ft. Scott joined Vinita in the figurative showers to reduce the Kansas State League to six.

Gus Alberts, at age forty-six a veteran of parts of three major league seasons, led the Indians on the field. To pay for the last part of the season, Bartlesville sold Larry Cheney, who owned the best record in the league with nineteen wins against four losses, to the White Sox on August 15. An August 12 report that the Kansas State League had followed the South Central League into oblivion when Parsons disbanded turned out to be false on both counts. Bartlesville finished its 110-game season.

Independence Coyotes	69	48
Iola Grays/		
Cherryvale Boosters	62	50
Parsons Preachers	60	50
Coffeyville Bricks	58	50
Bartlesville Indians	51	64
Chanute Browns	31	82
Ft. Scott Giants	35	18
Pittsburg Champs/		
Vinita	30	25

Once again, a minor league with Oklahoma teams failed to survive. Iola, Ft. Scott, Chanute would be out of Organized Baseball in 1907 and Vinita forever. Bartlesville led Coffeyville, Independence, and Parsons into a new league rising from the ashes of the South Central that would be called the Oklahoma-Arkansas-Kansas League.

OKLAHOMA-ARKANSAS-KANSAS LEAGUE 1907

OKLAHOMA-KANSAS LEAGUE 1908

1907

The March 5, 1907 edition of *The Daily Oklahoman* carried a headline "State League is Organized." The article stated that in the parlor of Oklahoma City's Lee Hotel president Joseph B. Roe of Shawnee and secretary Al J. Jennings of Lawton (treasurer was left vacant presumably due to lack of treasury) along with Charles Palmer of El Reno, Deacon White for South McAlester, and Bert McFadden representing Enid had agreed to form a new league. Additional target cities were Ardmore,

Chickasha and Muskogee. The piece concluded

The new league will start the season under the most favorable auspices, and each club is pledged to put up forfeit money of $200 to play out the season.

Ten days later it was reported that the New State League had granted six franchises to South McAlester, Enid, Lawton, Shawnee, Chickasha, and Muskogee. Roe stated that Ft. Smith wanted in and that if that city joined, Ardmore would follow. He denied that he was being ousted from the top job. With teams putting up $300 each, D. A. Duncan, the incumbent treasurer of the Oklahoma City Baseball Association, was named treasurer of the new league. This New State League never came together.

The Oklahoma league that played in 1907 was a continuation of the stronger clubs from the South Central and Kansas State leagues. The differences between the1907 and 1908 league were twofold: Parsons and Ft. Smith were dropped after the 1907 season and "Arkansas" was removed from the name. The 1907 Spalding's Official Baseball Guide states that the O-A-K was simply a name change of the Kansas State League.

Fred McDaniel continued as president while newspaper man Dan M. Carr of Bartlesville became acting secretary, both on a *gratis* basis. None of the people who joined with Roe's New State League pipedream were involved in either the Oklahoma-Arkansas-Kansas League nor the Oklahoma-Kansas League

Excessive rain forced Parsons (in seventh place) and South McAlester (in fourth place) to withdraw on June 1. A Blue Law in Arkansas

Fred McDaniel (1872-?), reared by an aunt and educated at the Cherokee Asylum for Orphans, came to Bartlesville in 1900 and later served as mayor from 1903-1908. Preliminary to statehood, he chaired the commission that would wind up the affairs of the Cherokee Nation government. Leading the O-A-K League was a continuation of his leadership of the 1906 Kansas State League.

Bartlesville's Boosters won both halves of the 1907 season and the only Oklahoma-Arkansas-Kansas League pennant. ABOVE: First Half Upper L-R: McClintock, Hutchinson, Love. St. John, Bradbury, Thomason. First Half Seated L-R : Bartley, Cheney, Campbell, White, Roth, Taylor. BELOW: Second Half Upper: McCullum, Reddick, Hodge, Foley, Lamb. Lower L-R: Killalay, Thomason (11), McClintock, Ed "Deacon" White, (9 not identified), Ed Pinkerton, (12 not identified).

barred Sunday baseball making it remarkable that the Ft. Smith club (in fifth place) lasted until August 16. To reduce the league to four, Tulsa (in last place) agreed to drop out of the pennant race provided it could play out the season against Bartlesville, Coffeyville, Independence and Muskogee. The foursome with tag-along Tulsa played through September 16. Bartlesville finished on top in both the first section ending August 16 (60-38) and the second section (24-13).

Howard McClintock of Bartlesville led the O-A-K with thirty-two wins against only six losses. Boosters' slugger Davey White, soon to appear for Oklahoma City, led with 135 hits while Fred Hutchinson scored eighty-four runs. Pitching dominated the O-A-K; the highest batting average was only .292 by Ernie Wilson of third-place Independence. The overall standings:

Bartlesville Boosters	84	51
Coffeeville Glassblowers	71	57
Independence Champs	68	63
Muskogee Redskins	63	70
Ft. Smith Soldiers	40	46
McAlester Miners	11	17
Tulsa Oilers	37	60
Parsons Preachers	10	19

Roy St. John stopped by to play shortstop for the 1907 Boosters during a seven season professional career.

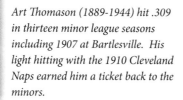

Art Thomason (1889-1944) hit .309 in thirteen minor league seasons including 1907 at Bartlesville. His light hitting with the 1910 Cleveland Naps earned him a ticket back to the minors.

1908

For 1908, Western Association president Doc Shively added the O-K loop to his duties. The Class D Oklahoma-Kansas League began the 1908 season in six cities —Bartlesville, Independence, Muskogee, Iola, and McAlester. McAlester and Iola disbanded during July. League fans were treated to back-to back no-hitters. Gene Packard of Independence threw a perfect game at Bartlesville on August 8. The next day Harry Killilay led Tulsa over Muskogee by a seven to one tally. Individual records were never compiled. Bartlesville would defeat Muskogee two games to none for the first half title, but would lose the finals to Tulsa in all three games. Because of records discrepancy, both Bartlesville and Tulsa could now claim the regular season title of 1908.

Ray Powell (1888-1962) played between his rookie season with Bartlesville in 1908 and 1936. He hit .294 in nineteen minor league seasons. Following a brief appearance in early 1913 with Detroit, he returned to the majors in 1917 where he was a regular outfielder for the Boston Braves through 1924. He managed in the Yankees' farm system 1939-1942 and last wore flannels in 1946 for Cleveland's class D club at Appleton, Wisconsin. He managed Shawnee's Western Association Robins in 1929 and 1930.

Joe Kelly (1886-1977) was a 1908 alumnus of the Oklahoma-Kansas League who hit .302 for Tulsa as a rookie outfielder. Between 1914 and 1919, he appeared in 376 major league games for Boston, Chicago and Pittsburgh in the National League. He played twenty seasons in the minors, sixteen of which were in classes A and AA. His last at bat was in 1930 as manager of the Oklahoma City Indians.

Bartlesville Boosters	71	50
Tulsa Oilers	69	55
Independence Jewelers	66	58
Muskogee Redskins	58	66
Iola Champs	32	34
McAlester Miners	17	47

Of the Oklahoma cities that were members of the O-A-K and O-K Leagues, only Muskogee and Bartlesville would be in Organized Baseball in 1909.

TEXAS-OKLAHOMA LEAGUE 1911-1914

Professional baseball along the Red River was first played in the Texas League as early as 1896 in the towns of Denison and Paris, then, after the Paris club failed, in Sherman. Another failed Paris team found a home in Ardmore, I.T. in 1904. While there were strong semi-pro teams in Denton, Denison, Sherman and Indian Territory towns including Ardmore, Tishomingo, Durant, South McAlester, and Coalgate among others, the first stab at forming a professional league of river cities was not taken until 1911.

While a member of the National Association of Professional Baseball Leagues and thus part of Organized Baseball, the Texas-Oklahoma League never appears in the directory of leagues that appeared annually in *The Sporting News* although the baseball Bible reported about it periodically. Record keeping was sporadic until C. O. Johnson became president before the 1913 season. There are not, therefore, official season statistics for 1911 and 1912.

1911

The driving force behind formation of the Texas-Oklahoma League was Wichita Falls electric streetcar and interurban entrepreneur, F. P. St. Clair. He convened representatives from Ardmore and Durant in Oklahoma and Sherman, Denison, and Gainesville in Texas at his home city during the last week of January, 1911. Wichita Falls, Ardmore, and Durant walked away with franchises. When the next meeting was held on March 24, D. A. Hatcox and J. M. Yarborough held the Durant franchise, the Cleburne Board of Trade got the rights in that town, Dr. C.R. Johnston and J. Stone owned the Gainesville slot, St. Clair's Traction Company held the Wichita Fall territory, and Emmett Roger's Ardmore Baseball Club owned that city's entry. A sixth franchise was being bid for by Lawton, Chickasha and Corsicana. The representatives elected St. Clair as president and Eugene A. Barnes, a past owner and manager of the Oklahoma City Mets, as secretary-treasurer.

Eugene Barnes at age sixteen stacked 2 x 12's on beer kegs to form the first baseball grandstand in Oklahoma City in July, 1889. He pitched for San Antonio in the 1899 Texas League, for the 1903 semi-pro Oklahoma City Mets, and the 1905 Tulsa Oilers in the Missouri Valley League. He owned the 1904 Oklahoma City Mets and 1921 Ardmore Peps of the Texas-Oklahoma League. He was a "neutral" officer in the new Texas-Oklahoma League.

Billy McCurren, who was trying to form a competing circuit of Lawton, Altus, Chickasha and Bowie, Texas, made an unsuccessful play for a Texas-Oklahoma franchise. In April, with the backing of a wealthy merchant and a bank president, Lawton received a club as did Altus and Bonham, Texas.

39

The league attracted some seasoned hands as well as some novices as field managers. Jimmie Humphries, who would run the Oklahoma City Indians for thirty-eight years, led the Bonham Boosters. Former major league catcher and founder of the Southwestern League, Emmett Rogers, headed the Ardmore Blues until replaced by George McAvoy, manager of the late Sapulpa club of the Western Association. Muggsy Monroe, a past mainstay for Oklahoma City and Guthrie, guided the Altus Chiefs until fired over trading away popular players. The Durant Educators began under local semi-pro player W. W. Washington who was followed by a pair of aging major leaguers and then

Jiggs Donohue (1879-1913) played all but five of his 813 major league games in the American League with the White Sox, Browns, and Senators batting .255. His final season in Organized Baseball began at Cleburne and finished with Galveston in the Texas League.

After twenty-three games behind the plate for the 1911 Ft. Worth Cats, Art Ritter moved down the line to Cleburne where he succeeded Jiggs Donohue. He led his club to the Texas-Oklahoma League pennant then duplicated the feat in 1912 in the revived South Central League.

Up from the semi-pro ranks, "Cap" Morris led Wichita Falls to Texas-Oklahoma League titles in 1911 and 1912. After the 1913 move of the Drillers to Hugo, he was released. He led Durant in 1914.

a duo of league and semi-pro journeymen players. Locals John Stone and George Morris captained Gainesville's Blue Ribbons. The Cleburne Railroaders' trip to the pennant was guided first by veterans Will Reed and former White Sox outfielder Jiggs Donohue and, finally, by Arthur L. Ritter who would also lead Cleburne's 1912 entry in a different league. Infielder and pitcher Fred "Cap" Morris followed veteran catcher Dick Naylor of Krum, Texas at the helm of St. Clair's Wichita Fall Irish Lads. Lawton's Medicine Men were managed by attorney C. O. Clark until a catcher from the disbanded Wellington, Kansas ball club named Ed Pinkerton came in on June 2 to preside over the club's final two weeks. Until Pinkerton, young Nebraskan William B. Metcalfe captained the team between the lines.

A *sine qua non* to success in the low minors was minimization of travel. The only route from one city to another was the railroad and, for very short runs, interurbans. Four of the Texas teams were on the Katy line running from Wichita Falls through Gainesville and the "Gate City" Denison to Bonham; Durant was just up the spur from Denison. The Missouri Pacific served Bonham and Sherman. The Wichita Falls & Northwestern as well as the Katy ran from the Falls to Altus and the Frisco from Altus to Lawton and Ardmore. The Santa Fe made a straight shot from its large yard in Cleburne to Gainesville to Ardmore. Getting around the Texas-Oklahoma circuit was no trouble.

Blue Laws forbidding labor on the Sabbath were the bane of baseball. Two examples:

- On May 14 Altus arrived in Durant only to learn that new District Judge A. H. Ferguson had ruled that professional baseball on Sundays violated the Oklahoma law against Sunday labor. Meanwhile, the Durant team coming directly from Wichita Falls was in Altus ready to play.
- Three weeks later, the Lawton and Durant clubs were arrested for Sabbath-breaking. Captain Metcalfe stayed behind as a prisoner of Bryan County pending court appearance.

The solution to Sunday baseball in two towns, Ardmore and Cleburne, was to locate ball parks outside the city limits. Sunday games drew the largest crowds, easily equaling the other days combined, and were the most profitable. Losing that big payday could well cause a franchise to fail.

Wagering was endemic in the low minors, especially in places not far removed from the frontier. President St. Clair issued a statement and admonition about gambling on May 18:

> We have learned that a great deal of betting has been practiced in [Wichita Falls] and at other parks in the league; and it must stop. If continued it will demoralize the sport, and besides it is not conducive to [a] clean sport such as baseball is, has been, and always should be. Not only from a moral standpoint are we making this announcement, but from a commercial standpoint as well, as the better element of the public will not continue to attend games where betting is practiced. At the outset it came to our ears that a little betting was indulged in and that it would cease to be, but it has been growing more frequent, if reports are true, and this announcement is made. We mean business and if betting is indulged in the parks in future we will make effort to prosecute the offenders.

The extent to which the league members observed it is never mentioned.

The first section of the schedule began April 25 and ran through June 7. The most notable feats of the first weeks came from the mound. Durant's J.R. McKee tossed a five-inning no-hitter on May 17 against Gainesville; the game was shortened due to travel. But for a scorer's refusal to change his mind on a questionable infield tap, Hinton rookie John Daugherty of Lawton would have had a nine-inning

gem against Ardmore on May 26. The end of the first section found Wichita Falls firmly in first place with Altus, Ardmore and Durant within one-half game of each other. Bonham, Gainesville, Cleburne and Lawton, in that order, formed the second division. Wichita Falls' success was in its team batting average of over .330; Altus was second at .287. Seemingly batting could compensate for poor glove work as second place Altus fielded a miserable .878. First half standings were:

Wichita Falls Irish Lads	29	9
Altus Chiefs	23	19
Ardmore Blues	24	20
Durant Educators	23	20
Bonham Boosters	19	24
Gainesville Blue Ribbons	17	23
Cleburne Railroaders	16	24
Lawton Medicine Men	15	27

As the June 16 *Lawton Daily News* reported "[N]ot a club on the circuit is more than paying expenses, win or lose and many of them are making up deficits by popular subscriptions. This can't last long." Nonetheless, a new schedule covering June 9 through July 7 was optimistically adopted.

There was a general acknowledgment among the other teams that Wichita Falls received favorable treatment and that to prevail in games there, the visitors had to "slaughter" the Irish Lads. As reported in Lawton, "[W]ith anything like a close score, the umpires always give the Wichita crowd the best of it and let them win."

Former Lawton player and Ardmore's center fielder, Hugh "Joe" McCullum, reported to his manager, Emmett Rogers, that he overheard President St. Clair say to an umpire "[y]ou know that Wichita Falls gets the edge on all close decisions." When this wound its way through the rumor mill to St.

Clair, he suspended McCullum for fifty days and fined him $50 (roughly half a month's pay). St. Clair telephoned Lawton manager Clark insisting that he not let McCullum play in the first game there; Ardmore played it under protest claiming the suspension was illegal.

Hugh McCullum (sometimes "McCollom" "McCullom" and also known as Joe McCollum") played in and around Oklahoma and Texas for over a decade with a number of teams: 1904 Corsicana, Paris and Ardmore, 1905 South McAlester, 1906 South McAlester and Webb City, 1907 Ft. Smith and Bartlesville, 1908-1909 Bartlesville, 1910 Arkansas City, 1911 Lawton and Ardmore, and 1914 Ennis, Texas where he led the Central Texas League in batting.

Chickasha, Oklahoma had enjoyed professional baseball as a member of the 1904 Southwestern League. A group tried to buy the Altus franchise with the intent of relocating; nothing came of it because, first, the league owners didn't like the rail connection and, secondly, Chickasha hadn't supported its last team. Shortly after losing at home to Wichita Falls on June 15 by a score of eleven to four, the Gainesville club disbanded. "Loose management" that soon ran out of operating capital was the reason for failure. Before the players went their several ways, they were kept together briefly awaiting word of whether Chickasha would take the Blue Ribbons. Muggsy Monroe, late Altus manager, was actively lobbying for the lead position if the club moved from the Red River to the banks of the Washita. Banker Ben Johnson was behind the attempt to return baseball to Chickasha but he could get no traction. The league was "drifting onto the rocks" and the first

visible sign of the impending wreck was the Gainesville failure. On June 16, the Texas-Oklahoma League had seven teams.

Gainesville disbanding most directly impacted Lawton of the all the remaining teams. The seventh place Blue Ribbons had been the only club that the Medicine Men had consistently beaten. Gainesville was due in Lawton for a four-game series over three days beginning June 16. Lawton couldn't withstand a three day hiatus without revenue. As things turned out, Lawton played its final game, "one of the prettiest and snappiest of the season," also on June 15 losing at Altus by a single run. The Medicine Men returned home, disbanded on the news that they would have no opponent or cash for the next few days, and scattered the following day.

Ardmore reorganized on June 14 with Rogers out and a new manager, a refugee from the Sapulpa club in the recently disbanded Western Association, George McAvoy, taking control on June 20. The league fathers produced a new schedule to accommodate a six-team circuit with games played before June 22 counting toward the first half race. The second half was to run to season-end in September.

As the second half began, Altus became the outlier with open talk of that club being moved to Hugo, Denison, or Corsicana to reduce travel expense. Altus disbanded for the first time on July 11. With Thomas "Dad" Campbell out as manager, the team came back together under the leadership of George Partain, who tried to place the Chiefs in Hugo or Greenville, only to finally wind up after July 19 as a semi-pro group playing from Honey Grove, Texas. *The Daily Oklahoman* predicted that the Texas-Oklahoma League would follow the Kansas State League into oblivion.

President St. Clair had been losing money

all season with his Irish Lads. The gates were not enough to pay the visitors' guarantees much less make expenses for the home team. He put his franchise on the block on July 20 and contemplated making them a road team for the balance of the season. With only five clubs left in the league, there was discussion of dropping Cleburne, now the outlier. That was never more than talk and in fact Cleburne won the pennant.

Ardmore was the next franchise to go *in extremis*. Following a series of games with Wichita Falls at the Comanche, Oklahoma, Fair, a poorly attended but enthusiastic town meeting was held. Realizing that if the Blues dropped out the Texas-Oklahoma League would fail, Ardmoreites scraped together $300 plus another $1,200 for salaries to finish the schedule.

The 1911 season was mercifully shortened to August 23. The five franchises still standing finished:

Cleburne Railroaders	36	20
Durant Educators	32	24
Bonham Boosters	31	26
Wichita Falls Irish Lads	25	26
Ardmore Blues	24	28

In a report from the *Dallas Morning News*, a runaway pennant race with Wichita Falls dominating the first half was considered to be the cause of the financial instability of the league and the cause for three of eight franchises failing along the way; "[i]t is not known whether the league will continue next season or not." The season ended in contention. Cleburne was declared the 1911 champion when, down by one game, Wichita Falls refused to play further claiming that Railroaders' pitcher Charlie Deardorff, who had tossed a seven-inning no-hitter at Bonham on August 15, was ineligible

and that the Irish Lads were owed for trips to Cleburne during the season. Texas League champion Austin challenged the Railroaders to a series to determine the champion of the Lone Star State. Cleburne declined the challenge because the players had already scattered. Art Naylor led with a .377 season batting average and 136 hits. Wichita Fall team mates swept the remaining hitting categories with Bill Brown scoring seventy-nine runs and Cliff Witherspoon sixteen rounder trippers. Hetty Green, who would see duty with Durant, had a league best eighteen and five record. Roy Grady of Durant was the only player from a team other than the Irish Lads to lead a category with his 181 strike outs.

1912

The members of the Texas-Oklahoma League did not formally dissolve the circuit but separately walked away. It was reborn at Durant on the Wednesday before Thanksgiving when a group met to promote a new, compact Texas-Oklahoma League composed of teams from Durant, Ardmore, and Hugo in Oklahoma and Denison, Sherman, Paris, Bonham, Greenville, McKinney, and Gainesville in Texas. V. E. Kendall of Durant was sent to visit those cities as the baseball missionary.

A threat appeared from the organizer of a potentially competing league who planned to include several of the Texas-Oklahoma targets. A meeting was hurriedly called to short circuit that attempt. The Texas-Oklahoma League was informally revived at Wichita Falls on January 29, 1912 with Durant, Ardmore, Denison, Sherman, McKinney, Wichita Falls, Bonham, and either Paris or Greenville forming the loop. In March of 1912, under the leadership of T. D. "Ted" Newcomb of Sherman, the league was reorganized. The 1912 season

Elijah "Jimmie" Humphries is best known as the secretary, business manager, and later owner of the Oklahoma City Indians from 1919 until the franchise was moved to Corpus Christi and He managed Bonham and Sherman 1911-1913, played for Paris and Durant in 1914, and managed McAlester 1915-1917. He came to Oklahoma City with Jack Holland's move of his 1918 Hutchinson club in the Western League. He purchased the Indians from Bill Veeck in 1951 for a box of cigars.

was to begin April 25 and end on July 28 for the eight-team line up. Four cities returned from 1911, all under new names: the Ardmore Giants, Bonham Tigers, Durant Hustlers and Wichita Falls Drillers. Newcomers were the Sherman Cubs, Denison Katydids, Greenville Highlanders, and McKinney, Texas, no-names. Familiar faces from 1911 were Jimmie Humphries at Sherman, George McAvoy at Ardmore, Fred Morris at Wichita Falls, and Hetty Green at Durant. E. E. Barclay, also of Sherman was elected secretary-treasurer. Umpires for 1912 were Lucky Wright of Houston, W.A. Sullivan of Galveston, L.A. McLouglin of Cleveland, Tennessee, Brooks Gordon of Callac, Missouri, and E. Nugent of Omaha. After the season began, Newcomb and Barclay stepped aside and H. L. Warren and R. A. Atkins, both of Greenville, replaced them at a special meeting on May 24 1912 at Sherman. C. O. Johnson and R. M. Finley, both of Durant, succeeded Warren and Atkins later in the season and would serve through the 1914 season.

The season began on April 25 for ninety-five games. Five days into it, Wingo Anderson of Bonham tossed the season's first no-hitter at McKinney for a nine to zero win.

BONHAM: A GOOD BASEBALL TOWN

Like Ardmore, Bonham, the seat of Fannin County on the Red River, fielded a team in the Texas-Oklahoma League in all six seasons of its operation (1911-1914, 1921-1922). The city's ball clubs were unique in that each operated under a different name (Boosters, Tigers, Blues, Sliders, Favorites, Bingers). Baseball was played in a small ball park in the middle of town.

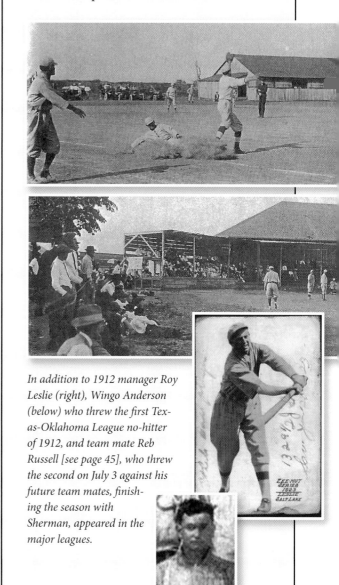

In addition to 1912 manager Roy Leslie (right), Wingo Anderson (below) who threw the first Texas-Oklahoma League no-hitter of 1912, and team mate Reb Russell [see page 45], who threw the second on July 3 against his future team mates, finishing the season with Sherman, appeared in the major leagues.

It was thirty-nine games into the season before the league lost members. On June 7, secretary Atkins' club, the Greenville Highlanders, with a record of fourteen wins against twenty-five losses, and the McKinney, Texas entry that had managed only six wins under three managers, disbanded. The league continued with six members. The short season finished on July 28. Wichita Falls was set to square-off against second half winner Ardmore. The seven-game championship series was shortened to three games when Ardmore manager and shortstop McAvoy was called up to the San Francisco Seals of the Pacific Coast League. When the Giants inexplicably disbanded on August 1, Wichita Falls was declared the winner. Unofficial statistics compiled by newspapers showed Ardmoreites George McAvoy topping the league with 68 runs and Art Naylor with 105 hits. Wichita Falls' Bill Brown had the highest average, .326, and manager Cap Morris led with nine homers. Bud Napier of Sherman had the best pitching record, twenty wins in twenty-seven decisions, while Reb Russell's 227 strike outs was most. Overall standings:

Ardmore Giants	62	32
Sherman Cubs	56	37
Bonham Tigers	53	35
Wichita Falls Drillers	52	38
Denison Katydids	44	49
Durant Hustlers	26	64
Greenville Highlanders	14	25
McKinney	6	33

League secretary Atkins selected a 1912 All-Star team. He listed Hayden Townsend of Sherman and Hornbuckle of Durant (and also Bonham) as receivers. The infield had two mangers, Bill Harper of Durant at third and Ardmore's George McAvoy at shortstop; slugger Charles Covington of Denison

and William Reed of Sherman filled out at first and second, respectively. He named an outfield of Collie Williamson from Sherman, Bill Brown from Wichita Falls, and Art Naylor of Ardmore. Buddy Napier of Sherman, Red Adams of Durant, Hetty Green from Denison, Ewell "Reb" Russell of Bonham, and Ovid Mullins of Wichita Falls were the dream hurling corps. Pennant winning Wichita Falls manager Fred Morris won top honors as a field general.

1912 DREAM TEAM

League Secretary and sports writer R. A. Atkins selected an All-Star team that included journeyman infielder Will Reed, future major leaguers Bud Napier and Reb Russell as well as Red Adams [see page 72] and Bill Brown [see page 129].

Reed *Napier* *Russell*

1913

In 1912 only a couple of teams lost money, three broke even and Denison had a $1,200 profit. All were owned by corporations.   For 1913 the league was back to eight members, Paris and Texarkana replacing Greenville and McKinney. On March 29, 1913 the league adopted a 108-game schedule instead of the ninety-five of 1912. Series were shortened to three games from four and the league divided into two loops: Texarkana, Paris, Bonham and Sherman in the east and Ardmore, Denison, Durant and Wichita Falls in the west. East clubs would play at west towns then west aggregations would take the train east, the whole idea being to reduce travel expense. Because the distance from Texarkana on the east and Wichita Falls on the west is some three hundred miles, the guarantee money paid to visitors would be $40 instead of the regular $30. This year only Durant and Bonham had ordinances banning Sunday baseball.

Opening day for 1913 would be on April 15 and the finale on August 8. Curiously, Bonham didn't make its first trip to Texarkana until two months and eleven days after the season began although Texarkana was at Bonham three times over the same period. At Denison a state of the art club house provided "every convenience possible for the players" including a locker for every player and three shower heads with hot and cold running water. At the pre-season meeting R.M. Finley and

J. W. Bailey represented the Durant Choctaws, DuPont Lyon and Jimmie Humphries the Sherman Lions, Fred Morris the Wichita Falls Drillers, and J. S. Patrick appeared on behalf of the Paris Boosters as did Dee Poindexter for his Texarkana Tigers, Dr. F.C. Allen was present for the Bonham Blues, for the Denison Blue Sox Fred Marcum and manager Aldridge "Babe" Peebles, and finally Morris Sass and Art Naylor for the Ardmore Giants. Field generals for the season start were Poindexter at Texarkana, Naylor for Ardmore, Claude Leslie at Bonham, Jimmie Humphries for Lyons' Lions at Sherman, Fred Morris returning to Wichita Falls, Stoney Jewell at Durant, Jack Jutzi at Paris, and Peebles, in the first of a five-season tenure, taking over Denison.

Two months into the season, President C. O. Johnson would raid his umpiring staff to provide a remarkably poor, struggling Ardmore club with a competent manager, veteran Brooks Gordon. He

Dee Poindexter played between 1902 and 1910 in the Texas League and Central Kansas League. He turned to managing in 1912 first with Tyler and then with Texarkana through 1913, finishing in the Central Texas League with Kaufman and Waxahachie in 1915 and 1916, respectively. His 1913 Tigers finished in third place.

Hailing from far south Texas, Babe Peebles was a player-manager for Denison in both the Texas-Oklahoma League (1913 and 1914) and Western Association (1915 and 1916) winning the pennant in each campaign. His 1917 Denison club finished in third place after local management clipped his wings by enforcing the league's salary cap and roster limit.

ED APPLETON
P.—Brooklyn Nationals
6

Ed Appleton (1892-1932) posted a 3.25 ERA in forty-eight appearances for the Brooklyn Robins in 1915 and 1916. As a sophomore for Sherman, he tossed the league's only no-hitter of 1913. Following military duty, he was five and five for Wichita Falls in the 1920 Texas League then spent the remainder of his career in class C and D leagues including stints with Ardmore in 1922 and 1923.

was able to pull the Giants out of the cellar only because Kid Speer's Durant Choctaws had two fewer wins and four more losses. Future Brooklyn Superba Ed Appleton threw the league's only no-hitter on July 6, winning by a score of four for Sherman and zero for Bonham.

Secretary Finley published unofficial statistics on July 15. Only ten players had batting averages above .300. Pitcher Ben Tincup led the pack bat-

Ben Tincup from Adair, I. T. (1893-1980) amassed a record of 251 wins against 199 loses in twenty-four minor league seasons. His last pitch was thrown at age forty-nine for the 1942 Fargo-Moorhead club of the Northern League. He spent 1914 and 1915 and parts of 1916, 1917, and 1918 with the Phillies. His last major league appearance was with the 1928 Cubs. He was with Sherman in 1912 and 1913 and managed Muskogee in 1938.

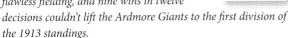

Liz Torrey played eight seasons in Organized Ball between his rookie year with the Nevada (Missouri) Lunatics of the Missouri Valley League in 1902 and his final season with the 1914 champion Texarkana Tigers. His bat, flawless fielding, and nine wins in twelve decisions couldn't lift the Ardmore Giants to the first division of the 1913 standings.

Sam Covington (1894-1963) was one of the baseball-playing brothers from Denison. He played in 1,833 minor league games between 1913 and 1927 as well as twenty games each for the 1913 St. Louis Browns and 1917-1918 Boston Braves. As a rookie he led the 1913 Texas-Oklahoma League with thirteen deadball home runs.

With a twenty and six record in his rookie season at Denison, Jim Haislip (1891-1970) of Farmersville, Texas earned a cup of coffee with the 1913 Phillies at season's end. He threw for Denison, Dallas, and Ft. Smith in 1914 and 1916 posting a 1.98 ERA in the minors.

ting .368. Texarkana catcher Al Ritter was next at .337. Pitcher Liz Torrey of Ardmore hit .323 and was flawless in the field. Through June 15, Ray Wakefield of Denison was tops with thirty-six stolen bases; at July 15 he had fifty-one; he finished with eighty. Sam Covington of Denison led in slugging with ten home runs, four triples, ten doubles and a .314 average.

At season end, Paris' .964 fielding percentage set the pace. The Oklahoma clubs were the worst: Durant .936, Ardmore .934 and .929 Hugo. The 1913 batting champion was Buddy Robinson of Durant at .312 with Paris' Ray Nagle just behind at .310. Sam Covington topped the circuit with thirteen home runs as Fred Nicholson of lowly Hugo led with 147 hits and ninety runs. Southpaw Joe Pate of Texarkana had the most wins with twenty-three. Jim Haslip and team mate Grady Higginbotham each won twenty while dropping only six at Denison for a league best .769 winning percentage. Sherman's Ben Tincup struck out 233 in 247 innings. The overall standings:

Denison Blue Sox	82	39
Paris Boosters	80	45
Texarkana Tigers	73	53
Sherman Lions	68	58
Bonham Blues	56	68
Wichita Falls Drillers/		
Hugo Hugoites	54	70
Ardmore Giants	43	80
Durant Choctaws	41	84

For the only season in its history, the league began and finished with eight members. There was one move, the Wichita Falls Drillers becoming the Hugo Hugoites on July 7. The smallest city in the league, Hugo would have league baseball until June 7, 1914.

1914

There was optimism and stability theretofore not experienced as the 1914 season began. There had been no franchise moves. Teams were under the same ownership. Johnson and Finley were back as league officers. The new umpires, George A. Mead of Portland Oregon, J. H. Carter, P. Roth, James H Murphy, and J. W. Moad, all had prior professional experience. A longer season, 126 games, was chosen.

The Hugo Scouts were the first to experience trouble. Heavy rains during the first home stand and the returning 1913 roster that just wouldn't jell under new manager Leo Ury made for a serious problem at the gate. By June 1, the club was $700 in the red plus it owed the league $550. A local effort to save the team failed. The Hugo Baseball Association turned back its franchise to the league office. With Ardmore now the outlier, the other clubs voted to drop it from the league on June 11. Denison was the big winner from the Hugo collapse, securing Tex Covington and future Hall of Famer Rogers

William "Tex" Covington (1887-1931) was Sam's elder brother. He won ten and lost seven for the 1911 and 1912 Detroit Tigers. Between 1907 and 1919, Tex won eighty against 105 losses. He last donned flannels in 1931 as manager of McAllen in the Rio Grande Valley League. He died in December of that year.

Hornsby. The McAlester club in the Western Association saw four Ardmore Indians join the hapless Miners. Sherman and Bonham held on until July 30. Denison, Paris, Texarkana, and Durant competed the season.

Three no-hitters were thrown in 1914. Red Adams of Denison had the first, an eight to one shellacking of Durant on June 7. Fritz Redford

of Bonham repeated the feat on June 22, with a seven to zero victory over Sherman. Dickie Kerr of Paris notched one of his twenty-three wins on July 25, embarrassing Denison by twelve runs to zero. Dickie Kerr's twenty-three win performance was the most while sophomore Robert Covington

Another pitcher from Denison, Robert Covington made his debut with Hugo in 1914 then finished that and the following two seasons with Denison posting forty-eight of his eighty career minor league wins. Following World War I, he threw for Petersburg, Virginia and finished pro ball in 1920 with the Western League's Oklahoma City Indians.

posted a .800 percentage with sixteen victories in twenty starts. Joe Neeley who divided the season between Bonham and Denison sent 198 batters back to the bench. Texarkana's Bill Stellbauer had the most hits, 151, and highest batting average, .351 while team mate C. H. O'Neal's seven round trippers was best. Ray Nagle whose .310 was second best in 1913 led with eighty runs. Texarkana bested Paris in four games for a pennant that would never be awarded.

The overall standings:

Paris Snappers	77	39
Texarkana Tigers	79	41
Denison Champions	68	49
Durant Gladiators	46	73
Bonham Sliders	47	58
Sherman Lions	30	75
Ardmore Indians	26	25
Hugo Scouts	19	32

Texarkana, Paris, Denison, and Durant met in early December to salvage the league for 1915. A new salary cap was set and Ardmore, McKinney, Sherman, and Bonham were invited to rejoin but showed little interest. President Johnson had

1914 Texarkana Tigers last champion of the pre-War Texas-Oklahoma League.

earlier absolutely refused to continue in his post and opined that the Durant merchants were exhausted and would not back a club again. A meeting was held on January 10, 1915 to consider the future. Denison and Paris wanted immediate release from the league to join the Western Association. Hoping Bonham would re-join, the members set January 15 as the drop dead date. The Texas-Oklahoma League officially went into mothballs on January 15. Denison, Sherman and Paris found homes in the Western Association for 1915. Ardmore would return to organized baseball when the 1917 Paris club sought refuge there as had its predecessor in 1904. Ardmore with Bonham would revive the Texas-Oklahoma League in 1921. Professional ball would not return to Texarkana until 1924. Hugo and Durant would never again have Organized Ball.

OKLAHOMA STATE LEAGUE 1912

Following the 1911 season, Oklahoma had but two members of Organized Baseball within its borders: the Ardmore Giants and Durant Choctaws of the Texas-Oklahoma League. The demise of the first edition of the Western Association left Sapulpa, Muskogee and Tulsa homeless. The genesis of the first Oklahoma State League was grounded in providing baseball in Oklahoma City for the 1912 campaign. How the new Capital almost missed that season deserves brief mention.

Oklahoma City had moved up to the Texas League in 1909 with R. E. Moist, prominent coal dealer, leading the Oklahoma City Base Ball Association as seventy-five percent shareholder. The three-season adventure was fraught with controversy, rancor, and litigation. The first point of contention was the guarantee to visiting teams. Within Texas it had always been $50. With Oklahoma City and Shreveport, however, it was double for visits there because of the travel distance. When Moist's club refused to pay the full $100 to visitors, those shorted simply recouped when the Indians came to their cities. There was bad blood between the Texas clubs and the two new outlanders. As Texas League historian W. E. Ruggles observed "[O]ut of state prejudice fanned Shreveport and Oklahoma City ire against Texas opposition. Field fights were common."

The other had to do with who owned the Oklahoma City ball club. Moist owned three-fourths of the shares of Oklahoma City Base Ball Association but held the Texas League franchise in his own name. On July 13, 1910 Moist sold the Texas League franchise to owner of the Night and Day Bank, Abner Davis described as "a stormy petrel of the Oklahoma courts" and one of the most colorful scoundrels in early Oklahoma. Davis successfully beat Oklahoma prosecutions for bank fraud and two separate federal indictments for mail fraud.

Tripartite litigation quickly began with Moist suing for payment, Davis claiming fraud, and the minority shareholders of the Association asserting they had been abused. Over the winter, Billy Kelsey, 1909 manager of the Indians, was appointed receiver of the franchise. As things finally wound up on April 1, 1911, Davis got

Litigious at the drop of a hat, Abner Davis was one of the most interesting white collar crooks of early Oklahoma, eluding federal and state prosecutors in Oklahoma and Tennessee. His Night and Day Bank failed but was one of the first that did not keep banker's hours.

the ball club, Moist got $7,500, the minority $4,120 and the receivership $1,300.

On February 3, 1912 Davis sold the operation to a group from Beaumont. As part of the agreement, he retained territorial rights to play Organized Baseball in Oklahoma City up until the day before the 1912 Texas League season began. As the Texas League was showing him the door, Davis announced that he was calling a meeting to form an Oklahoma league.

Thwarting the plans of local movers and shakers, in February, 1912, Davis announced that he would not give up his right even if Oklahoma City was awarded a Class A Western League franchise. His thinking was that he had lost $7,000 in the Texas League and that with the greater distances a Western League club would lose $15,000. Instead

Davis decided to apply for membership in the Mid-Continent League, after speaking with J. B. Bartlett of Tulsa who was organizing the loop. At the time, Tulsa, Bartlesville, Muskogee, and Ft. Smith were in and Oklahoma City, Guthrie, Shawnee, Enid or Lawton were prospects. A week later the Mid-Continent people rejected Davis' application, awarding it instead to A. E. "Doc" Monroney, Billy Kelsey, Davis' bitter enemy, and civic leaders including John Shartel, owner of the streetcar line that served the former Delmar Gardens where the ball park was located. To prevent Davis from blocking Monroney, the Mid-Continent members selected a season opening date two weeks after the Texas League started and after Davis' territorial rights expired. Davis countered with a threat to back out of the sale to Beaumont and keep the Texas League in Oklahoma City or seek his own Western League club.

Leo Meyer was an assistant under Oklahoma's first Secretary of State and then served as State Auditor from 1911-1913. A leader in the State's Jewish community, he was president of the Guthrie Base Ball Association before the Capital was moved to Oklahoma City. He was the only Jew to hold elective office in Oklahoma until 1994.

George "Billy" Kelsey (1881-1968) was Abner Davis' baseball nemisis. A light-hitting catcher, he played for Oklahoma City in 1908 and managed the city's first entry in the Texas League. When Davis sued the seller of the franchise, the court appointed Kelsey as receiver of the ball club to preserve it for 1911. He had appeared in two games for Pittsburgh at the end of the 1907 season. Before returning to his native Ohio for good, he managed the 1915 Tulsa entry in the Western Association.

Believing he had been doubled-crossed, Davis moved forward with his Oklahoma State League naming J. M. Postelle as president. His league, which would have smaller cities — El Reno, Guthrie, Anadarko, Chickasha and Enid— , fought a territorial battle with the Mid-Continent group over Oklahoma City and Shawnee. When J. H. Farrell, secretary of the National Association, ruled in Davis' favor, the Mid-Continent group retrenched.

Their choices were either merging into Davis' league as Farrell had strongly suggested or moving forward as a small town six-team loop. Their non-negotiable point was that El Reno, Anadarko and Enid would not be members of any consolidated league. Davis rejected the peace overtures from Tulsa. Davis did invite individual clubs from the eastern side of the State to make application for seats in the Oklahoma State League. The Mid-Continent's back was broken when the National Association recognized Davis' league and newly-elected State Auditor Leo Meyer became president of it with Okmulgee, Tulsa, Muskogee, and McAlester joining Oklahoma City, Guthrie and Anadarko. Holdenville would fill out the league.

The Anadarko, Holdenville, Guthrie, Okmulgee, and McAlester franchises were owned by local associations. Three were individually owned: Oklahoma City, by Abner Davis, Muskogee by former Carlisle Institute football and baseball star, Vick Kelly, and Tulsa by future Hall of Fame member Jake Beckley. Playing field managers were a solid

Jake Beckley (1867-1918) still holds the all-time record for chances and put outs by a first baseman. He was elected to the Hall of Fame in 1971. He was a fixture in the National League from 1888 through 1907 when he managed Tulsa in the Oklahoma-Arkansas-Kansas League and later led the 1910 Bartlesville club. He was awarded the Tulsa franchise in the new Oklahoma State League where his Terriers were in second place when the league was declared dissolved.

Herman "Chick" Leuttke played second base in Kansas and Oklahoma between 1904 and 1914 including 1909 and 1910 with Guthrie. Popular with the fans, he was selected to lead the no-names between the lines for the 1912 campaign where his team tied the Oklahoma City-Eufaula bunch for last place with fifteen wins in forty-eight outings.

Frank Gardner had led strong semi-pro teams at Okmulgee. He was the logical choice to head his city's first venture into league ball.

"A consistent all round fielder" according to Texas League historian William Ruggles, Jerry Kane made his debut in the Three-I League in 1904 and finished at Ft. Worth in 1913. In between he played seven seasons in the Texas League. He made three attempts as a team owner, none successful. His 1912 McAlester Miners failed when the league succumbed. After landing the Ft. Smith franchise in the newly constituted 1914 Western Association, he soon moved it to McAlester and, floundering financially, quickly sold it to local interests. His attempt to revive the orphaned Joplin ball club in Guthrie ended with the team disbanding after just ten days. He finished the 1914 season, his last, playing second base for Tulsa. He died in 1946.

group with William Reukauff for Oklahoma City, Herman "Chick" Leuttke at Guthrie, Vic Kelly, at Muskogee, Howard Price at Tulsa, Frank Gardner at Okmulgee, Jerry Kane for McAlester, Ray Ellison at Anadarko, and veteran Jimmy Bouldin leading Holdenville. A post-season series against the champion of the Texas League was proposed and, failing that, one against the winner of the Texas-Oklahoma League.

The season began April 30 on a high note with parades and large crowds at all the home openers. The fans at Okmulgee were treated to Powell Burnett's no-hitter against visiting Muskogee. Back in the Capital, Davis Field, on South Robinson at a bend in the North Canadian River near the Santa Fe tracks, was nearing completion but the Patterson Streetcar Line was inadequate to the task of transporting fans. From the outset, Oklahoma City, with a population approaching 70,000 was presumptively the cornerstone of the league. The other members with populations of from 25,000 (Tulsa) to 2,200 (Holdenville), were assumed to be the weak links. The success or failure of the Oklahoma State League hinged on the acumen of litigious innovative banker —his Night and Day Bank was open an unheard of thirteen hours daily— Abner Davis.

Schedule of Oklahoma State Baseball League, 1912

	At Anadarko	At Okla. City	At Guthrie	At Tulsa	At Okmulgee	At Muskogee	At McAlester	At Holdenville
Anadarko	READ	May 3, 4, 5 May *30, *30, 31 Sept. 1, *2, *2	May, 15, 16, 17 June 16, 17, 18 July 27, 28, 29	May 12, 13, 14 June 28, 29, 30 July 24, 25, 26	June 10, 11, 12 July 12, 13, 14 Aug. 8, 9, 10	June 13, 14, 15 July *4, *4, 5 Aug. 5, 6, 7.	May 21, 22, 23 July 15, 16, 17 Aug. 17, 18, 19	May 24, 25, 26 July *1, 2, 3 Aug. 20, 21, 22
Oklahoma City	Apr *30, May 1, 2 June 1, 2, 3 Aug. 29, 30, 31	THE	May 12, 13, 14 June 25, 26, 27 Aug. 26, 27, 28	May 27, 28, 29 June 22, 23, 24 Aug. 14, 15, 16	June 13, 14, 15 July *1, 2, 3 Aug. 5, 6. 7	June 10, 11, 12 July 21, 22, 23 Aug. 8, 9, 10	May 24, 25, 26 July 9, 10, 11 Aug. 20, 21, 22	May 21, 22, 23 July 18, 19, 20 Aug. 17, 18, 19
Guthrie	May 27, 28, 29 June 22, 23, 24 Aug. 23, 24, 25	May, 18, 19, 20 June 28, 29, 30 July 24, 25, 26	HERALD	May 3, 4, 5 May *30, *30, 31 Sept. 1, *2, *2	May 21, 22, 23 July 21, 22, 23 Aug. 17, 18, 19	May 24, 25, 26 July *1, 2, 3 Aug. 20, 21, 22	June 10, 11, 12 July 12, 13, 14 Aug. 8, 9, 10.	June 13, 14, 15 July *4, *4, 5 Aug. 5, 6, 7
Tulsa	May 18, 19, 20 June 19, 20, 21 Aug. 26, 27, 28	May 15, 16, 17 June 16, 17, 18 July 27, 28, 29	Apr *30, May 1, 2 June 1, 2, 3 Aug. 29, 30, 31	FOR	May 24, 25, 26 July 9, 10, 11 Aug. 20, 21, 22	May 21, 22, 23 July 18, 19, 20 Aug. 17, 18, 19	June 13, 14, 15 July 6, 7, 8 Aug. 5, 6, 7	June 10, 11, 12 July 15, 16, 17 Aug. 2, 3, 4
Okmulgee	May 6, 7, 8 July 18, 19, 20 Aug. 2, 3, 4	May 9, 10, 11 July 6, 7, 8 Aug. 23, 24, 25	May 15, 16, 17 July 15, 16, 17 Jul 30, 31, Aug 1	June 7, 8, 9 July *4, *4, 5 Aug. 11, 12, 13	THE BEST	May 3, 4, 5 May *30, *30, 31 Sept. 1, *2, *2	May, 15, 16, 17 June 16, 17, 18 Aug. 29, 30, 31	June 28, 29, 30 July 27, 28, 29
Muskogee	May, 9, 10, 11 July 6, 7, 8 Aug. 14, 15, 16	May 6, 7, 8 July 15, 16, 17 Aug. 2, 3, 4	June 4, 5, 6 July 9, 10, 11 Aug. 11, 12, 13	June 7, 8, 9 July 12, 13, 14 Jul 30, 31, Aug 1	Apr *30, May 1,2 June 1, 2, 3 Aug. 24, 25, 26	AND LIVEST	May 27, 28, 29 June 21, 22, 23 Aug 26, 27, 28	May 12, 13, 14 June 25, 26, 27 Aug. 29, 30, 31
McAlester	June 4, 5, 6 July 21, 22, 23 Aug. 11, 12, 13	June 7, 8, 9 July *4, *4, 5 Jul 30, 31, Aug 1	May, 9, 10, 11 July 18, 19, 20 Aug. 2, 3, 4	May 6, 7, 8 July 1, 2, 3 Aug. 23, 24, 25	May 12, 13, 14 June 25, 26, 27 Aug. 14, 15, 16	May 18, 19, 20 June 28, 29, 30 July 27, 28, 29	SPORTING	Apr *30, May 1, 2 June 1, 2, 3 Sept. 1, *2, *2
Holdenville ...	June 7, 8, 9 July, 9, 10, 11 Jul. 30, 31, Aug 1	June 4, 5, 6 July 12, 13, 14 Aug. 11, 12, 13	May 6, 7, 8 July 6, 7, 8 Aug. 14, 15, 16	May 9, 10, 11 July 21, 22, 23 Aug. 8, 9, 10	May 27, 28, 29 June 21, 22, 23 Aug. 26, 27, 28	May 15, 16, 17 June 16, 17, 18 Aug. 23, 24, 25	May 3, 4, 5 May *30, *30, 31 July 24, 25, 26	NEWS

*Holiday

This schedule is split in two seasons, the first season commencing April 30 ... June 30. The second season commences on July 1, and closes on Labor Day, September 2, 1912.

The Oklahoma State League dissolved eight days before the end of the first half-season.

With the gate so poor at Davis Field that home games were transferred to Guthrie, the league forfeited Davis' franchise on May 26 and president Meyer assumed management of the club. He promised acquisition of new players and work on improving fan delivery. He fired manager Reukauff and made pitcher Leo Langley field captain. A winning combination between the lines couldn't be put together. Meanwhile the other members of the league were underwriting baseball in the Capital when the business plan had been just the opposite: Oklahoma City receipts were supposed to have bolstered the small markets.

Leo Meyer took over the Oklahoma City franchise after ousting Abner Davis and his manager Bill Reufauff. An attempt to sell tickets to Davis Park —on the river on South Robinson with inadequate streetcar connections— involved a contest for a diamond ring. The promotion failed and the league disbanded two weeks after this advertisement was published.

BE A
Baseball Booster

In order to insure a better class of baseball for Oklahoma City the remainder of the 1912 season and still better next year, it is necessary that money be raised immediately with which to carry the Oklahoma City club through the present season and protect local territory for next year.

To do this, the Oklahoma City franchise, which now has control of the Oklahoma State League Booster Baseball tickets, good for any two championship games of baseball played in Oklahoma City this season.

$150 Diamond Ring

is to be given away FREE as a reward to the Young Lady selling the greatest number of these tickets between June 7 and July 4.

A Winning Team is to be the lot of Oklahoma City from this on. Buy tickets and use them today, and then get more tomorrow. Help your young lady friends and enjoy good baseball.

OKLAHOMA STATE LEAGUE OF BASEBALL CLUBS

A month into the season Wynn of Muskogee was leading in batting with a .414 average. Tulsa's Gabriel was hitting .404 while Robison of the doormat Oklahoma City Senators was at .380. Other team leaders were Burge of Holdenville at .359, Pierce of Okmulgee .357, McAlester's Wren .342, Moneymaker, who began the season at Tulsa then was traded to Guthrie, hit at a .338 clip while manager Tom Reed topped Anadarko at .304.

Meyer reported on June 20 that all the members except Oklahoma City had plenty of money to complete the season. The other members were willing to keep Oklahoma City playing even if that dented their bottom lines. They felt, Meyer said, that Oklahoma City couldn't be lost.

The demise of the Oklahoma State League was precipitated by politics. Boone Hite, interim president of the Anadarko ball club after Mayor William Plum had skipped town, left for the Democratic National Convention in Baltimore without leaving money to pay the wages of the players, then three days delinquent. Tom Reed telephoned Meyer

Tom Reed was a big, rawboned first sacker from Pittsburg, Kansas who also worked as a miner. The Western Association, where he played from 1903 through 1910, brought him to Oklahoma in 1909. In the Oklahoma State League, he succeeded Ray Ellison on May 9 and broke the news to Leo Meyer that the Anadarko club was disbanding.

on June 21 to let him know that the Indians had broken camp and it was every man for himself. The Muskogee club had been tottering and could just have easily been the league's last straw. The remaining members couldn't afford to keep Oklahoma City afloat. Meyer unilaterally declared the Oklahoma State League defunct on June 22. Players began signing with other clubs in other leagues.

There were no official statistics. *The Muskogee Phoenix* reported that a Muskogee player surnamed Wynn, who later landed briefly with Dallas, was hitting .460 when the music stopped and that Ben Tincup had 163 strikeouts. At dissolution, the standings were:

Okmulgee Glassblowers	38	10
Tulsa Terriers	33	5
Anadarko Indians	24	23
Holdenville Hitters	21	23
McAlester Miners	21	25
Muskogee Indians	19	24
Oklahoma City Senators	15	33
Guthrie	15	33

Two days later, the remaining owners rescinded Meyer's dissolution order. J. B. Bartlett, late of the Mid-Continent league, became president while the team representatives —White of Muskogee, Gardner of Okmulgee, Beckley of Tulsa, Leuttke of Guthrie, Howard Price of Enid, H. L. Vinson of Holdenville, and E. A. Daniels of McAlester— approved the sale of Oklahoma City's place to H. B. Ernest. All players were declared league property regardless of whether they had signed on with others. The Anadarko team was placed in Enid. The only games played before the second half were a best of three playoff between Okmulgee and Tulsa. Okmulgee won the first two games to settle the first half.

The second half of the season began June 28 with Ernest moving his club to Eufaula. No exhibitions would be played in Oklahoma City. Davis Park would remain empty through the 1913 season except for local sandlot games. In their inaugural the former Senators dropped a twelve to four decision at Okmulgee. On July 1, at Eufaula about 500 new fans watched McAlester tap manager Langley for seven runs. Things looked good for one day. Okmulgee's management lacked faith in the future of the Oklahoma State League and the players lacked faith in management over failure to make the June 30 payroll. On July 1 the seven top players were sold to Kansas City and the remainder to Kewanee of the Three-I League. At the time, Okmulgee was growing at over a 300% clip, faster than Tulsa or Oklahoma City. Its loss was a set back the league couldn't withstand. The accelerant to the blaze, though, was William R. Reukauff's, the fired, former manager of Oklahoma City, July 2 lawsuit against the league, its president Meyer, the franchise holders, and their presidents. He made a money claim for salary, bonus, and share of player contract sales and, demonstrating that the league was a money-losing proposition as presently run, sought a receiver. No public reports about the league follow. If his object was revenge, he got his pound of flesh. The name "Oklahoma State League" would not be uttered favorably again until 1920.

William Reukauff, a professor and former baseball player for St. Edward's College in Austin, first crossed paths with Abner Davis as he negotiated an option to buy the Oklahoma City franchise in the Texas League in December, 1911. When that fell through and the club went to Beaumont, Davis called on him to assemble his club in the new Oklahoma State League. He was fired when the league took over his team four weeks into the season. As with virtually everyone Davis touched, Reukauff finished in court suing the league, president Meyer, and the individual owners for salary and the percentage of revenue from sale of player contracts Davis had promised. How the litigation ended is academic as even a victory would have been Pyrrhic.

WESTERN ASSOCIATION 1914-1917

1914

Following the collapse of the 1911 incarnation of the circuit, the former member cities outside of Oklahoma were without league baseball for 1912 and 1913. Joplin, Springfield, and Ft. Smith were too small for the Class A Western League, too remote for the Class B Central League or Texas League, and too large for the new Class D Kansas State League. Sapulpa would be outside Organized Baseball for a decade. Tulsa and Muskogee first signed on with the newly formed Mid-Continent League then flipped to Abner Davis' Oklahoma-only league. The irascible Davis, who had sold Oklahoma City's Texas League franchise to Beaumont in 1911, assembled a new 1912 league—the Oklahoma State League— to host his new Oklahoma City team then saw his team forfeited and the nascent circuit collapse before the end of June. In 1913, only Ardmore, Durant, and after mid-season, Hugo enjoyed professional baseball.

Two promoters, former T.C.U. baseball coach, W. C. Holliday of Ft. Worth, and journeyman minor leaguer Larry Milton of Carthage, Missouri, made stabs at stirring up interests for a new Class C league. Holliday was first. Holliday had twice before tried to get a new league off the ground. Following a trip to cities that would comprise a new circuit, he arrived in Oklahoma City on December 1 to an enthusiastic welcome. Three days later an organizing meeting was held in Muskogee with the intention of operating a six-team league. Some familiar names attended. Mid-Continent League organizer, Judge Joseph B. Bartlett of Tulsa, and Muskogee's former player-manager, George 'Kid'

W. C. Holliday had enjoyed success as coach of the Texas Christian University baseball team including vanquishing professional ball clubs such as the 1912 Ardmore Giants. He was hired to manage Guthrie's Oklahoma State League entry but lasted only two days and was fired before the season began. He then outmaneuvered Larry Milton to land the Oklahoma City franchise in the new Western Association. As things unfolded, Holliday was all hat and no cattle. He found a mullet in Ft. Worth, S. D. Hunter, to whom he dumped the operation as he and seven signees shuttled off to Muskogee. On May 19, the owners seized the Muskogee club and sent Holliday packing. He was not heard from again.

Larry Milton (1879-1942) started 1903 with a one game look-see by the St. Louis Cardinals then retreated to Kansas City and Omaha in the Western League. Excepting 1909 with Little Rock, between 1904 and 1910, he threw in the Western Association, managing the 1910 Sapulpa Oilers there.

Speer, were joined by Holliday and legates from Joplin and Shreveport. Supposedly the territorial rights had been secured from the National Association. The participants agreed to complete secrecy lest a competing group arise. Somehow Larry Milton learned of the effort and quickly moved to undermine it.

Milton arrived in Oklahoma City in mid-January hand-in-hand with popular former Oklahoma City Mets outfielder (1905-1907) Arlo Scoggins. He advanced what was essentially Holliday's plan with Doc Shively as president. It came to nothing. On February 14, it looked like another season of sandlot ball in the Capital City.

Three days later, Tulsa city employee and former Western Association outfielder and manager, Howard Price, chaired a meeting with representatives from Springfield, Tulsa, Oklahoma City, Ft. Smith and Joplin to make preliminary plans. The next week a formal meeting was called with future St. Louis Brown and Chicago Cub Scott Perry and

Tulsa third-sacker W. J. Gourley active in the Tulsa effort, Jerry Kane for Ft. Smith, W. F. Meagher of Muskogee, coal millionaire A. J. Baker from Joplin, and Holliday for Oklahoma City. On March 1, the Western Association was formally reorganized with A. J. Baker as generalissimo, holding the offices of president, secretary and treasurer.

Entrepreneur and mine owner A. J. Baker underwrote baseball in Joplin only to see his 1909 Joplin team moved to El Reno then his 1914 Miners collapse in late June. Each time he had to relinquish office, the first as vice-president to J. H. Shaw and the second as president, secretary, and treasurer to W. P. Hill.

A player salary cap of $1,200 per month and a "forfeit" deposit of half that amount per member were agreed. The franchises and owners were: Judge J. B. Bartlett and Price in Tulsa; Kane in Ft. Smith; Meagher in Muskogee; Charles B. Serage in Joplin; C. A. Ludlow in Pittsburg, Kansas; and Holliday. Baker hired William West, Charles Porter, and Doug Hall to arbitrate games. Five days into the season after watching a terrible display of umpiring, Baker fired West and hired Fred Austin.

Within two weeks Kane had moved his franchise to McAlester. A miners' strike in Pittsburg forced Ludlow to sell his franchise to R. M. Mack of Springfield. At the next owners' meeting on March 30, the magnates approved Mack's move to Ft.

Smith. J. E. Letcher of the Tulsa Commercial Club of Tulsa was elected league vice-president.

At Oklahoma City, Holliday continued his public relations campaign announcing that he didn't want to take a single dollar of local capital. A lease of a triangular tract bounded by Exchange Avenue, Tena Street (now S.W. 7th) and the North Canadian River just southwest of the old Colcord Park —that had been torn down and the land subdivided into Packingtown lots—was secured and Layton & Smith engaged to design a 3,500 seat grandstand. Holliday made a trip back to Ft. Worth ostensibly to recruit players for his new manager Heine Maag from Galveston and returned with a dozen plus a new cash partner, S. D. Hunter of Ft. Worth.

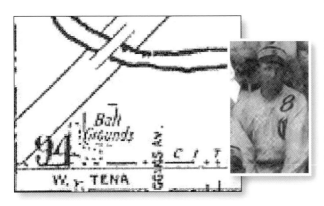

Southwest Seventh Street (formerly Tena Avenue) and Exchange Avenue was the approximate location of S. D. Hunter's 1914 ball park. Following World War I and the relocation of Jack Holland's Hutchinson, Kansas franchise, Western League Park was built at this location. The 1923 flood ended baseball there. In 1924, Holland built a new facility at Northwest Fourth and Virginia on the streetcar line across from the water works.

Holliday hadn't gotten around to turning a spade full of dirt before on April 18 he announced that he had sold out to Hunter and that he, both as bench manager and new owner, along with seven players were headed for Muskogee. With less

than two weeks before the season opener against McAlester, Hunter had to get a field and ball park ready. He did it and so did all the other owners. Muskogee secured a tract in downtown where a ramshackle grandstand was erected. Baker built a $17,000 palace in central Joplin. A "small army of workmen" hustled to complete a 4,000 seat facility near Tulsa's central business district. Ft. Smith and McAlester each had new ball parks.

Problems in the league rose quickly. Within six weeks, all save Oklahoma City and Ft. Smith had changed ownership.

Holliday promptly ran the Muskogee operation into the ground. On May 19, the other owners (with Hunter absent) took away the Holliday franchise, appointing infielder George McAvoy interim

Henry "Heine" Maag was a seven-season Texas League veteran and one of the most popular players and managers of the first decade of the last century. "A sparkling defensive player, good everywhere, but probably best at second base. . . ." according to Ruggles. Holliday signed him from Galveston to take over the 1914 Oklahoma City ball club. His 1914 Boosters won the pennant in a playoff. His 1915 Senators finished second to Joplin but vanquished Muskogee in six games for the championship of Oklahoma.

leader until he departed for a cup of coffee with the Phillies. A syndicate headed by local oilman M. J. Lamme stepped in. C. C. Ellis took over day-to-day management.

Underfinanced and ineptly managed, McAlester soon fell into trouble. Jerry Kane was ousted on June 14 and, after making an aborted ten-day effort at resurrecting baseball in Guthrie, ended up playing first base for Tulsa. E. A. Daniels led a new group of owners who hired Johnnie Henley from the umpiring ranks to lead the Miners.

The Joplin operation was the next casualty.

Druggist E. A. Daniels came to McAlester from Pennsylvania in 1908. He acquired the McAlester franchise from Jerry Kane in the early part of the 1914 season and was involved with it through 1917. He moved to Oklahoma City and established a chain of drugstores. He owned the McAlester ball club in the revived post-War Western Association becoming president in 1922. That same year he took on the post of president of the new Oklahoma State League and served in that capacity until it disbanded in July of 1924.

Oklahoma City Boosters	37	21
Tulsa Oilers	34	22
Ft. Smith Twins	34	23
Muskogee Mets	30	27
Joplin-Webb City Miners	20	38
McAlester Miners	18	42

The Boosters faded in the second half while Muskogee crafted a .620 winning performance in the July 1-September 7 section. In fact, the only changes in finish were that Oklahoma City and the Mets exchanged places while McAlester surrendered the cellar to Henryetta.

Muskogee Mets	44	27
Tulsa Oilers	40	27
Ft. Smith Twins	39	29
Oklahoma City Boosters	38	31
McAlester Miners	29	37
Henryetta Boosters	15	54

According to president Baker "[p]oor management of the team killed the game at Joplin." On June 26, just four days before the end of the first half of the split season, the league took over Joplin, appointing Ben Blanchette to lead the orphaned Missourians. It was generally assumed that Sapulpa, Okmulgee or Bartlesville would succeed Joplin. When the owners next met on July 9, Kane showed up with a $500 guarantee deposit and became the new proprietor. Guthrie gave shelter in the form of free use of a ball park but no local buy in. Following a disastrous first homestand, the as yet unnamed Guthrie aggregation disbanded. Those players who did not take free agency and flee were melded with a good semi-pro club from coal mining center Henryetta to become on July 21 the "Boosters."

With all the turmoil, including his home town losing baseball, Baker threw in the towel on July 2. Working in the background, Oklahoma City's Hunter held the league together until attorney W. P. Hill of McAlester took the league reins that he would hold until the middle of the 1916 season.

On the field Oklahoma City took the first half lead on May 30 and never relinquished it.

The Senators' Glenn Dameron topped the circuit with a .357 batting average. Muskogee players Harry Thompson and Ed Palmer led in hits and home runs with 155 and twenty-one, respectively. Tulsa had the run-scoring champion with Lee Morris' 105 as well as the best pitcher, Nelson Jones who won twenty-nine of thirty-seven. Shaking off their second half lethargy, Oklahoma City copped the first pennant of the new Western Association by taking four of six games from Muskogee. The victory was not without controversy. Muskogee was accused of having too many players on the payroll and fielding players under contract with other clubs.

1915

The first change for 1915 was sale of the Oklahoma City club to a group with Col. E. M. Duncan as the managing secretary and Joe Wylie as figure-

1915 Oklahoma City Senators. Upper L-R: Heine Maag, Larry Gierhart, Likowski (pitcher), John King, Darnell (pitcher), Ray Fagan, E. M. Duncan business manager. Middle L-R: Glenn Dameron, Jerry Naylor, Robert Allen, Dennis. Seated L-R: L. Hebert, Pete Killduff, Bob Dowie, Floyd Hall. Killduff hit .270 in five National League seasons. Three future Major Leaguers not shown in the photo were Johnny Schulte, Fred Eunick, and Frank Thompson.

head president. Duncan would run the operation though the 1917 season. The seller, S. D. Hunter, had been a leader in the Western Association and justly credited with saving it when he acquired the Oklahoma City franchise from W. C. Holliday just as the league was on the verge of disbanding. Roy W. Purpus was the new owner of Tulsa. The Western Association added three Texas cities from the defunct Texas-Oklahoma League —Denison, Paris and Sherman— to expand to an eight team circuit that was now centered in eastern Oklahoma and east Texas. Player disputes marked Denison's entry. Not only did it assert that it was successor to Henryetta and the owner of its players but also had purchased the contracts of the defunct Durant franchise from the Texas-Oklahoma League.

The Federal League played its first season as an outlaw major league in 1914. The battle with the American and National Leagues was bitter and extended beyond the 1915 season, culminating in the Supreme Court of the United States' ruling that baseball was exempt from the proscriptions of the Sherman Anti-Trust Act. One of the new Federal League owners was wealthy Tulsa oilman Harry Sinclair who had purchased the Kansas City Packers. He wanted a development league to feed the Packers and other Federal teams. The logical target for him was the Western Association. Shortly before the March 1, 1915 pre-season meeting, Sinclair made an attractive overture to make the Western Association an outlaw minor league to pair with the Colonial League that had aligned with the Federals.

OUTLAW BASEBALL

Newly wealthy oil tycoon Harry Sinclair picked up the failing Covington (Ky.) Blue Sox of the new Federal League as they moved to Kansas City to become the Packers; catcher Ben Ragsdale who played for the 1904 Ardmore Territorians is eighth from right. Sinclair added the Newark Peppers to his portfolio. He planned to gain a toe hold in the New York City area and purchase the New York Giants. By February, 1916 Sinclair was done with baseball and directed his money-losing to horse-racing.

Covington Blue Sox

Federal League Newark Program 1915

The owners rebuffed him, electing wisely to remain in Organized Baseball. The Federals were gone in 1916. The Western Association played that season.

At that meeting, Hill, who had stabilized the Association so that the 1914 season was completed and guided it through reorganization and ownership changes over the winter, was re-elected president, Jack Letcher of Tulsa became first vice-president, and Ft. Smith's J. Roy DeRoss secretary-treasurer. A single season schedule beginning April 13 and ending on August 28 was adopted.

The absence of Sunday baseball in Ft. Smith complicated scheduling and put Denison on the road for twenty-four consecutive days. Dit Spencer of Denison, Harry Womack of Minco, Oklahoma, R. W. Pontius of Dodge City, R. H. Morgan from the

McAlester attorney W. P. Hill stepped into A. J. Baker's shoes as Western Association president in July 1914. He held the post until July 17, 1916. He moved his family to Tulsa soon after.

Texas League, who played in the Western Association in 1914, and J. W. McNulty from the Class AA American Association were hired as umpires. A rule against taking players on optional assignment from teams in higher classifications and prohibiting buy-back agreements was adopted.

Fan dissatisfaction at Muskogee dated back to mid-1914 despite success on the field. Lamme's management did not include honest bookkeeping. When he missed the May 15 payroll, Hill forfeited the franchise and Secretary DeRoss intervened directly; an audit disclosed money missing and unaccounted for. A new ownership group headed by R. B. Blakeney

was awarded the franchise after making up the payroll and reimbursing Oklahoma City for the guarantee money for a series played at Muskogee.

Heavy rains and poorly attended games played in mud plagued the Western Association during the first six weeks of the 1915 season. Ft. Smith, McAlester and Sherman all nearly disbanded because of the weather losses. The failure of the cotton crop set back the local economies of Paris and Denison. At the mid-season meeting, Hill offered his resignation but the owners prevailed on him to remain in office.

Babe Peebles' 1915 Denison Railroaders, Champions of the Western Association. Upper L-R: Fred Nicholson*, H. Merritt, Walt Kinney*, Rogers Hornsby*, Everett Sheffield. Middle L-R: Leo Hellman, Wray Query, Babe Peebles, David Glenn, B. Brooks. Seated L-R: William Campbell, John Harper, Kid Speer*, Robert Covington, Edmonds. * Appeared in a major league.

Denison won the first game of the season, took the lead on May 8, clinched the pennant on August 27, and won the season finale to finish with a .589 percentage and give Babe Peebles another pennant to match the Texas-Oklahoma one he won for Denison in 1913.

Surprisingly, none of the league leaders were from Denison. Muskogee's John Robinson led with 160 hits for a .323 average. Clyde McCarty of Ft. Smith scored the most runs, 104. Slugger Otto Breese from McAlester exploded for an unheard of thirty-four homeruns. The Senators' Ray Fagan posted an extraordinary 1.06 ERA while winning all thirteen decisions. The top winners were Roy Clements of Tulsa and Dick Robertson of Ft. Smith. L. G. Daniels of Paris led with 228 strikeouts.

The great problem confronting Hill in the last six weeks of the season was dealing with frivolous protests, enforcing the $1,400 monthly salary cap that the owners had largely honored in the breach, and ferreting out optioned players. Oklahoma City rallied as the season drew to a close and was hot on Denison's heels. The who's who of Denison telegraphed president Hill alleging that Muskogee was throwing the last series of the season to propel the Senators past the Railroaders. The umpire for the series, R. H. Morgan, verified that Muskogee played hard and opined that the Denison protest was baseless. Hill agreed. It later was disclosed that Denison had a $2,400 monthly payroll and two of its stars were on option: Fred Nicholson from Detroit and pitcher David Glenn from Houston.

While finishing last, McAlester under the leadership of Jimmie Humphries won twenty of twenty-six during August and played close to .600 ball from the date he took over on July 12. Owner Purpus at Tulsa was pleased with the season and began

working for a higher classification for the league. Under Blakeney's ownership, Muskogee moved from seventh having won only twenty of forty-nine to a fourth place finish above .500. Paris was well-pleased with the better quality of baseball compared to the Texas-Oklahoma League and optimistic about 1916 despite having had all of the profitable exhibitions and five straight home games rained out, attendance slipping to a quarter of 1914's, a depression in the cotton market, and a revolving door of players and multiple managers. All of the clubs showed a small profit or broke even except for champion Denison. While nearly every club exceeded the fourteen player limit, Denison broke the bank with high monthly payrolls approaching $2,400, twice what was legal. Denison's attendance dropped to the lowest in its time in Organized Ball. The last two games as well as the final doubleheaders were rained out. Cotton that supported Denison's railhead was in the proverbial tank. The only salvation was sale of Rogers Hornsby to St. Louis for a tidy profit. All of this notwithstanding, the business community had stepped up to underwrite the final five weeks of the 1915 season as well as setting aside seed money for the next season. The final standings:

Denison Railroaders	76	53
Oklahoma City Senators	76	62
Sherman Hitters	70	65
Muskogee Mets	68	66
Paris Red Snappers	66	66
Tulsa Producers	63	71
Ft. Smith Twins	61	75
McAlester Miners	57	79

Two days after the season ended, Oklahoma City and Muskogee played a best of seven postseason series to determine the championship of

Oklahoma that includied September 2 and Labor Day field "novelty contests" among the players. Oklahoma City won in six games.

1916

Interviewed after the 1915 season, president Hill was justifiably proud of completing 1915 without loss of a franchise in spite of the tight money caused by the European War, reduced attendance league-wide, terrible weather, and an expensive outside-produced schedule that placed a heavy burden on some teams, especially Oklahoma City and Ft. Smith. The good news was that all franchises were in place for the next season. The difficult issue facing him for 1916 was the division among the owners whether to seek class C status. Hill preferred Class D and said so. The National Association settled that issue at its November meeting when the leagues represented refused to promote the Western Association. Secretary Farrell granted the Association a waiver of the Class D limit of thirteen players and $1,300 per month salary cap provided the owners were unanimous in raising either or both.

The annual league meeting was held in Hill's hometown of McAlester on December 19, 1915. The first item of business was refusing Hill's resignation. The offices of president and treasurer were combined and Hill was elected to it. J. W. Bell of Paris became first vice president while J. Roy DeRoss and Jack Letcher stood as alternates. Charles Brill, sports editor of *The Daily Oklahoman*, was made league secretary. It was rumored that Harry Sinclair, who had added the Newark Feds to his sports empire, would be purchasing Tulsa if he successfully acquired the New York Giants (he was not). Drafting a schedule fell to a committee headed by Oklahoma City's E. M. Duncan. His task was

complicated not only by Ft. Smith's Blue law but also by the new interurban between Sherman and Denison. The latter required that those cities not be scheduled at home on the same dates. He succeeded with adoption at the February, 1916 meeting in Denison of a 140-game unitary campaign begin-

J. W. Bell of Paris, Texas presided over the Western Association from mid-July 1916 until the league went dormant in January, 1918. He stepped in as business manager of the Paris Orioles of the Sooner State League following the 1957 season.

ning April 20 and concluding on September 4. The acknowledged weak team in the league, Paris, received a huge set back when on March 21, 1916 a fire decimated the town, taking the entire downtown and several of the better residential neighborhoods. Nonetheless, the Paris ball club renamed the "Survivors," was on the field on April 20. Muskogee had thirteen players back and ready to compete. Denison, whose 1915 club batted .259, returned most of its champion lineup under Babe Peebles' leadership and was the odds on favorite to repeat.

President Hill made it plain before the season began that he was going to resign just as soon as the owners settled on a successor. The owners would dawdle for two months. While they fiddled, Oklahoma City's Saratoga Park was literally under the waters of the North Canadian. The Senators fell into the red with missed dates, high salaries, and over forty players rotating through the clubhouse. Gambling had never gone away from the game. In early July, *The Daily Oklahoman* reported that "[m]ore money is bet in Oklahoma on major league games every week than the governor draws down in salary." Wagering got worse when federal law banned off track betting on horses. In the pool halls across the country, baseball replaced the nags as the medium for betting. The Western Association lost a leader when R. M. Finley, who had been active in the Texas-Oklahoma League before leading Paris, Sherman, and Denison to the Western Association, resigned on July 2. More turnover was to come. Franchises were ignoring the player and salary limits.

Hill resigned once and for all at the July 6 meeting but announcement was withheld until the July 17 meeting at Muskogee when Paris' J. W. Bell took over for the duration of the Association's life and Brill added the title of vice-president. The main topics were the umpires and the remainder of the season. Dit Spencer quit after a head injury from a pop bottle had hospitalized him. Remaining arbiters had other problems. Morgan got mixed up nipping a Sherman rally against Denison with a two-out inning. Pontius was the *casus belli* of a near riot at Oklahoma City.

Almost immediately, Bell was confronted with the failure of his hometown Survivors. In fact, this event precipitated announcement of Hill's resignation originally scheduled for August 1. He thought Bell better able to handle it. Following the fire, Paris had enough in the bank to complete the season had everyone else played by the rules. In fact, the Survivors could not be competitive on the field because they couldn't offer salaries of the kind offered by the other teams. Bell shopped the club

to Ardmore, Joplin, and Springfield, none of whom were interested. He appointed a board of three Paris trustees who raised enough to pay off club debts and sold George Clark, future Red Sox shortstop Turkey Gross and veteran hurler Cy Watson to supplement league financial support and finish the season. If the fans did not support the team, they would become a league-owned orphan. Hill meanwhile moved his practice and family to Tulsa.

After a day when League teams scored sixty runs on ninety-four hits, Tulsa jumped out to a lead it held until June 1. A Producers' losing streak coupled with Denison catching on fire put the Railroaders on top. After the failure of the Paris franchise, the league split the season with Denison far ahead:

Denison Railroaders	60	29
Tulsa Producers	53	40
McAlester Miners	52	40
Sherman Lions	45	46
Muskogee Mets	43	51
Ft. Smith Twins	41	50
Oklahoma City Senators*	39	52
Paris Survivors	34	59

Oklahoma City was also called the "Bearcats."

The last forty-five games were played in a new semi-season.

Tulsa Producers	27	18
McAlester Miners	27	18
Denison Railroaders	26	20
Oklahoma City Senators*	25	21
Paris Survivors	22	24
Ft. Smith Twins	20	26
Muskogee Mets	20	26
Sherman Lions	16	30

It finished in a tie. Future Major Leaguer Ross Youngs of Sherman led the league with 195 hits,

103 runs, and a .362 batting average. Pete Adams of Ft. Smith, Harry Moore of Tulsa, and Ed Hopper of Muskogee each hit twenty-two home runs. Walt McKinney of Denison led with twenty-two wins while team mate H. M. Watson led with a .700 winning percentage. McAlester had the strikeout king, Rollie Naylor with 228, and ERA champ, Rolla Mapel with 2.03.

As Tulsa finished the full season one-half game ahead of McAlester, the Producers got to square off against Denison. Unable to gain an advantage by a fictitious protest to J. H. Farrell (who said he'd never seen it), Tulsa dropped the playoff series four games to two. Tulsa continued to protest and claim it was cheated out of the title. In point of fact, Denison's manager Aldridge Peebles did cheat by having been above the player caps and salary limits all season. Nonetheless, the owners awarded Denison the pennant at their November 1916 meeting.

1917

The threat on the horizon for J. W. Bell was not the war in Europe or the Mexican revolution to his south, but the expansionist aspirations of the Class A Western League to the north. The owners of that circuit were eager to bring Oklahoma City and Tulsa within their fold, shedding Topeka and Wichita on the way. Bell also had trouble in his neighborhood with Denison weakened from overspending, Sherman questionable for 1917, and Paris still not weaned from league support. As he left for the National Association meeting in New Orleans, the president of the Western Association did not know what cities would be members of his league or if the Western Association would play in 1917. By early December, it appeared that 1917 would be played with the same lineups as 1915 and 1916. Committee chair Duncan began drafting a schedule with plenty of Sunday doubleheaders for presentation to the owners in January.

Peebles' last pennant winner, 1916 Denison. Rear L-R: Jerry Darcy, Fred Nicholson*, H. Merritt, Walt Kinney*, Rogers Hornsby*, Everett Sheffield. Middle L-R: Leo Hellman, Wray Query, Aldridge Peebles, David Glenn, B. Brooks. Seated L-R: William Campbell, John Harper, G. N. "Kid" Speer, Robert Covington, Edmonds. Hornsby spent 1916 as a rookie with the Cardinals.
*Appeared in a major league.

The first challenge of the new year was the situation at Denison. The Railroaders had won two pennants under Babe Peebles by flaunting the rules and playing in the financial red to the tune of $1,600 in 1916. Bell brought things to a head when he visited the Gate City to see if there was the commitment to underwriting the 1917 campaign. A new board of directors rejected the past cheating, handcuffed Peebles and committed to raising $6,600. That was good enough for Bell.

Al Tearney was president of the Three-I League and later the Western League.

The dean of minor league presidents, Al Tearney of the Three-I League observed in early January that "minor leagues were absolutely lacking in business methods." He described the Western Association exactly. In 1914 official records were not compiled; what *The Daily Oklahoman* produced was used. The 1915 records were only partially official because scorers were lax in sending in score sheets for compilation. The eight franchises spent $125,000 to operate in 1916. Accounting and recordkeeping were poor. Bell set a goal to bring 1917 costs to under $100,000. The biggest initiative in that direction was Bell's revolutionary directive that players pay their own way to spring practice. In the past, anyone who wanted to tryout could get a free ticket. Bell's rule eliminated those who were not confident in their abilities and, more importantly, preserved operating funds to carry franchises through the early part of the season.

Bell hired Frank Nealey and Ray Cahill of

St. Louis and Charles Schaffer of Chicago for the umpiring staff; Ralph Pontius from 1916 would fill out the quartet. Duncan continued working on a schedule paying particular attention to the mileage each team would travel on road trips; some teams had spent all their profits on rail travel. During the past two seasons, McAlester (3,087) and Denison (3,318) had traveled the least while Oklahoma City (4,887) and Tulsa (4,299) were the road warriors.

With Denison in, Bell had to issue an ultimatum to Sherman to put up its guarantee money by February 16 or lose its franchise. It was the impetus needed as the problem in Sherman was not lack of enthusiasm. Billy Batsell was elected president of the nameless ballclub; A. S. Saul continued as secretary and business manager. Sale of 1916 batting

Ross Youngs (1897-1927) hit .322 in ten seasons with the New York Giants (1917-1926) and was elected to the Hall of Fame in 1972. At Sherman in 1916, he led the league in average (.362), runs (103), and hits (195).

leader Ross "Pep" Youngs to the New York Giants provided capital for the new season. A new downtown ball park was anticipated on the assumption the voters would approve a bond issue. Failing that, Lyons Park would be used where, safely beyond the city limits, Sunday ball could be played.

Paris ostensibly was set financially but had problems signing players. Manager Speer and veteran catcher Dick Crittenden were signed, and veterans Bernie Everdon and Hubert Dennis acquired from Oklahoma City were the nucleus of a mound staff. Most of the position players under reserve were holding out. It looked as though 1917 would see Paris with a very young nine.

Dick Crittenden made his debut in 1907 with Ottumwa and, after two years of semi-pro, returned to league ball with Larned, Kansas and St. Joseph in the Western League. He came back south in 1915 after a sojourn in the Pacific Northwest with Tacoma and Helena. He was with Paris in 1915, 1916, and 1917 when the club moved to Ardmore. When Kid Speer abandoned the Ardmoreites, they became a road team that Crittenden managed the remainder of the season. He finished his eleventh season in 1921 dividing time between Drumright and Henryetta in the post-War Western Association.

Bernie Everdon played for three Oklahoma teams: Okmulgee in 1912, Oklahoma City in 1916, and Ardmore in 1917.

The owners called a special meeting for March 4 at which they adopted a 154-game schedule including eight doubleheaders. Duncan had done a masterful job of leveling travel. Denison would travel the least at 3,807 miles while the top traveler would be McAlester at 3,978. The season would begin April 12 and end traditionally on Labor Day.

The United States formally declared war on the Imperial German Government on April 6. On opening day, Bell ordered all the teams to provide military training and instruction for the players. All teams except Denison claimed to be stronger than the 1916 versions. Openers were at Ft. Smith against Tulsa, at Denison against Oklahoma City, Muskogee at Paris, and Sherman at McAlester. The salary cap was raised to $1,365 to accommodate players acting as road secretaries. Rosters had to be cut to fourteen by May 1.

The field was competitive. Between May 2 and 13, the lead changed hands eight times. On May 10, the Paris franchise was formally transferred to Ardmore, a city that had been awaiting a Western

Association berth since 1914. There was speculation that Paris' move presaged transfers or forfeitures of the other two Texas clubs. Okmulgee, Bartlesville, and Sapulpa were ready to pounce if either faltered. In first place on the date of transfer, the newly christened Ardmoreites dropped their first game at Oklahoma City and were in third with nineteen wins and sixteen losses when they squared off against McAlester for the first professional game in Ardmore since 1914. The A's were poor hosts as they took the Miners by a five to two tally before 2,000 fans on Ladies Day. It was all downhill from there. The Ardmore team became an orphan at the end of July and finished with eleven players and a last place record of forty-one wins against eighty-six losses after leaving Paris.

On rumors that the Western Association was close to disbanding, the Western League sent emissaries to Oklahoma City and Tulsa and extended invitations for 1918. Secretary Charles Brill resigned

Charles Brill (1888-1956) was the sports editor for The Daily Oklahoman *and served as secretary and league statistician. He was also a published historian of the Indian Wars.*

RUNAWAY MINERS

The wartime McAlester team ran away with the Western Association pennant in 1917. The ball club sported three future major leaguers. Frank Thompson (1885-1940) spent 1920 with the St. Louis Browns before being returned to Phil Ball's farm club at Tulsa. Madill's Ray Johnson (1895-1986) was 1-5 with the 1918 Philadelphia Athletics. He began managing in 1928 then joined the Chicago Cubs system in 1934. He finished his career in 1944 in Wrigley Field as the Cubs' field general. Rags Faircloth (1892-1953) had a 2.52 ERA and forty-six wins in five minor league seasons. In his only two innings in the Show, as a 1919 Phillies twirler he yielded five hits and two earned runs before getting a one-way ticket to the semi-pro jungle.

Johnson *Faircloth*

Thompson

1917 Western Association champions McAlester Miners. L-R: Orin Masters, Frank Thompson*, Jimmie Humphries, James Stewart, A. E. Bailey, Johnny Nutt, C. N. Phillips, Ray Johnson*, Cecil Griggs, Frank Herriott, Oscar Palmer, J. L. Rags Faircloth*, Emmett Mulvey, O. O'Neil.
*Appeared in a major league.

on reports that president Bell had accused him of selling batters' statistics. Meanwhile, Bell wished to cut short the season while Tulsa, Ft. Smith and Oklahoma City wanted to finish on Labor Day. A meeting that would determine the future of the league was held on July 30 at McAlester. The four large cities wanted to play out. Ardmore, McAlester, Denison, and Sherman wanted to end the misery. Bell surprisingly sided with the large towns and cast the deciding vote. In so doing he made peace with Brill who returned as secretary and statistician.

Military conscription began in July. If a team could not continue because of loss of players to the Colors it had either to recruit amateurs, sign free agents from some of the many class C and D leagues that had folded, or surrender its franchise. Denison, Ft. Smith and Muskogee lost players to the first draft call. Enlistments and conscriptions thinned out the fan base and money became tight. Consequently, attendance and revenues were down across the league. The southern tier of teams was all waiting for one to drop out. A team that voluntarily quit lost its territorial protection but one dropped by a league retained it.

As the season drew to a close, the Western Association and Blue Ridge Leagues were the last class D circuits playing. President Bell on his final

J. P. Scott had purchased the Tulsa club in 1917. He worked to put together a league for 1918 but the War effort was too much of an obstacle.

tour of the league opined that the Western Association would not play in 1918. He stated that the decision to continue the season had been a mistake. The business people around the circuit who had backed baseball were financially exhausted and could not be expected to ante up again. The president of the Tulsa club, J. P. Scott, countered Bell with his knowledge that a new league of the northern tier teams and refugees from the Western League was likely. All the while, McAlester and Ardmore were

setting a record by playing a nine inning game in just thirty-six minutes. Ernie Clabert of Muskogee had a record-setting season leading the league with 177 hits, 101 runs, thirty-four four-sackers. McAlester's Emmett Mulvey had the best average at .320. Charlie Robertsons twenty-six and six season made him the best of the pitchers. Walt Kinney, 1916's wins leader, had 260 strike outs. The final standings

McAlester Miners	95	57
Muskogee Reds	89	69
Sherman Browns	80	72
Denison Railroaders	79	75
Ft. Smith Twins	77	82
Oklahoma City Boosters	72	80
Tulsa Producers	68	84
Ardmore Ardmoreites	41	86

Western Association All-Stars barnstormed against the Dallas Giants.

The Western Association did not have a championship series but an All-Star team did play a series against the Texas League champion Dallas Giants.

Col. Duncan actively promoted a new Class B league to be staffed by undrafted free agents. As events transpired for 1918, there would be only five minor leagues below the class A level. Duncan was somewhat clairvoyant as the Hutchinson, Kansas club of the Western League did move to Oklahoma City on June 2, 1918. That team played as the Indians until the league disbanded on July 7.

At the Western Association meeting in November 1917 there was a split. The Association was insolvent due to the members not having paid assessments. Oklahoma City, Tulsa, Ft. Smith, and Muskogee would seek affiliation with another circuit in a higher classification. Ardmore and Sherman were definitely out. Denison and McAlester did not expect to play but would if there was still a league.

The Western Association was officially laid to rest on January 20, 1918. It would rise again in 1920 under J. E. Letcher with only Ft. Smith of the old members joining the new incarnation.

Col. E. M. Duncan kept baseball in Oklahoma City through 1917.

THE CITIES

PART TWO

ALTUS

ALTUS CHIEFS
TEXAS-OKLAHOMA LEAGUE
1911

SEASON	TEAM NAME	MANAGERS	WON	LOST	PERCENTAGE	FINISH
1911	Chiefs	Muggsy Monroe	31	44	.413	Disbanded July 18
		Thomas "Dad" Campbell				
		George Partain				

Altus was one of the oldest settlements in the Oklahoma Territory.

Unlike other towns in southwest Oklahoma, Altus was originally chartered under Texas law in 1886 as a part of Greer County which was later awarded to Oklahoma in 1896. When the Frisco railroad came from the east and the Wichita & Northwestern arrived from the south, Altus became a thriving cotton crossroads.

Altus was the last city to be awarded a franchise in the Texas-Oklahoma League. The *Altus Weekly News* reported on March 30 that a group of businessmen were soliciting $1,500 to build a ball park and join a professional league. O. J. Jeffrey was the president of the local baseball association. Muggsy Monroe, who had close to a decade's experience in semi-pro ball, including stints with the 1903 Oklahoma City Mets as well as with Guthrie and Muskogee in the Western Association, was hired as field manager. With no affordable space available in the city, a ball park was built on the outskirts of town. This location did not help attendance but solved the problem of Sunday baseball ordinances.

Rick "Red" Adams (1878-1955) was 2-5 in eleven games for the 1905 Washington Senators. His professional career began in 1901 in the Pacific Northwest League. He returned to his Paris home the following season and competed in the Texas League, Southern Association, Western League and Eastern League until 1911 when Houston cut him. Joining Altus in 1911, he finished his career with Durant and Denison in the Texas-Oklahoma League. His record was 169-125 in 280 minor league mound appearances.

Muggsy Monroe was nearing the end of his career when he took the reins of the Altus Chiefs.

Alex Malloy (1886-1961) lost all six starts during his 1910 tryout with the Browns. He was brilliant, however, in classes C and D winning thirty-four of forty-eight decisions. His last season was 1913.

Altus was the last stop on outfielder Dick Latham's odyssey that began in 1898 with Ft. Worth. Aside from Altus, he stayed near the Gulf coast playing with Galveston, Orange, Lake Charles and Beeville as well as in the semi-pro ranks. His career average was .267. Ruggles describes him as a "[h]itting outfielder, the beau ideal of his time."

On opening day, a parade led by Mayor Orr and the Altus Merchants Band with the Altus and Lawton players in open automobiles and fans in cars, buggies, on horseback and on foot began at Main and Maple, processed around the courthouse square and then to the new grandstand. After thirty minutes of remarks, Mayor Orr threw the first pitch to Mayor-elect Kirby and the umpire yelled "play ball" to the 549 in attendance. Altus swept the first series and, with about one hundred fans joining the Chiefs on the Frisco, descended on Lawton where they took two of three from the Medicine Men at new Koehler Park. Behind former major leaguers Red Adams and Alex Malloy, the Chiefs spent much of the early part of the season near the top of the standings. On May 8, before 4,000 fans, 3,000 of whom were on special excursion trains from Wichita Falls and Wellington, Kansas, Altus

dropped a four to zero contest to Wichita Falls in a game where all of the visitors' runs were scored on the Chiefs' six errors. Poor glove work was behind the club's position in the standings: a decidedly bush league .878 percentage at May 10. The Chiefs' strength was at the plate. Dick Latham was hitting .450 while Altus native Ed Kizziar at .322 and John Frierson at .304 backed him up. Young catcher

The season with the Chiefs was John Frierson's first of twelve in league ball. He was with Ft. Worth, Galveston, San Antonio and Houston in the Texas League for eight seasons between 1912 and 1918 and in the Southern Association in 1919 and 1920. He last played in 1923 for Sherman in the class D Texas Association.

Hornbuckle came over after Lawton cut him. Pacific Coast League hurler Fred Bergman was added to the mound staff as well as veterans James Bates and Robert "Farmer" Ray.

Robert "Farmer" Ray (1886-1963) spent 1910 in the St. Louis Browns' starting rotation that included the erratic Hall of Famer Rube Waddell. Ray had a 4-10 record for a last place team that lost 107 of 154 games. Alex Malloy and Marc Hall were teammates there. He found himself in Altus the next season. After the Chiefs disbanded, he sold his services to Hartford. From 1912 until his last season in 1916, he played in Texas at Houston, Sherman, and Denison. His minor league record was 76-75 in seven seasons.

While the May 12 tie at Bonham before a "large crowd of enthusiastic fans [who] squabbled frequently" was "one of the most sensational games of the season," on May 14 there was no game. The Chiefs mistakenly took the train from Bonham to Durant for a Sunday game only to learn that Sunday baseball was illegal there. The Durant Educators meanwhile had taken the train to Altus from Wichita Falls. Durant headed east. After dropping two of three weekday games played at Durant, the Chiefs swept the home team to begin an eleven-game winning streak that came to an end on May 31 at Cleburne. The first half of the season ended on June 7 with Altus in second place sporting a record of twenty-three wins and nineteen losses.

On June 1, a group from Chickasha, hearing that the Altus franchise was struggling, made a pass at purchasing the club but apparently was rejected. Beginning the second half, the Chiefs took four of five from Lawton home and home. On June 14,

after winning "one of the prettiest and snappiest games of the season" from Lawton, club president O. J. Jeffrey relieved Muggsy Monroe of his field captaincy. The given reason for the termination was that Monroe didn't send in a reliever for the Chiefs' ace Malloy after he had given up ten walks. The real reason was that Monroe had traded away the most popular player: Ted Sherwood for Lawton's C. E. Alberta, both shortstops. As fate would have it, this Altus win was the Medicine Men's final game; they dissolved two days later when their next opponent, the Gainesville Blue Ribbons, did not appear for the June 16 series. The Texas-Oklahoma suddenly was a six-team league. A new schedule was drawn.

Thomas "Dad" Campbell, whose minor league career began in 1903, was hired as manager on June 16 and delivered three of four games at Wichita Falls. The Chiefs then dropped eight straight to the Irish Lads and Cleburne followed by three more with an intervening victory at Bonham. Despite a report that the Chiefs had disbanded on July 11, they appeared on the field on July 12 under new manager George Partain and romped over Bonham by a score of twelve to one; as it turned out, it was Altus' last win.

What was left of the franchise disbanded again on July 15 with a record of three wins and eighteen losses. The *Altus Daily News* reported that the team "just blew up." McMahan signed with Wichita Falls briefly. Frierson left for Bonham.

On the 16th, the "whole town" turned out and

Having spent his first five seasons on the east coast, Bill McMahan fled to Waco following the collapse of the Chiefs. He finished his playing days there in 1914.

businesses closed as Bonham returned the favor of July 12 twelve to three. That would be the last professional game played in Altus. The "Outcasts" as the team was now known traveled to Durant for the scheduled games. They dropped their last league game to the Educators ten to four. Meanwhile, Partain was frantically looking for a new home in nearby Hugo or Greenville, Texas. His efforts were fruitless. William Hillis, Ardmore's business manager, had forwarded train tickets for the Outcasts to begin a series on July 19 with the Blues. When he received word from league president St. Clair's office that Altus had lost its franchise, he pulled the tickets. Now an independent ball club the late Chiefs instead rode to Hugo for a game against the local semi-pros and, reportedly, on to Honey Grove, Texas, equidistant from Bonham and future Texas-Oklahoma League member Paris.

Counting the games played under the first, eight-team second half schedule, the Chiefs finished with thirty-one wins and forty-four losses and a three and twenty record in the official league second half.

ANADARKO

ANADARKO INDIANS OKLAHOMA STATE LEAGUE 1912

Anadarko called itself "Queen of the Washita." Shown is a new colonnade on Main Street.

Anadarko was born of the 1901 lottery for some of the unalloted Comanche, Kiowa and Apache reservation lands. Called in early literature the "Queen of the Washita," the city had close to 5,000 camped in "rag town" just outside the former reservation. Following draw of the lottery, the new city of Anadarko boasted 2,190 residents at Statehood and added another 1,200 by the 1910 Census. The first business has always been agriculture with the Indian Agency second in importance.

Anadarko had produced outstanding semi-pro teams since its birth. The 1911 club was particularly strong. When news of the formation of a professional league came to Anadarko, civic boosters led by Mayor William M. Plum — who would skip the U.S.A. around May 15 after his creditors began involuntary bankruptcy proceeding against him— appointed Ray Ellison and Jim Menifee to bring home a franchise. That was granted at the mid-March meeting.

continued on page 76

SEASON	TEAM NAME	MANAGERS	WON	LOST	PERCENTAGE	FINISH
1912	Indians	Ray Ellison	24	23	.511	Disbanded June 21
		Tom Reed				
		Ted Price (after disbanded and moved to Enid June 28-July 2)				

A READY-MADE LEAGUE TEAM

The 1911 club won forty-six and lost only four.

RIGHT:
Tanner

ABOVE:
Isom

RIGHT:
Kahl

Jasper

White

Oram

Ray Ellison   Cotton Ellison   Phil Dayton

Liese

Billings

Anadarko fielded among the best semi-pro nines in Oklahoma. Both brothers Cotton Ellison and Ray Ellison played for the independents. A number of those players had toiled for Lawton the previous season in the Texas-Oklahoma League. The roster was filled out by John Isom, former Cleveland Nap Nick Kahl (1879-1959), veteran Texas Leaguer Arch Tanner, Davey White from the Oklahoma City club, and former Boston National Leaguer Fred Liese (1885-1967). Future big leaguer Hi Jasper (1886-1937) joined Tanner and Lee Oram on the mound. Rookie Josh Billings (1891-1981) a phenom from Oklahoma A & M, discovered that his talents were on the other side of the plate where he caught for Cleveland and the St. Louis Americans from 1913 through 1923. He played in the minors for another dozen seasons and managed into the 1940s.

Abner Davis, who was behind the formation of the Oklahoma State League, was suspected of syndicate ball, i.e. having interests in multiple franchises in the same league. The one club he was open about was the Oklahoma City Senators led on the field by Will Reukauff. The Senators had visited Anadarko for a pre-season exhibition and came away with a five to zero victory behind rookie Joe Williams' two-hitter while his support committed no errors.

Under the direction of Ray Ellison, a ball park was raised in the Kite Addition. The Indians opened the April 30 festivities with a parade led by the Anadarko Brass Band followed by the Mayor and business leaders, then the players marching from the City Hall west on Main Street to Fourth Street where all crossed over to Broadway then north to the playing field. There, Mayor Plum threw the first pitch to league president and State Auditor Leo Meyer. Manager Ellison's first line up had Montgomery from Hobart at third base, brother and Texas-Oklahoma League veteran Cotton Ellison in center field, Tom Reed, who would become manager on May 9, at first base, Fred Liese, who had appeared with the Boston Braves in 1910, in right field, rookie James Hartline from Altus at shortstop, another rookie, Isom, at second base, Oklahoma City castaway Owen Gallagher behind the plate, and George "Bugs" Stone, a 1911 Lawton Medicine Man who finished that season with Durant in the Texas-Oklahoma League, on the slab. Verden's Phil Dayton from the 1911 Anadarko semi-pro champions, was backup catcher. Davey White, down from Oklahoma City, soon took over a place in the outfield. Nick Kahl won shortstop. Tom Casey, Hi Jasper, Lee Oram, Archie Tanner, and a Texan named George Crevenstine joined Stone to form a pitching corps. The Indians were gracious hosts before 459 paying fans (and another thousand watching from outside the field) as the Senators walked away with a seven to one victory. Hi Jasper, who would wear the flannels of the White Sox, Cardinals, and Indians, returned the favor before 145 Anadarkans with a four-hit whipping of Oklahoma City to even the series. The Cityans won the rubber game eight to three scoring five runs on Oram's wildness.

May 3 was the Senators' turn to host. This time the players rode in the parade that included Governor Cruce. Josh Billings, the Oklahoma City *wunderkid* from Oklahoma A & M, was wild and the Senator's dropped the opener six to one and, following a rainout, the second as well seven to six. Quickly released by the Senators, Billings joined Anadarko.

The Indians then returned home for a three day series against Okmulgee where Stone ended the Glassblowers' eight-game win streak that had begun on the first day of the season. Following a home series played in Muskogee, Anadarko appeared in Tulsa, and Guthrie. Of the ten games played around rainouts, Anadarko won five and dropped five including a near no-hitter at Muskogee by Ben Tincup; Davey White's solo home run was the only hit. Back home for series with Tulsa and McAlester, also split three/three, they took two at Holdenville then back home swept Guthrie.

With Oklahoma City under new management, a home and home resulted in three wins for each including the Senators' sweep of the Decoration Day twin bill. At home until June 9, the Indians let McAlester and Holdenville ride away with only a single victory each.

League leader Okmulgee hosted Anadarko for three beginning June 11 with Stone, Crevenstine and Tanner suffering losses. At Muskogee again the teams split the first two then the Creek Nation

The grandstand of Ellison's design the Indians used was eventually moved to the Caddo County fairgrounds and continued as the home of championship semi-pro teams.

Indians slaughtered Anadarko twenty-six to four in a dust storm. Guthrie was a poor host winning both of the games played. The last professional game played in Anadarko was an eight-up tie with Tulsa on June 20.

Boone Hite, interim president of the Anadarko ball club after Mayor William Plum had skipped town, left for the Democratic National Convention in Baltimore without leaving money to pay the wages of the players, then three days delinquent. Tom Reed telephoned Meyer on June 21 to let him know that the Indians had broken camp and it was every man for himself.

With no league games scheduled on the 21st, president Meyer unilaterally dissolved the Oklahoma State League on June 22. Two

Tom Reed from the Oklahoma City club succeeded Ray Ellison as manager on May 9. He broke the news to Leo Meyer that payroll had not been made and the Indians were disbanding.

days later, the remaining owners rescinded Meyer's dissolution order. J. B. Bartlett, late of the Mid-Continent league, became president and declared the Anadarko club was moved to Enid under the management of Ted Price. The reorganized league ran from June 28 through July 2 when a receivership was asked over the league.

A CROOKED MAYOR: THE STORY OF WILLIAM M. PLUM

At age twenty-six he joined 50th Iowa Volunteers for duty in the Spanish-American War but never left Des Moines. He came to Anadarko to make his fortune. He was involved in real estate speculation and private lending funded by a $500,000 line of credit with the National Reserve Bank of Kansas City. He had all appearance of success serving first as Caddo County Sheriff and then as the first Mayor of Anadarko for two terms. On May 15 he vanished leaving one letter resigning as Mayor and another to his wife saying she would never see him again. A few weeks later, he was spotted in Jamaica on his way to a new life in Brazil. He returned to his father's residence in Iowa sometime in late November. From there Mrs. Plum and the Sheriff of Caddo County returned him on Christmas Eve. He was reportedly convicted of embezzlement and sent to prison.

ARDMORE

ARDMORE   TEXAS LEAGUE   1904

ARDMORE   TEXAS-OKLAHOMA LEAGUE   1911-1914

ARDMORE WESTERN ASSOCIATION 1917

SEASON	TEAM NAME	MANAGERS	WON	LOST	PERCENTAGE	FINISH
1904	Territorians	Billy Hughes	3	7	.300	4 of 4
1911	Blues	Emmett Rogers	49	58	.458	5 of 5
		William Hillis				
		George McAvoy				
1912	Giants	George McAvoy	62	32	.660	1 of 8
1913	Giants	Art Naylor	43	80	.350	7 of 8
		Whitey Hewitt				
		Louis Pelkey				
		Brooks Gordon				
1914	Indians	Brooks Gordon	26	25	.510	dropped June 11
1917	Ardmoreites	G. N. "Kid" Speer	41	86	.323	8 of 8
		Dick Crittenden				

Founded in 1887, Ardmore, I. T. was named by a crew of the Santa Fe who named the stations on the route north after towns on Philadelphia's Main Line. North of Ardmore was Berwyn (now Gene Autry), Wynnewood and Paoli. The view is looking west. The date is circa 1910.

1904

The rail and cotton center of the Indian Territory, Ardmore, Pickens County, I.T., named by an A.T. & S.F. crew after one of the Philadelphia Mainline suburbs, had a baseball pedigree going back to near the time of its founding in 1887. First town teams then semi-pro aggregations that took on all comers as well as playing in a league outside of Organized Baseball, the citizens of Ardmore had grown accustomed to winners. The best of the Ardmore semi-pros was the 1904 Indian Territory League Territorians that bested a very good South McAlester club for the championship.

While the Territorians were compiling a record of twenty-six wins, eight losses and two ties, the Texas League doormat the Paris Parasites were withering on the vine. The day after Ardmore was crowned as the best in the Indian Territory, the Parasites disbanded with most getting on the train headed west where they would join the Texas League's newest member, the Ardmore Territorians.

WESTBOUND PARASITES

When the Paris Parasites of the Texas League disbanded under the command of former Guthrie manager Billy Hughes, Hugh McCullum, the "Pitching Parson" J. Argus Hamilton, affable Earl Zook, and Bucknell University star and future New York Highlander Walter Blair (1883-1948) took the train west on August 3 to Ardmore where they joined the strong Ardmore Territorians to reconstitute the Texas League's fourth team.

McCullum

Hamilton

Zook

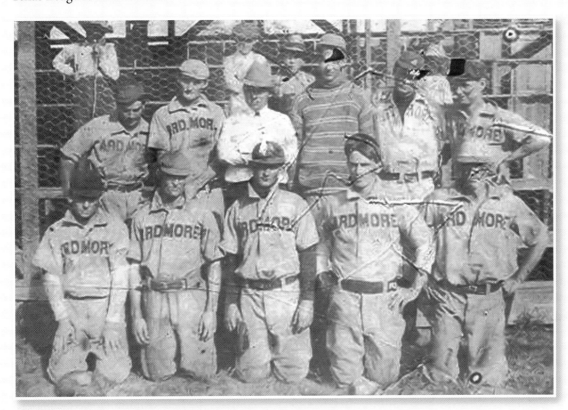

Blair

Ardmore Territorians: Top L-R: Ben Ragsdale, John Stone, business manager Gifford, John Harris, John Bibbs, Ed Savage. Lower L-R: Bill Redmon, Clyde Nichols, William Clayton, Walter Dougherty, Banks Moulder. The season was cut short on August 15 after only one league game had been played in Ardmore.

The Territorians, improved with league players like Hugh McCullum, Argus "the Pitching Parson" Hamilton, Earl Zook, future major leaguer Walter Blair, and manager Billy Hughes, a 1885 Philadelphia Athletic, taking on seasoned clubs like the Ft. Worth Panthers, Dallas Giants, and the Corsicana Oil Citys.

Within twenty-four hours of arriving, the new Territorians faced off at Chickasaw Park against the league-leading Ft. Worth Panthers. The Cats took the match not because of any flaws by pitcher "Long" John Harris or sixteen-year old Billy Clayton's homerun but by multiple bobbles on the field. The second game was rained out.

With twelve home games scheduled to follow ten on the road, the Ardmore club hit the rails bound for Dallas where, on August 8th the Territorians notched their first victory on nine Giants' errors by a score of ten to seven. A trip to Corsicana produced two more wins behind the pitching of Bob Teas and Banks Moulder. The last stop before the August 16 final homestand was Ft. Worth. With rumors flying that the Texas League was about to fold, the Cats took a single game on the thirteenth and a double header the following day. Those turned out to be the last three contests of the Territorians' professional season. The owners indeed decided to shut down operations. While Corsicana was taking eleven of nineteen games from Ft. Worth to claim the 1904 pennant, the Ardmore nine reverted to semi-pro status, winning ten more games before a finale on August 28 at the new home for Sunday baseball, Lorena Park that was safely beyond the city limits. Six seasons would pass before professional baseball would be played again in Ardmore.

1911

Emmett Rogers had been in baseball since he broke in with Hot Springs in 1887 and was the youngest player in the major leagues when he appeared for the 1890 Toledo Maumees. He migrated to the Oklahoma Territory where he was owner of

Emmett Rogers, seven years after launching then losing the Oklahoma City Mets of the Southwestern League, organized the Ardmore Blues in the new Texas-Oklahoma League. He lost that franchise in June, once again because of poor management and fan support.

Harry Williams (1890-1963) joined the Blues toward the end of the 1911 season. After a good 1912 season at Galveston, the Yankees bought him on June 23 where he saw duty in twenty-seven games. He made the team in 1914, playing fifty-nine games. He was sent down to Lincoln of the Western League on June 30, 1914, never to again appear in the Show.

the 1903 semi-pro Oklahoma City Mets and appeared behind the plate for the 1904 Guthrie Blues. As the sole owner of Ardmore Baseball Club, he received one of the charter franchises of the newly formed Texas-Oklahoma League. A team was cobbled together that included former Territorian Hugh McCullum and future New York Yankee Harry Williams. The newly-named Blues set up shop at the existing baseball facilities, Chickasaw Park, four blocks from Main Street, and on Sundays the grandstand at Lorena Park at the terminus of the Ardmore Railway Line just south of the Maxwell farm, three years later to become Dornick Hills Country Club, legendary designer Perry Maxwell's first golf course. The field conditions were deplorable. *The Daily Ardmoreite* of June 4 reported

The innerds [sic] of both of the baseball parks are in horrible condition. Local and visiting players pronounce the infield of the park on South Washington the worst in the circuit and the Lorena grounds are equally bad . . . . The rise near first base makes ground hit balls in that direction very uncertain.

Ardmore got off to a fast start with W. L. Gordon, future major leaguer Fred Nicholson, and

Rookie W. L. Gordon got off to a fast start. He spent the rest of his career with Durant and Denison then finished in the Middle Texas League.

Thomas "Slats" Wilson (1890-1953) was the Blues main catcher for most of the 1911 campaign. A rookie with the Blues in 1911, Wilson spent 1912-1916 behind the plate for the Galveston Pirates of the Texas League before being sold to Beaumont where he finished his career. He appeared once at the plate for the Washington Senators on September 8, 1914.

Western Association veteran C. M. Porter hammering the competition. Thomas "Slats" Wilson was behind the plate until recalled by Galveston. Even though the Blues played above .500 ball, the poor facilities and remarkably poor officiating repelled fans. The local business community stepped in to prop up the franchise, banishing Rogers from the front office. A slump dropped the Blues to fifth place prompting a headline "TEAM IN BAD SHAPE with Pitchers Overworked and Crippled

George McAvoy (1884-1952) managed Sapulpa of the Western Association to third place in 1910 and left his Oilers with a 32-21 record when that league exploded on June 19, 1911. He was quickly hired to replace Emmett Rogers. He finished the 1911 season with Ardmore and led the 1912 Giants to the playoffs. After a stint with San Francisco in the Pacific Coast League,

he became the regular second sacker for Ft. Worth. McAvoy was called up from Muskogee to appear as a pinch hitter in one game with the Philadelphia Phillies on July 7, 1914. He finished the season and his baseball career at Scranton. He played as George Carey with Galveston in 1920.

Infield and Outfield." After sweeping series with the T-O's cellar dwellers, the Blues climbed back to second. At that point, Rogers was forced out and, following the collapse of the Lawton and Gainesville operations, George McAvoy took the reins in a now six-team league. Ardmore finished the first half of the season in third place with twenty-four wins against twenty losses.

Financial problems caused by poor attendance continued to plague the Blues. Ardmore dropped to last place when Altus disbanded on July 18, leaving the league with five members. The Blues supplemented their lost Altus dates with exhibitions. Ardmore's return to baseball ended with a stumble across the finish in last place for the second half with twenty-four wins against twenty-eight losses.

1912

The Texas-Oklahoma League for all practical purposes dissolved following the 1911 season. It was resurrected at the impetus of a group from Durant and by the leadership of Ted Newcomb of Sherman. McAvoy ended up with the Ardmore operation, changed the name to "Giants," and commenced assembling a strong ballclub. Ardmore Baseball Association assumed ownership with McAvoy in control. A quick start put the Giants in the lead of the league race but, again, the locals failed to support the club. Following an offer to move the franchise lock, stock, and barrel to another state, a new stock company was formed headed by John S. Owens, William Hillis, and Morris Sass.

The Giants dropped the first half to Wichita Falls. McAvoy supplemented his ballclub with refugees from the Greenville and McKinney clubs that folded in early June and option players from the

Texas League. Jerry Naylor, who would star for Durant in 1913 and 1914, caught. Louis Pelkey, lured away from the Newton, Kansas, team, held down first base. Wilder Gray from the 1911 Blues played at the keystone. R. L. Woodward owned third base while manager McAvoy covered the shortfield. Veteran Art Naylor joined Buddy Robinson, on option from Austin, and Richard Sullivan in the outfield. A pitching corps of veterans Roy Allen and Sis Hopkins combined with newcomers J. L. Caldwell, Charles Deardorff, Dean Goss and rookie spitballer Rube Towers, teamed with the position players to cop the second half title. In all, the Giants won sixty-two and lost thirty-two.

Wilder Gray played eleven seasons in the minors between 1904 and 1914. He came to the Blues on the bounce from the Tulsa Railroaders of the defunct Western Association and was a regular for Ardmore in 1912 and 1913 until traded away to Superior of the Nebraska State League.

Roy "Snake" Allen began a playing career in 1912 that would run through 1925. He won ten of twenty-five decisions for a poor 1913 Ardmore club. Promoted to the Texas League, he found himself with the Kansas City Blues in 1919. From 1920-1924, Allen was a mainstay for Oklahoma City's Western League Indians. He last played for San Antonio in 1925.

A best-of-seven playoff with Wichita Falls was truncated to best of three when manager McAvoy was called up to the San Francisco Seals of the Pacific Coast League. The Giants took the first game in eleven innings but dropped the next two to the Drillers. McAvoy led the league with sixty-eight runs while Art Naylor had the most hits with 105.

1913

McAvoy abandoned Ardmore to become the Ft. Worth Cats' second baseman who, according to Texas League historian William Ruggles was "[a] capable and versatile infielder when at his best but far from consistent." As senior man on the roster, management named Art Naylor to lead the 1913 edition of the Giants. Spring drills were inauspicious as players showed up badly out of shape and local enthusiasm for baseball seemed on the wane. The manager started his young cousin Rollie Naylor, eventually a fixture on the Philadelphia Athletics' mound staff, in the opener then, after giving up fourteen hits, pulled and released him. Naylor's charges lost eleven of the first twelve games when he surrendered.

Pelkey from the 1912 Giants took over the team for three weeks. Eddie Palmer joined the Giants on his way to a date with the Philadelphia Athletics in 1917. On June 7, as it appeared that Hugo would seize the Ardmore franchise, the season record stood at seventeen wins against thirty-eight losses.

Alarmed at the prospect of Ardmore failing, Texas-Oklahoma League president C. O. Johnson reached into his umpiring staff for veteran Brooks

"Good field, no hit" aptly describes Southerner Louis Pelkey. Following six seasons in the Sally League with Savannah (where Shoeless Joe Jackson was a team mate), Pelkey headed west to join the Newton, Kansas club. He played against Ardmore in 1912 spring exhibitions and, liking what he saw, jumped to the Giants a month into the season. Batting .223 in 1913 as well as taking over managing the Giants when Art Naylor was fired, for 1914 he moved up to McAlester in the Western Association, later that season landing a job with Henryetta. With a last-place team, in his last game as a professional, Pelkey moved from the outfield to behind the plate to catch Don "Crazy Snake" Flinn, a future Pittsburgh Pirate and another fielder playing out of position.

Eddie "Baldy" Palmer (1898-1983) broke into Organized Baseball as a nineteen year-old rookie with the 1912 McAlester Miners of the Oklahoma State League. He signed with Ardmore for 1913. Palmer joined the Philadelphia A's at the end of the 1917 season batting .212 in sixteen games. He played eight years in the Texas League and then served as an umpire there for another eight years. "One of the steadiest of second basemen, good hitter of the free swinging type. . . .One of the best liked . . .by both players and fans for genial disposition and good sportsmanship."

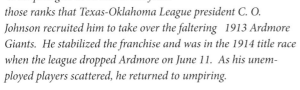

Catcher Brooks Gordon was only twenty-one when he added "manager" to his duties in 1905. He played and managed in the Texas League through 1910 winning three pennants along the way. Ruggles praised him as "[a] superb catcher and coach of pitchers, handicapped by having lost half of one foot in a rail accident." He turned to umpiring in 1911 and it was from those ranks that Texas-Oklahoma League president C. O. Johnson recruited him to take over the faltering 1913 Ardmore Giants. He stabilized the franchise and was in the 1914 title race when the league dropped Ardmore on June 11. As his unemployed players scattered, he returned to umpiring.

Gordon and installed him as the Giants' new field leader. He promptly shook up the roster and within two weeks had sold Naylor and mound ace Deardorff to Sherman. The Giants escaped the cellar but just barely. The August 1 edition of *The Daily Ardmoreite* led with 'CONTINUE RACE TO CELLAR Ardmore Seems Determined to Finish in last-Place This Year.' The headline was not prophetic only because the Durant Choctaws lost two more games than the Giants.

1914

Gordon returned with the best players from 1913 and augmented them with future major leaguers Roy Leslie and Cotton Tierney as well as steady veteran Joe Fenner.

Three weeks into the season, re-named as the "Indians," Ardmore had hold on second place and was challenging for the top spot. Field success notwithstanding, business manager John Hoffman struggled to make payrolls. The Indians were in

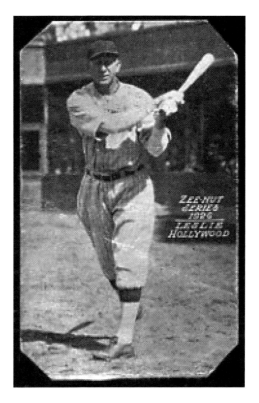

Roy Leslie (1894-1972) was an eighteen year old manager of Bonham when he broke into league ball in 1912 and continued through 1913. He signed with champion Ennis of the Middle Texas League after Ardmore disbanded on June 11, 1914. Leslie appeared at the tail end of two seasons with different teams: seven games with the Chicago Cubs in 1917 and twelve games with the 1919 St. Louis Cardinals. He was the Phillies' regular first baseman in 1922. After spending 1923-1926 in the Pacific Coast League, he returned to Texas finishing as the manager of Tyler in 1929.

Cotton Tierney (1894-1953) was a rookie with Tyler and Dallas in 1912. He climbed the minor league ladder until Tulsa sold him to Pittsburgh at the end of the 1920 season. He got into twelve games with the Pirates and then remained with them through 1923. He also appeared for the 1924 Boston Braves and 1925 Brooklyn Robins. He last played for Shawnee in the Western Association in 1929 and finished in Organized Baseball the next year managing Joplin.

Joe Fenner was a steady hitter with six seasons' experience when he joined the 1914 Ardmore Indians. After Ardmore was booted, he signed with Belton where he was hitting .455 before moving down the road to Austin where he hit .310 in the Texas League to end the season. 1916 was his last campaign, batting .296 for Ennis in the Central Texas League.

trouble but not nearly as bad off as the Hugo Scouts who had moved from Wichita Falls in late July of the previous season. On June 11, the league owners jerked Hugo's franchise and decided to reduce the league to six. To reach that number, Ardmore, with a twenty-six and twenty-five record, was dropped. The Indians won their last game behind Tom Weeks' two-hitter against the Durant Gladiators. The core of the Indians migrated to McAlester of the Western Association. The rest scattered.

On July 30, the Texas-Oklahoma became a four-team loop that would go dormant until 1921.

Foley White (?-1955) was one of the three White brothers who appeared for the 1906 South McAlester Miners (see page 152). Ardmore was the last stop on his professional itinerary, dividing catching duties with manager Brooks Gordon.

1917

The Paris ball club called itself the "Survivors" after the March 21, 1916 fire that leveled much of the town. Baseball was played and the 1916 season completed. It was not long into the 1917 season, however, that the damage done the year before plus falling cotton prices, and tight money after America's entry into the Great War combined to make league baseball untenable in Paris. J. W. Bell engineered the transfer of the franchise on May 10 to a city that had been promised league baseball in 1915 and had been waiting in the wings: Ardmore, Oklahoma.

Sheldon Tyer was the Carter County Clerk and chair of the Ardmore Draft Board when he led the effort to land the floundering Paris franchise in the Western Association. He also was the organizer of Ardmore's 1924 entry in the Oklahoma State League.

Head of the local draft board and County Clerk Shelton Tyer collaborating with W. C. Waggoner landed the ball club. A place to play was needed in eight days. The angel was the Ardmore streetcar line whose car barn was located at Lorena Park north of the city. The grandstand that had hosted baseball on Sundays since 1904 was moved near the car yard and christened "Putnam Park" in honor of the Ardmore Railway Company's manager.

Renamed the "Ardmoreites," the home debut was made on May 18. In the first division with a sixteen and twelve record when the move was made, before 1,800 fans the Ardmore club whipped visiting McAlester five to one behind the pitching of veteran Bernie Everdon. The season was downhill from there. By June 8 the club had fallen to fifth with a percentage under .500 for the first time

ANOTHER PARIS CLUB MOVES WEST

Ardmore's first professional team came from Paris, Texas and its last one before 1921 also came from that city. Paris' Western Association team never completely recovered from the 1916 fire that destroyed the heart of town. It was something of a wonder that the aptly-named "Survivors" finished 1916 and no surprise when they pulled up stakes on May 10, 1917 and headed for Ardmore. Initially called the "Wanderers," Ardmore's new team's new home was the old grandstand at Lorena Park, north of the city limits, at the terminus of the streetcar line; location solved the problem of Sunday baseball but didn't help weekday attendance.

"Kid" Speer who had a cup of coffee with Detroit in 1909, had led the 1916 Survivors and brought them largely intact to Ardmore.

Regulars included Frank Allison, Floyd Hall, Richard Kauffman from the Kansas City Blues, and veteran backstop Leslie "Drap" Hayes, who managed Chickasha and Henryetta in the Western Association as well as Ardmore's first 1924 club. He took his last at bat in 1929 as playing manager of Miami.

Renamed the Ardmoreites, Speer abandoned his team at the end of July. Under Dick Crittenden (page 67), the club finished the campaign as a road team.

Terminus of the streetcar line.

Allison

Speer

Hall

Kauffman

Hayes

and was soon to tumble to sixth. The larger towns with Bell's deciding vote overcame the smaller cities' move to truncate the season. Instead of ending in July, the season would continue into September. By July 9, the Ardmoreites had taken over the cellar with forty-two wins in ninety-four starts. Over the next three weeks, only six more were added to the win column. At that point manager Speer would take a leave of absence and turn over the team to veteran catcher Dick Crittenden who promptly

fled Ardmore for the security of daily guarantees as an orphan team. Winning only one game the first twenty days of August, the eleven remaining Ardmoreites struggled to season's end. Speer reappeared for the last day of the campaign as the team split a double header at Tulsa to end the season with fifty-seven wins against ninety-eight losses. With the military draft and wartime restrictions, the Western Association suspended to be revived in 1920 without Ardmore.

CHICKASHA

CHICKASHA SOUTHWESTERN LEAGUE 1904

SEASON	TEAM NAME	MANAGERS	WON	LOST	PERCENTAGE	FINISH
1904	Indians	W. M. Hazlett	13	24	.351	*

* May 1-5 Shawnee Indians   June 24-July 29 Shawnee Orioles   August 1-5 El Reno

August 17-September 5 Shawnee Browns

A street scene from Chickasha circa 1905. It was the rail and mercantile center of the western Chickasaw Nation.

Pete Hauser (1884-1935) was a member of the Cheyenne tribe who attended both the Haskell Indian School and Carlisle Institute where he shared the football backfield with Jim Thorpe. Along with Ben Tincup, Hauser is a member of the American Indian Athletic Hall of Fame.

Banker and baseball enthusiast W. M. Hazlett elbowed his way into the new Southwestern League by persuading the Oklahoma City, Enid, and Guthrie owners to boot Wichita. A schedule was set with the assumption Hazlett would operate from Chickasha but when the season opened on May 2 in Enid, the visiting team was the Shawnee Indians. His team completed the first trip with a pair of wins and the same number of loses. When the train home reached Chickasha, the Indians departed to become the other Queen of the Washita's representative and the only professional club in the Indian Territory.

A parade of the teams, a band, and 300 fans processed to the unfinished Rock Island ball park to watch the maroon and green-clad Indians dismantle the Oklahoma City Mets by a lop-sided score of nineteen to two in a rain-shortened contest. The opening line-up had Tommy "Butch" Kern (Kearns) behind the plate, Carlisle Institute star Pete Hauser at first base, Cousins on second, Ben Grant on third, Lawton's Tarr at shortstop, with William Weller, Ben Bennett, and Doc Andrews in the outfield. Ed Betch and Clyde Loughmiller, who began the season with the semi-pro Ardmore club, were the mainstays on the mound.

With the Indians in third place only because Guthrie had only three wins three weeks into the season, following a shellacking at Oklahoma City, Betch and Loughmiller went AWOL causing a forfeit the next day as Chickasha had fewer than ten players in uniform. Andrews had to take the mound and managed to vanquish Guthrie on June 6 in sixty-five minutes. Meanwhile, Hazlett signed Lawton's Ed Pokorney and local boys Henderson and DeRoss.

"Wee" William Weller played for Oklahoma semi-pro and league clubs, including Chicka-sha and Lawton, during the first decade of the last century.

Ed Pokorney (1880-?) was one three brothers —Milton and Otto were the others— from Lawton who played professional baseball between 1904 and 1916. He is shown here with the 1904 Guthrie Blues. He reached the AA level, the rung below the major leagues, with Toledo.

Jay "Doc" Andrews (1876-1925) had been in the game since 1894 when he found his way to the Twin Territories where he saw duty with both Chickasha and Oklahoma City before moving east to Nashville. He last took the field in 1914 but was in the dugout as a manger through 1921.

Rapidly Hazlett's financial situation became a cause for concern. The club needed $200 per month to operate. On June 3, a local committee of C.M. Fechheimer, R. Stephens, James Pettyjohn, Hugo Roos, and W. F. Grandee was formed to solicit the merchants and businessmen for support. By June 15, the Indians were firmly ensconced in last place with a record of fourteen wins against twenty-five losses even after a sweep of Guthrie. The next stop was Enid. In "an exhibition of rotten ball playing" and "errors galore" the Evangelists vanquished Chickasha. On the return to home, the Indians took an exhibition from the Ft. Sill soldiers. On June 20 the last professional game played in Chickasha until 1920 saw Andrews blanking Enid eight runs to nil. The team, unpaid, refused to appear for a series beginning June 21 in Oklahoma City. On June 22, the following article appeared in the *Chickasha Daily Express*.

CLUB DISBANDED

The Chickasha baseball team has gone to pieces. The history of the team has been a checkered one and it would be difficult to go into all the details that lead to its downfall. The principle [sic] trouble was lack of support. The crowds that attended did not bring in sufficient funds to support the team. Various mistakes in management increased expenses and decreased receipts.

When Hazlett quit the team, a large debt was hanging over it. The citizens who undertook to raise a fund sufficient to guarantee the support of the club worked hard but they found difficulties that could not be overcome and had to abandon their efforts.

At the present time the indebtedness to the players is $140. This amount should be raised and paid to them at one [sic]. Besides this amount there is other indebtedness that should be looked after.

The most famous Minco ringer was Hall of Famer Walter Johnson who received $250 to pitch an exhibition against the Geary town team. Familiar names for Minco were Ned Pettigrew, Ben Brownlow, Red Davis, Arch Shelton, Willie Weller, and Tom Campbell. Geary pros included Clyde Geist, Sled Allen, and Floyd Hall. Minco won six nil behind Johnson's two-hitter.

Minco, Oklahoma was both a polo and semi-pro baseball power-house before World War I. The 1909 team pictured won seventy-seven and lost but seven (including two to Texas League opponents). With a couple of exceptions, all the players lived near Minco year round. They also hired ringers such as the Hauser brothers, Pete and Emil, from Carlisle Institute.

The Chickasha ballpark was on Grand Avenue across from Oklahoma College for Women on the same property where USAO's baseball team plays. The streetcar began service in 1910 and ran behind Trout Hall. A contemporary report stated "[d]espite the cold, threatening weather, baseball bugs from almost the entire state packed University park from extreme left to right fields. Every seat in the grandstand and bleachers was taken. From start to finish it was one continual ovation for Johnson." Shown are the streetcars delivering fans to the contest.

The league left the franchise with Hazlett but moved it to Shawnee effective on July 1; the team "suspended" in the interim.

During the time without professional baseball, there was plenty of semi-pro activity. During the Teens and Twenties, it was not unusual for major league stars to appear for a game or two with town teams. This happened at University Park in Chicka-sha on October 25, 1914.

On a cold, windy day before a full house from across Oklahoma, a Minco nine full of Western Association stars blanked Geary's ball club behind the Washington Senators' Walter Johnson's two-hitter.

DURANT

DURANT   TEXAS-OKLAHOMA LEAGUE 1911-1914

SEASON	TEAM NAME(S)	MANAGERS(S)	WON	LOST	PERCENTAGE	FINISH
1911	Educators	W.W. Washington	65	46	.586	2 of 8
		Joe Connor				
		Ben Brownlow				
		Bill Harper				
		Hetty Green				
1912	Hustlers/ Choctaws	Hetty Green	26	64	.289	6 of 6
		Leslie Mitchell				
		Charles Deardorff				
		Bill Harper				
1913	Choctaws	Stoney Jewel	41	84	.328	8 of 8
		George "Kid" Speer				
1914	Gladiators/ Indians	Fred Morris	46	73	.387	4 of 4
		Bert Humphries				

Founded in 1873 and named after French-Choctaw settler Dixon Durant (originally "DuRant"), the Magnolia City and seat of Bryan County is the capital of "Little Dixie." Like nearly all southern county seats, there is a memorial to Confederate soldiers on the courthouse grounds. Curiously, when it came time to divide up institutions for the new state, Durant lost the Confederate Veterans Home to Ardmore. As a consolation, Durant got Southeastern State Normal College.

Of the sixteen cities that hosted teams in the first iteration of the Texas-Oklahoma League, only charter member Durant began and finished all four seasons. Durant's nines toiled under five different names in two ball parks. The 1913 season opened with only Durant and Ardmore of all the cities and towns of Oklahoma, including the Capital and Tulsa, enjoying Organized Baseball. It was business people in Durant who revived the league after a difficult 1911 season and a Durant man led the league as president from 1912 through the league's demise after the 1914 season. Durant fans supported teams that played below .400 ball for three consecutive seasons. Before league baseball, Durant had fielded champion teams in the semi-pro Indian Territory League. After the Texas-Oklahoma League folded, it remained a good baseball town and continued to support sandlots clubs as well as the semi-pro G.I.'s of the 1940s and 1950s.

1911

D. A. "Doc" Hathcox was the promoter who secured a franchise in the newly formed Texas-Oklahoma League. By mid-February, he had secured $400 of the $1,000 needed to make the league guarantee and erect a ball park in time for spring drills on April 1. For city boosters, a professional team was a "splendid advertisement." Durant League Baseball Club was formed with Hathcox at the helm to operate the new venture. W. W. Washington, a long time Durant semi-pro, joined Hathcox in securing a roster. A $600 ball park was built six blocks from the business district, just beyond the city limits at the east end of Main Street across mineral bayou and three blocks east of the new East Ward School. The new grandstand was sixty feet across the front and seated approximately five hundred.

The temporarily-named Invincibles christened new league park on April 12 with a fourteen-inning scoreless tie against Muskogee's Western Associa-

Morrison Hall built in 1910 was the first campus building. The new Durant league team was named the "Educators" because of the college. Prominent early Southeastern graduates were oilmen Lloyd Noble and Waco Turner.

tion Redskins. Washington signed an opening day roster headed by former New York Highlander catcher Joe Connor in his sixteenth professional season. Young Reedy Jennings' entry of "Educators" —because Durant was the academic center of Little Dixie— won the team naming contest.

The season opened on April 25 at home before two thousand fans. With the first Durant batter, Harry Burge, knocking the first pitch beyond the high outfield fence, Durant went on to score nine runs against visiting Cleburne; Burge added a triple and double for nine total bases. After trailing leader Wichita Falls for the first two weeks of the season, the Educators hit a slump with Connor

With the exception of two games with the 1895 St. Louis Cardinals and three with the 1906 Ft. Worth Cats, Joe Connor (1874-1957) had spent his entire career east of the Mississippi River with most seasons played in New England before he took over the Durant club in the 1911 Texas-Oklahoma League.

J. R. McKee from the Central Kansas League threw the league's and Durant's first no-hitter on May 28, 1911, a game shortened to five innings when darkness fell.

Rookie Lindy Hiett began a ten season career with the Educators that included twenty win seasons in 1913 and 1914. Ruggles said of him "[a] tall, slight righthander handicapped by never pitching for a consistent winning club."

replacing Washington. The club finished the first half season with twenty-three wins against twenty losses in fourth place but only one-half game behind second-place Altus. One of those wins was

J.R. McKee's May 28 darkness-shortened no-hitter at Gainesville; only five innings were played as the teams didn't take the field until 5:00 p.m.

The local ministerial alliance in a city that seemed to have ongoing revivals of different stripes came out in favor of weekday but not Sunday baseball. The result was an ordinance against Sabbath-breaking. The ball park was constructed beyond the city limits emulating Cleburne's solution to the Sunday problem. Hathcox was publicly vocal in favor of Sunday ball because that day made the franchise financially viable. The powerful Baraca Sunday school class of First Methodist Church countered a Sunday baseball petition drive by arranging for the sheriff to enforce the recent order of new District Judge A. H. Ferguson enjoining Sunday ball under a state law. It had been anticipated that their hand would be played when Altus came to town on May 14. Instead, signals were crossed with Altus arriving in Durant and the Educators landing in Altus. When Lawton came to town to play the next scheduled Sunday game, both teams were arrested following the game. Lawton captain William Metcalfe remained behind as a hostage while his team traveled on to the next series. The morality police also cracked down on wagering. Five, including the sheriff's son, had been arrested for gambling at the ball park on May 1. That incident and others in every league town prompted President St. Clair to issue an epistle general on the subject.

Durant began the second half fast, winning ten against two losses. A new second half schedule with pre-June 22 games counting in the first half standings placed Durant at thirty-three and twenty-two, a firm second-place finish. As the new second half began, local leaders intervened in the business of Durant League Baseball Club on June 29. Court

As a twenty-four year old third baseman, Ben Brownlow (1886-1944) was Durant's third manager of 1911. His playing career ran from 1909 through 1927 including nine seasons in the Texas League. "Average hitter but very capable fielder at any infield or outfield position" according to Ruggles. He was killed in a cotton gin accident.

Clerk William R. Collins succeeded Hathcox as president, haberdasher E. V. Kendall became secretary, with W. E. Utterbach, T. L. Cox, W. B. Pettey, and Charles Woodward filling out the board of directors. Their first act was to furlough Connor for health reasons and appoint Ben Brownlow as interim captain. The league had shrunk to six teams after Gainesville and Lawton collapsed in rapid succession on June 17. Bill Harper succeeded Brownlow; Hetty Green, who had spent most of the season with Wichita Falls and led the league in wins and winning percentage, followed him. A number of players had come through the Educators' clubhouse including future manager Stoney Jewell.

By season end on August 23, only Elmer Brooks, Harry Burge, and pitcher Henson were still around from opening day. The final game against

Bert Corzine broke in with Durant in 1911 and played his entire career in Texas-Oklahoma League cities. His ERA for his last two seasons was 1.71 for Sherman in the Western Association.

J. K. Armstrong joined the Educators from the Clay City, Kansas club where he was batting .291. He held down first base.

Bonham before a large crowd was described as "in reality a farce" by the *Bryan County Democrat* as the Boosters shelled outfielders-cum-pitchers Pat Patterson and Buddy Robinson for eight runs in five innings while the Educators managed only two hits, stranding six. Once again, Durant finished second with thirty-two victories against twenty-four defeats. This time, though, Cleburne topped the remaining five clubs; Altus had dropped out on July 11. Duncan League Baseball Club like the other members of the league wilted. The first season had been financially precarious. There was a real prospect that there would be no league ball in 1912.

1912

Durant League Baseball Club's president Collins called a mass meeting for November 28, 1911 to examine the past season and make arrangements for league baseball in 1912. As no "boozers" or "has beens" were to be included for 1912, "only good, clean, and young men who are interested in the game and want to get higher" would be recruited. With half of the 1911 members out of baseball, the imperative to reorganize became urgent. V. E. Kendall was dispatched to prospective franchisees: Ardmore and Hugo in Oklahoma, Denison, Sherman, Paris, Bonham, Greenville, McKinney, and Gainesville in Texas. The first organizational meeting was February 2 in Wichita Falls with Durant, Ardmore, Denison, Sherman, Bonham, Wichita Falls and McKinney in; Hugo did not send a representative. Locally, C. O. Johnson was elected president of the new Durant Baseball Association with William Head secretary. Johnson returned from the next league meeting with a ninety-five-game schedule over a season running from April 25 to July 28. The resurrected league added Greenville

as the eighth member. A new name, Hustlers, was selected and a sample new uniform —grey, green stripes, black lettering, white stockings, and black belt— was placed in the Stone-Kimbrell Drugstore window. A new ball park was erected in town closer to the business district. Hetty Green came to terms and was named manager. The players in camp were, according to *The Sporting News*, "weak-hitting" and the outfield was "poor." The bright spots were behind the plate with Ada rookie John Kaiser and local semi-pro Lewis Mitchell, returning keystone Oscar Eppling, and Native American pitchers Nelson Jones and McDaniel.

The wealthiest woman in the world noted for her parsimony, the "Witch of Wall Street," was Henrietta or "Hetty" Green (1834-1916). Texas-Oklahoma hurler L. M. Green was called Hetty with such frequency that his given name has been lost. He debuted in the 1909 Kansas State League where he was won twenty-two of forty-two decisions in two seasons. He spent the rest of his career shuttling among the Western Association, Texas-Oklahoma, and Texas Leagues including 1912 with Durant, Denison and Dallas, 1913 at Wichita Falls and Hugo, and 1914 with Hugo, Tulsa, and Henryetta. Green was Durant's fifth manager of 1911 and first of 1912.

The Hustlers dropped the first game of 1912 to Sherman by an eight to two count. It was a harbinger of a poor season. Deardorff, who had lost the opener, and manager Green were the pitching staff. Outfielders regularly took the mound. It was not until May 16 and 17 that Durant strung together consecutive wins. One month into the season the Hustlers had

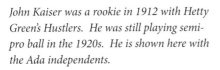

John Kaiser was a rookie in 1912 with Hetty Green's Hustlers. He was still playing semi-pro ball in the 1920s. He is shown here with the Ada independents.

Oscar Epling was another refugee from the Kansas leagues. He held down second base for the 1911 and 1912 Durant teams.

Charles Deardorff began his career in the Northeast Arkansas circuit in 1909 then moved up to the Texas League for two seasons. He began 1912 with Durant and was the team's third manager until Bill Harper returned and traded him to Ardmore who sent him to Sherman. He began 1913 with Sherman and finished with Durant.

The Hustlers didn't live up to the name so were rechristened the "Choctaws" for the second half. After the Oklahoma State League exploded on June 22, a number of new free agents were looking for work. The Choctaws inked outfielder Guiton Scott, catchers Oscar Palmer and Hornbuckle plus pitchers L. M. Gierhart, J. Campbell and veteran Sis Hopkins. They sent Green to Denison for $100 and two players including future Federal Leaguer Orie Kerlin. Green showed the Choctaws that they should have kept him when he three-hit his former team mates on July 2.

Bill Harper (1889-1951) twice served "in relief" as manager of Durant. He preceded Hetty Green in 1911 and followed Charles Deardorff in 1912. He began his professional career at age twenty-two with the 1911 St. Louis Browns for ten days during which he pitched nine innings. He threw for Decatur in the Three-I League in 1912, 1913, and 1914.

won only seven games. On May 25, Bonham threw a no-hitter at the Hustlers. They finally defeated Sherman on May 29 to run the season to eight wins and twenty-five losses. At this point, Green turned over the team to catcher Mitchell who then passed along the captaincy to Deardorff. Despite the poor showing, McKinney's no-names had managed to win only four contests to keep Durant out of the cellar. The Hustlers handed McKinney its fifth and sixth wins on June 3 and 6. The following day McKinney played its last, dropping a nineteen to eight game to Durant; the no-names finished their foray into Organized Baseball with six wins and thirty-three losses. On June 8, Greenville and McKinney disbanded, reducing the league to six. The first half ended for Durant with ten wins and thirty-two defeats. On the bright side, the Hustlers signed Greenville's manager and third baseman Bill Harper and ace pitcher and future big leaguer, Rick Adams (see page 72).

The Choctaws signed rookie catcher Oscar Palmer late in 1912 and he remained on the roster into 1914. He was sold to Bonham, then Sherman and, when those clubs disbanded, landed a position with Henryetta in the Western Association. After World War I, he appeared for Oklahoma City, and Pawhuska in the new Western Association, and Parsons, Cushing, and Sapulpa in the 1921 revived Southwestern League.

Nothing came of a proposal from A. L. "Dad" Ritter to merge his league-leading Cleburne club of the South Central League and continue the season in Durant; his Railroaders disbanded on July 17. Durant got off to a fast start in the second half but a fortnight later were in last place with four wins and eight losses. With nearly a complete turnover of its personnel, the Choctaws began to play good baseball but with the season ending July 27 it was

Orlie Kerlin (1891-1974) came to the 1912 Hustlers from Denison. At the time he was a student at Louisiana State University. After seasons of semi-pro ball in Texas, he signed with Pittsburgh in the new Federal League after being discovered by Rebel Oakes, the Pittsburgh manager who was from Homer, Louisiana. He failed to get a hit in his only trip to the plate for the 1915 Pittsburgh Rebels. He returned to his Homer, Louisiana home where he worked in a family hardware store, ran a saw mill, and served as the town undertaker.

A catcher from German country in south Texas, Adolph Knaupp had appeared in the Texas League before landing at Denison. He was sold to Durant near the end of the 1912 season.

too late. Win number eleven and loss twenty-seven came by way of forfeits. Red Adams won the last match-up of the season against archrival Ardmore. A battery of J. Campbell and Adolph Knaupp, acquired from Denison, took the season finale at Durant by a score of two to one.

Weak-hitting is the best description of the 1912 team. W. L. Tucker led the Choctaws with a .300 batting average. Next was manager Harper at .267, then Gordon at .256, at .250, and Hornbuckle at .222. None of the rest of the players hit above .200.

1913

C. O. Johnson had become the President of the Texas-Oklahoma League toward the end of the 1912 campaign. J. B. Smith succeeded him as prexy of Durant Baseball Association. Beside season ticket sales and selecting a manager, the operation had to reconfigure the ball park to solve complaints about noise. The grandstand and bleachers were switched from the southwest to the northwest corner of the property.

The 1913 crew was guided by Oklahoma City's Stoney Jewell who played in the 1911 Educators' infield. Red Adams, J. Campbell, A. Edens, W. L. Gordon, and Jerry Naylor had been reserved from the 1912 aggregation. Bill Horrill, at Lyons, Kansas the previous season, won the first base position. R. M. Woodward would share second base with manager Jewell. Edens would again cover third base while Arch Shelton held down shortstop. Buddy Robinson from the 1912 Ardmore club, Thomas Robinson who managed Holdenville in 1912, Cole Hooper, Calvin Bryant from the 1911 Educators, Hennessey, and Clark would roam the outfield. John Herman joined Naylor as backup catcher. Veteran George "Kid" Speer, John Younkman, Cramer, Taylor, G. Chapman, and Rube Towers, also an Ardmore alumnus, and G. W. Long, joined Campbell and Adams to form the mound staff. New uniforms for 1913 were identical to the Texas League Dallas Giants. That was the only resemblance. Dallas won ninety-two games in 1913.

The season opened at home on April 17 with an eight to five win for the Choctaws over Ardmore. Durant shelled future Philadelphia Athletic Rollie Naylor for fourteen hits in his professional debut. It was downhill from there. In an eighteen-inning loss to Paris, the umpire, Vitter, showed such favoritism

CHOCTAWS SHOULD BE BETTER THAN THAT

Midway through the 1912 season, the Durant team changed its name to Choctaws from Hustlers apparently because the club was deep in the cellar at the season mid-point and hadn't shown much hustle. The name carried over to the 1913 club that finished eighth wining only forty-one of 125 games. Oklahoma Cityan Stormy Jewell with nearly a decade in semi-pro and league ball was signed as manager after Harper's departure. Jerry Naylor was back for a second season after a sojourn at Ardmore and would catch in 1914 as well. G. W. Long was 15-20 for Muskogee and McAlester in 1915. John Herman played two seasons at Durant then joined Muskogee and Tulsa in the 1915 Western Association. Frank Taylor joined former major leaguer Red Adams to form the core of the pitching staff. Texan W. F. "Monk" Johns covered third base for the Choctaws. The steadiest Durant player was Buddy Robinson who played part of 1912 and all of 1913 and 1914 in the City of Magnolias. Veteran pitcher G. N. "Kid" Speer took over from Jewell for the second half of the season.

Jewell

Naylor

Herman

Long

Taylor

Robinson

Johns

to the Boosters that he even suggested whom to call in for relief. A month into the season, Durant's record was five wins against twenty-four losses. Then the Choctaws went on the longest winning streak of the year —five games— to raise victories to double digits. By July, the Choctaws and manager Jewell parted ways. He joined the Paris club and with that a number of transactions followed. Third baseman Jimmy Wicks was sold for $300 plus the Booster's third sacker, Dailey. Pitcher John Younkman went to Paris for $400. George Harper was released and signed. Paris finished second.

George "Kid" Speer, who had a brief appearance with the Detroit Tigers in 1909, took over the Choctaws for the second half of the season. Like 1912, the Durant players did not hit. Buddy Robinson went on a tear improving his .238 average at July 15 to .312 by season end. Only two other regulars, shortstop Edens and third baseman Monk Johns, hit at or above .250. Two hurlers accounted for nearly half the team's wins, twelve for Adams, eight for Campbell; each lost twenty, nearly half the loses. No Durant pitcher had had a winning record for two seasons.

Most of the 1913 starters were reserved for 1914. There was hope for a high finish in 1914.

1914

J. W. Bailey had succeeded J. B. Smith as president of Durant Baseball Association. C. O. Johnson remained as league president. The newspaper announcement for a mass meeting a week before the season opener included the words "Durant will not hug the cellar this year." The ball park was placed into top condition.

Fred Morris, who had led Wichita Falls to the 1911 and 1912 pennants, had been released from

the helm of the Hugo Scouts and was looking for a team to lead. Speer, who finished the season leading the Choctaws, was working his way back to the Show —unsuccessfully as it turned out— having been signed by the Ft. Worth Cats of the Texas League. Durant was looking for a leader out of the depths of the Texas-Oklahoma League. Morris was hired. He had the core of a team in place. Buddy Robinson, A. Edens, Thomas Robinson, Wallace

After taking his Wichita Falls club to the 1911 and 1912 crowns, the team that moved to Hugo in 1913 failed to make the first division. With ownership thinking he had lost his touch, Morris found himself unemployed in February, 1914. Vowing Durant would not suffer through another losing season, Morris took over the team freshly rechristened as the "Gladiators."

Ralph Heatley first appeared in a paid-to-play setting when he joined the 1914 Gladiators. He played through 1922 reaching Milwaukee of the American Association in 1916. His best success was as a manager. He took Bristow to the Oklahoma State League title in 1923 and was just out of first place when the league failed in 1924.

Murie, Charles Lockhart, J. Campbell, John Herman, Jerry Naylor, Ralph Heatley, L. M. Gierhart, and Jimmie Humphries were back. Rookies Henry Erwin, Virgil Hughes, and Roy Floyd joined them as did veteran Lucky Wright. There was reason to be optimistic.

The opener was a festive affair with a parade of both the Gladiators and Sherman's Lions, Lyday's brass band, fifty or sixty cars, and a second line of fans processing to the ball park. Following remarks by Judge J. M. Hatchett, nine local ladies "played one sixteenth of an inning." The game was a slugfest with thirty-one hits, nine errors and twenty-nine runs. The Gladiators were on the short end of a fifteen to fourteen stick.

Paris, Texarkana, and Denison set the pace. On June 11, the insolvent Hugo franchise was returned to the league. To avoid an odd-numbered league membership and the scheduling problems that entailed, the owners decided to drop Ardmore as well. In their last game, the Indians behind their ace, watchmaker Thomas Weeks, shut out the Durant nine five to zero. Durant being the only Oklahoma club remaining was "an honor that justly belongs to this city, as Durant was responsible for creation of the Texas-Oklahoma league." Even with the addition of Ardmore's third baseman L. E. Carey.and top pitcher, J. Ray Francis, a six team league did not help out Durant.

The Texas-Oklahoma League nearly ended on July 30 when Sherman threw in the towel and Bonham refused to play in a four-team league as did Durant which offered to disband in deference to the Bonham organization. League president Johnson rallied the local fans to continue and Durant Baseball Association agreed after some concessions were made. Now called the Indians, Durant was in the

When Ardmore was dropped from the Texas-Oklahoma League, veteran L. E. Carey was signed. He was soon sold to Austin

Rookie J. R. (Ray J.) Francis (1893-1934) was the top pitcher for Ardmore and then turned in a strong performance for the Gladiators. Working his way up via Seattle, he spent 1922, 1923, and 1925 in the American League with the Senators, Tigers, Yankees, and Red Sox. He pitched in the minors another seven seasons.

familiar cellar. They remained there, cementing their hold with a last day loss of a double header to Denison. Durant's energy for baseball waned as the oil boom grew. League ball was never to return.

Bert Humphries (1880-1945) replaced Morris late in the season. Between 1910 and 1915 he amassed a 50-43 record with a very respectable 2.79 ERA for weak teams: Phillies, Reds, Cubs. He led the National League in winning percentage (.800) in 1913. He threw in the Florida State League 1921-1924, retiring to Orlando.

EL RENO

EL RENO PACKERS   WESTERN ASSOCIATION
JULY 4, 1909 - JULY 31, 1910

SEASON	TEAM NAME	MANAGERS	WON	LOST	PERCENTAGE	FINISH
1909	Packers	Bill Burns	16	46	.258	8 of 8
		Bailey Vinson				
		Newton Fisher				
1910	Packers	Art Riggs	65	43	.602	dropped July 31

A major yard of the Rock Island railroad and the home of El Reno Packing & Provision Co. as well as an entire packing town, El Reno in 1909 with a population of approximately 7,000, had more than doubled in size since the 1900 Census and had even added 2,050 residents since the 1907 Statehood enumeration. The leading force in the community in 1909 was the Commercial Club, a league of businessmen headed by H. S. Engle, that functioned rather like a combined Chamber of Commerce and Rotary Club. El Reno had many of the badges of prosperity and growth but it lacked one: a league baseball team.

When mining center Joplin, Missouri failed to support its Class C franchise in the Western Association, the Commercial Club snapped it up on July 2 paying the $500 league entry fee and paying off the attendant debts. League President Doc Shively ordered the change immediately. The Commercial Club dispatched Bailey C. Vinson, a local, experienced semi-pro baseball man, to Muskogee with a dozen uniforms borrowed from the semi-pro

El Reno had become a meat packing center soon after it became the maintenance hub of the Chicago, Rock Island & Pacific Railroad. It had doubled in size in the decade following the 1900 Census. The town had become a city.

club. On July 3, 1909 the El Reno Packers in Joplin uniforms dropped the day's game at Muskogee by a score of ten to zero. Vinson shadowed first baseman and manager Bill Burns pending selection of a new field leader. A stock association with fifty shareholders was formed to own and operate the franchise. The canvass raised $2,500 including $1,000-$1,500 to construct a ball park. Its officers and executive committee were H.S. Patterson, president; A. L. Cromer, secretary; A. T. March, treasurer; Ed LaVan, J. P. Gutelius, and Charles Bergen, committee members. Meanwhile a committee of the Commercial Club visited local businesses to

Peach's Park was at the edge of town, a mini-Delmar Gardens located on the grounds of what is now Legion Park. The top of the baseball grandstand is shown.

The Southern Hotel was the first home of the Packers after leaving Joplin. Today it contains apartments for senior citizens.

assure that they would close for the home debut on the afternoon of July 9.

One of the most popular recreational venues was Peach's Park opened in 1903. A smaller version of Delmar Gardens in Oklahoma City, like its big sister it was home to the local ball park —— in fact, baseball is still played on its grounds at what is now Legion Park. The grandstand where the Packers played was on the west side near Morrison Avenue, visible from the park lake. Peach's Park would be the home of the Packers.

The Packers arrived from Muskogee on the morning of the ninth and were shuttled to the Southern Hotel. The opposing team, the Bartlesville Boosters, arrived at 1:30 p.m. and was put up at the Kerfoot. Acting Manager Vinson with input from Burns, selected a line-up with veteran Loren Brown behind the plate, Bill Burns at first base, Howard Speck at second, Joe Levine on third, Frank Leudes at shortstop and an outfield of Harry Landes, Tex Farrell, and Jack Ryan.

Before 3,000 appreciative fans, behind W. S. "Doc" Pollard's pitching and home runs by Brown and Landes, the El Reno bunch took Bartlesville by a score of five to three. There was no box score in the *El Reno Daily American* the following day. The Commercial Club failed to engage an official scorer.

Two businesses in town kept the fans up to date on the Packers at home and on the road as well as the Western Association race. The Smoke House —tobacco, not barbeque— on South Bickford compiled and posted the line scores each

South Bickford. The Smoke Shop, padlocked on July 22, 1909, is along the street.

VIEW FROM THE CELLAR

Despite a dismal performance, one of the 1909 Packers had been to the Show and another was headed there. Ike Fisher (1871-1947) who appeared as the Phillies' catcher for nine games in 1898, relieved local manager Vinson on August 8.

Mike Balenti, a team mate of Jim Thorpe and Pete Hauser at Carlisle Institute would appear briefly for the Reds in 1911 and hold down shortstop for the 1913 St. Louis Browns.

Bill Burns was manager of the Joplin club when the Commercial Club in El Reno brought it south. New field leader Bailey Vinson of El Reno shadowed him to learn how to manage a league team. Position players who would return in 1910 were Harry Landes and Joe Levine.

Young outfielder Clarence Willingham would return to the semi-pro ranks after an interlude with the 1911 Lawton Medicine Men. Pitchers John Beltz and Doc Pollard would also return in 1910. Howell "Pat" Crowson, on loan from the Texas League Oklahoma City Indians, was recalled and spent the last part of 1909 and 1910 in the new State Capital.

Fisher

Burns

Balenti

Willingham

Pollard

Levine

Beltz

Crowson

Landes

evening until July 22 when it was padlocked for violation of the Oklahoma Prohibition Ordinance that was effective with Statehood in 1907. This was part of a campaign by the County Attorney to dry up El Reno. He sued every building owner in town to enjoin them from leasing to anyone who manufactured, sold, or served intoxicating liquor. The other place that supplied official scores before the next edition of the *Daily American* was the apparently more respectable Brunswick Billiard Parlor on South Rock Island.

After several days of decision-making and the floating of names like J. B. O'Connell of the Oklahoma City Indians, and Lou Armstrong of the Wichita Western League club, the baseball association's management decided to make Vinson manager for the remainder of the season. Pitcher Willbank was released and Beltz optioned to El Paso. Vinson signed outfielders John Henley and Hershel Finney, and picked up pitchers Pat Crowson and Bill McClintock on the bounce from Oklahoma City. Local attorney Fred Gillette, a star at the University of Kansas, suited up for a game. The third of the Balenti brothers, Mike, who starred with Jim Thorpe on the 1908 Carlisle Institute football team, began play on July 22. Max Addington, second baseman, joined the Packers in early August and was followed by local amateurs Billie Simpson, a left-handed pitcher, and Clarence Willingham, an outfielder.

Vinson was glad to relinquish his field duties to Tennessean Newton "Ike" Fisher on August 8. That date only Farrell, Burns, Landes, Levine, Pollard, Ludes and Brown were left from the roster that played on July 9 in the opener. The Packers were out of the pennant race the day they moved from Joplin and things did not get better. The club was twenty and forty-three in Joplin and sixteen and forty-six in El Reno to finish with a .288 winning percentage forty-four games behind champion Enid.

1910

The Commercial Club took the franchise with the understanding that for 1910 the other league owners could move it. With the success at the gate and support of a losing team, the Western Association owners decided to keep the Packers where they were.

For the 1910 season, management hired Arthur Riggs of Arkadelphia, Arkansas to manage and hold down first base. From 1909 were Loren Brown, Harry Landes, Joe Levine, John Beltz, and Walter Pollard. New faces were outfielders Herman Benham, Lewis Summa, and Bert James, Senter Rainey at first, second sacker Claude Leslie, and pitchers

John Kimball, "Wild" Bill Luhrsen, Hank "Rube" Robinson, Floyd Perritt, and diminutive Harry Womack. Other than some tryouts during the season, only fourteen players appeared in Packer flannels in the second season.

The Packers began with home and home series against first Guthrie then Enid, with El Reno hosting the latter two sets. The Packers swept Guthrie as guests and at home while splitting the Enid series three games each. Returning to the road on an eastward swing, the Packers divided six games with Sapulpa including a thirty-one hit performance fueling a twenty-eight to six route of Larry Milton's Oilers. The El Reno bunch won only one of three at Muskogee but took two of three at Tulsa. Back at home, the Packers swept Muskogee and Tulsa. El Reno was within one game of first place.

Frontrunner Joplin came to town for the first showdown of the season. After exchanging wins, Joplin took the rubber game on eight Packer errors. After winning two at Bartlesville, El Reno copped the first and second games with the Miners taking the seven-inning game of a doubleheader. At May 27, both El Reno and Joplin had twenty-three victories but with more ties, Joplin had lost thirteen to the Packers' fifteen.

El Reno continued to play good baseball but took a few licks. Guthrie's Louis Listen, a rookie who had been cut by Sapulpa then El Reno, from Central Normal College in Edmond, silenced El Reno bats in the first game of the June 7 doubleheader for a seven to zero no-hit shutout in his first professional decision. After dropping a doubleheader at home to Bartlesville, El Reno played in streaks winning four or five, losing one or two then begin another string of wins. Rube Robinson exacted a measure of revenge on July 8 when he tossed a no-hitter at Guthrie. Robinson's gem was one of only five games the Packers won during next fortnight. Meanwhile, Okmulgee, formerly Muskogee, was setting a then-twentieth century record with nineteen consecutive losses (eclipsed in 1961 by the Phillies' twenty-three) while Joplin tied the Chicago White Sox for the then Organized Baseball record of nineteen consecutive wins (broken by 1916 New York Giants with twenty-six straight victories).

Okmulgee and Tulsa disbanded on July 22. The next week in the Western Association was confusing. By July 26, Guthrie and Okmulgee were out of the standings with Tulsa replacing the former State Capital. The Packers took a series from Tulsa between July 26 and 28. Traveling to Bartlesville, El Reno took the games played on the 29th and 30th. The July 31 game was ostensibly "cancelled by agreement" but in fact the Boosters were broke and couldn't pay the visitor's guarantee much less player salaries. The Bartlesville club disbanded and scattered. The Packers took the train home. They were scheduled to begin a series at Joplin on August 1.

Robinson   *Luhrsen*   *James*   *Riggs*   *Perritt*   *Listen*

TURN AROUND: THE BEST TEAM THAT NEVER FINISHED

New manager Art Riggs kept the best from 1909 and embellished with a trio of past and future major leaguers. Hank "Rube" Robinson (1887-1965) threw a no-hitter at Guthrie on July 8. After 139 major league games between 1911 and 1915 for the Pirates and Cardinals and a brief sojourn with the 1918 Yankees, he pitched thirteen seasons for his hometown Little Rock Travelers. "Wild Bill" Luhrsen (1884-1973) was 3-1 with a 2.48 ERA in his three weeks with the Pirates in 1913. He hurled for Sherman in 1915. Bert James (1886-1959) hit .286 in five days with the Cardinals as the end of the 1909 season following a good but not great season at Waco and Shreveport. The .314 average he posted in 1910 was a career best. Arkansan Art Riggs, who was the target of Western Association president Tom Hayden's treachery in 1911 respecting his Ft. Smith franchise, won with pitching. Rookie Floyd Perritt was 55-32 in five Texas League seasons. Another rookie who was not looked at closely enough, Louis Listen, exacted revenge for being released with a 7-0 no hitter against the Packers on June 7.

Enid manager R. E. "Snapper" Kennedy actively worked with Enid owner J. H. Shaw to forfeit the El Reno franchise after Bartlesville disbanded on July 31. The effect was to leap frog his Railroaders into second place. Shaw made the unilateral call that both Bartlesville and El Reno had refused to play and should, therefore, forfeit their respective places in the Western Association. In the case of the former, the deed was already accomplished. El Reno, on the other hand, was solvent, had a loyal fan base and community, and securely held second place with a record of sixty-five wins against forty-three losses for a .608 winning percentage. Only sixteen games remained in the season. Shaw's "double cross" had the effect of clinching the pennant for Joplin and moving his Enid Railroaders into second place. The season concluded on August 16 with four ball clubs left standing.

It would be a dozen years before professional baseball was again played in El Reno.

EUFAULA

EUFAULA   OKLAHOMA STATE LEAGUE   1912

SEASON	TEAM NAME	MANAGERS	WON	LOST	PERCENTAGE	FINISH
1912		Leo Langley	2	2	.500	8 of 8

Eufaula was as unlikely a place to move a professional baseball team as was Maud to where the 1929 Muskogee club fled. The county seat of McIntosh County, it had actually declined in population from Statehood to the 1910 Census from 974 to 307. It was on the Katy line so connections through Oklahoma City were good.

The official records do not recognize Eufaula as a member of Organized Baseball. The reason, presumably, is that the Oklahoma State League is treated as having officially ended on June 22 when president Leo Meyers declared it dead. But there was an afterlife and Eufaula was part of it.

On June 24, the remaining owners rescinded Meyer's dissolution order. J. B. Bartlett, late of the stillborn Mid-Continent league, became president while the remaining owners approved the sale of Oklahoma City's place to H. B. Ernest who quickly moved the late Mets to Eufaula. All players were declared league property regardless of whether they had signed on with others.   On the way to their next stop and a new home, Ernest's nine played an exhibition against the McLoud town team to raise some much needed cash.

The second half of the season began June 28. Ernest announced that no exhibitions would be

Eufaula's Team. This photo of the 1912 Oklahoma City Senators was taken near the beginning of the Oklahoma State League season as Bill Reukauff, who was fired on May 26, appears. Upper L-R: Richard Atkins, Red Reynolds, Louis Listen, Oscar Gay, Douglas, Myrick, Harry Steakley. Middle L-R: Robison, Babe Green, Boyce, Clark. Seated L-R: Brown, Hartman, Crawford, Reukauff, Fair.

After breaking in with Lyons, Kansas in 1910, pitcher Leo "Joe" Langley joined the team shortly before the league took it over and Leo Meyer made him manager. He does not appear again in Organized Baseball records.

played in Oklahoma City. In their inaugural on June 28, the as yet unnamed Eufaula nine dropped a twelve to four decision at Okmulgee. The next day the score was closer, six to five, and the roles were reversed with Eufaula on top. The Okmulgee team refused to play on June 30. At Eufaula on July 1 about five hundred new fans or at least curious onlookers crowded the baseball grounds to watch the McAlester Miners tap manager Joe "Leo" Langley for five runs in the seventh inning to spoil the only league game played there by a score of nine to three. An Independence Day doubleheader with nearby rival Holdenville was scheduled, preceded by an Indian stickball game. Things looked good for four days.

Okmulgee's franchise was broke and the shareholders were nowhere to be found to pay off the players for both salary and playoff money. The owners took the easy way out and on July 1 sold off all the players to teams in other leagues. With Tulsa and Muskogee on the ropes and with two thoroughly untested new cities in the circuit, losing Okmulgee was a set back from which the league couldn't recover.

The one and only Oklahoma State League game played at Eufaula was, as fate would have it, the last. The Holdenville doubleheader was never played. Eufaula would never again host a professional sports franchise. But the town can say that it was once on the baseball map.

GUTHRIE

GUTHRIE BLUES · SOUTHWESTERN LEAGUE 1904
GUTHRIE SENATORS · WESTERN ASSOCIATION 1905
GUTHRIE SENATORS · SOUTH CENTRAL LEAGUE 1906
GUTHRIE SENATORS · WESTERN ASSOCIATION 1909-1910
GUTHRIE · OKLAHOMA STATE LEAGUE 1912
GUTHRIE · WESTERN ASSOCIATION 1914

SEASON	TEAM NAME(S)	MANAGERS(S)	WON	LOST	PERCENTAGE	FINISH
1904	Blues	Ernest Jones	56	44	.560	1 of 4
		Billy Hughes				
		Frank Overby				
		Thomas Neal				
1905	Senators	Argus Hamilton	66	70	.485	5 of 6
		Ben Bennett				
1906	Senators	Ben Bennett	18	55	.247	disbanded July 21
		James Geer				
		J. W. Faulkner				
1909	Senators	Howard Price	70	55	.560	3 of 8
1910	Senators	Howard Price	47	73	.392	4 of 4
1912		Chick Leutke	15	33	.313	8 of 8
1914		Jerry Kane	2	10	.167	disbanded July 21

The first baseball game in the Unassigned Lands was played in Guthrie on June 30, 1889 before the organization of the Oklahoma Territory. That was a time when the only law among the thousands of stake-claimers, fortune hunters, and entrepreneurs was the U. S. Cavalry. The bluecoats' tents were in plain sight of an improvised diamond. That first ball yard was just west of the Santa Fe tracks in the Cottonwood Creek bottom, a place later occupied by Lincoln School.

The opponents were the Guthrie town team that included some of the soldiers and the aggregation from Oklahoma City, that would host a repeat match on July 4. Attorney Frank Dale, later Chief Justice of the Oklahoma Territorial Supreme Court, served as umpire. The game was back and forth until the home club pulled out victory in the bottom of the ninth.

Frank Dale was an honest man. He was so fair that he was selected as umpire of the first baseball game played in the Oklahoma District. Dale came to Guthrie at age thirty-nine on the train from Wichita on the day of The Run. He was appointed a Judge of one of the Territory's three judicial districts by President Cleveland and later served as Chief Judge of the Supreme Court of the Oklahoma Territory. Following Statehood he was a distinguished member of the Bar. He died in 1930.

1904

The season opener for the Blues was at Colcord Park adjacent to the grounds of Delmar Gardens, a popular entertainment venue one mile west of the business district in Oklahoma City on the unpredictable North Canadian River. Manager Ernest Jones' line-up was largely made of semi-pro alumni. Brewington was behind the plate with Harry Adams and Jack Hoffmeister in relief forming the battery. Captain Billy Hughes held down first, slugger Charles Barry was at second with popular veteran

DOING A LAND OFFICE BUSINESS

Guthrie was, like Oklahoma Station forty miles south, a way station on the Santa Fe line to Purcell in the Chickasaw Nation. When the shot was fired that began the Land Run on April 22, 1889, Guthrie, named after a Kansas judge, burst into prominence as the home of the field office of the United States Land Office (now the Bureau of Land Management) where a claim had to be registered in order to receive a Patent, a deed to land from the United States. The Unassigned Lands or Oklahoma Country (see page 6) was an unorganized district of the United States with no government, only the authority of the U. S. Army and whatever order the occupants spontaneously created.

The phrase "doing a land office business," while not originating with Guthrie, was certainly an accurate description of what was going on.

The Organic Act of May 2, 1890 created the Oklahoma Territory that included Guthrie as the Territorial Capital.

Guthrie was a town of tents and prefabricated building brought in by the settlers.

Each morning a line of people who had "staked" a claim to a quarter section waited to be recorded.

The 1904 Guthrie Blues. Upper L-R: Emmett Rogers, Ed Pokorney, Red Werner, A. G. Jefferies, Charles Barry [Berry]. Lower L-R: Ben "Dad" Bennett, Pat Flaherty, Thomas Neal, Harry Adams, Loren Brown, Muggsy Monroe. Seated L-R: Ned Pettigrew, Alex Dupree.

Ben "Dad" Bennett at third and Campbell covering the short field. Manager Jones, James Smalley and Ernest Metz comprised the outfield. The result of the afternoon's slugfest was a one-run loss caused by catcher Brewington, in disgust at the umpire's call, throwing the ball on to the field allowing the winning run to score. Guthrie lost the next two before continuing the first road trip at Enid with Billy Hughes named the new manager.

The Blues made their home debut at Island Park (now Mineral Wells Park). Chickasha came to town and despite a triple play, came out on the short end of the first two contests by scores of ten to two and seven to three. The Indians turned the tables on the Blues on Sunday in a fifteen to nil romp.

After fifteen games, the Blues had only won four. A local committee headed by Judge G. C. Horner intervened and ousted Jones to place the team on a firm financial footing. Popular Billy Hughes lost his ownership interest but remained as field leader. While monthly subscriptions of $150 had been gathered, the May 31 payroll was missed and the players had to pay their way for the Blues' next series at Chickasha. On June 8 there was another intervention. Those present formed Guthrie Base Ball Association with D. F. Smith as president,

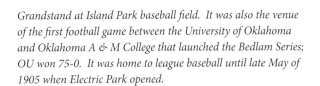

Grandstand at Island Park baseball field. It was also the venue of the first football game between the University of Oklahoma and Oklahoma A & M College that launched the Bedlam Series; OU won 75-0. It was home to league baseball until late May of 1905 when Electric Park opened.

Harry Palmer vice-president, Carl Havinghorst treasurer, Corb M. Sarchett secretary, and Earl Croston corresponding secretary. Directors were Frank Overby and O. E. Metcalfe among others. More was subscribed and Hughes and his charges were directed to return to Guthrie for the next series and their back pay. At June 12, Guthrie at seventeen wins against twenty losses was hitting a winning stride as a battered Oklahoma City faltered. At Enid, the Blues dropped the last game of the first half to the champions four to three. Meanwhile, on June 18 Frank Overby took over field leadership as Hughes convalesced en route to taking over the Texas League Paris Parasites who later became the

Ardmore Territorians. O. E. Metcalfe succeeded to the presidency.

Notwithstanding owner Walter Frantz's agreement to the second half schedule that called for baseball on Sunday, he refused to bring the Evangelists to Guthrie for the opening series on July 1. The problem was solved by Frantz selling the franchise to league president W. J. Kimmel and manager Howard Price, neither of whom had qualms about playing on the Sabbath. Guthrie picked up two in the win column due to forfeits. Guthrie's president D. Fatima Smith succeeded to Kimmel's post

The instability of the Shawnee franchise and its faux move to El Reno confused things over July. Guthrie played several exhibitions games against Southwestern League and semi-pro competition as the Enid "Backsliders" missed the first dozens dates of July. At July 30, Guthrie was in second place with fifteen wins against eleven losses. So that El Reno would not be saddled with Shawnee's six and fifteen record, president Smith by fiat recalculated the standings by throwing out various games so the at August 5 Guthrie was on top with wins in ten of fifteen counted games. A new schedule running through October 1 was adopted. Then El Reno turned out to be a fabrication. The league halted play until August 12.

Another schedule was adopted when a new Shawnee club joined the Southwestern. The Blues managed to play fifty-three innings in four days including Harry Adams tossing twenty-two consecutive innings. The other clubs, particularly, Oklahoma City complained loudly of Guthrie poaching players such as Ed Pokorney from Shawnee and Ned Pettigrew and Bill Beeker from the Mets. Things worked out until the third version of Shawnee's club disbanded on September 5. Stand-

Ned Pettigrew (1881-1952) began his baseball travels as a Bloomer Girl on a barnstorming team in 1903 (each women's ball club had two or three male players in drag). Guthrie was his first league ball. He played through 1921 in the Western Association, Western League, Three-I League, and Southwestern League. He managed Chickasha, Bartlesville, and Cushing in the 1920s. His last assignment was as manager of Hobbs, N. M. in 1937. He could claim major league status because of his two unsuccessful trips to the plate on April 23 and 24, 1914 for the new Buffalo Buffeds of the Federal League.

William Beeker posted a 53-54 record for Shreveport and Mobile between 1906 and 1909. Guthrie was his second professional job after appearing for Oklahoma City in 1904. He ended his career with Lawton in the 1911 Texas-Oklahoma League.

ings are not available for the remainder of the season beyond *The Daily Oklahoman's* report that Guthrie jumped to first place at September 27 after a five-game sweep at Enid and on the following day stating that Guthrie had clinched the pennant. The Blues won the cloth but the Mets got the cash when Oklahoma City won the post-season exhibition for a $100 purse.

1905

Over the winter the Southwestern League self-dissolved. Enid and Shawnee ended up out in the cold. Guthrie and Oklahoma City, however, were embraced by the new Class C Western Association. Guthrie Base Ball Association, now owned by Tom Neal, hired pitcher *cum* schoolmaster, J. Argus Hamilton, the "Pitching Parson, to manage the

Argus James [sometimes J. A.] Hamilton, nicknamed the "Pitching Parson" because of his status as a Methodist minister, began playing league ball for Dallas in 1902 and was a member of the Paris Parasites when the team came west to Ardmore in 1904. Between seasons he was the school master at Stonewall, I. T. He assembled the initial Guthrie Senators roster for 1905 in the Western Association. When the franchise was pulled from his partner Thomas Neal, he moved north to Vinita where he threw for the Cherokees in the Missouri Valley League. The next season found him in the Virginia League.

1905 Senators. Hamilton had thrown in the Texas League and in 1904 was with Paris, Ardmore, and then jumped to Dallas. The Guthrie Association also had new leadership in the form of Heinz Braun as president and Havinghorst as secretary.

Hamilton assembled a veteran roster. The pitchers were Hamilton, Benny Henderson, Walter Queisser, Harry Womack, and Jack Forrester. From Indianapolis came Walter's brother Art Queisser to form a battery and Loren Brown as backup. Back from 1904 were Charles Barry, Ned Pettigrew, and Muggsy Monroe. Newcomers were J. W. "Red" Downs, Tex Jones, Charles Graves, and G. E. Dalrymple.

With league president D. M. Shively in attendance, Mayor Duke served up a fat pitch that Police

Walter Queisser (1885-1954) was the pitching half of a brothers battery from Indianapolis. In his rookie season with Guthrie then Leavenworth, he won twenty-two games dropping sixteen. He continued in the minors through 1912.

Chief Cates crushed to begin the 1905 season at Island Park before a full house. Guthrie wore their new maroon flannels. The visiting Wichita Jobbers spoiled the evening, however, by a score of eleven to five. The clubs went on to split the four-game series. Guthrie was off to a far better start than 1904.

Guthrie resident Ben "Dad" Bennett had been a fan favorite in 1904. After he broke his leg, two thousand paying fans attended a benefit Fats versus

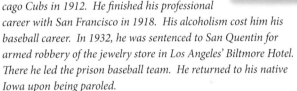

Jerome "Red" Downs (1883-1939) was part of the 1904 Ft. Scott team that was brought to Guthrie. Following a .319 performance with the Senators and after the franchise moved to St. Joseph, Downs signed with Topeka where he had another good season. He was the Detroit Tigers regular second baseman in 1907 and 1908, playing alongside Ty Cobb. He played three seasons for Columbus and Minneapolis in the American Association then got his second chance in the Show with Brooklyn and the Chicago Cubs in 1912. He finished his professional career with San Francisco in 1918. His alcoholism cost him his baseball career. In 1932, he was sentenced to San Quentin for armed robbery of the jewelry store in Los Angeles' Biltmore Hotel. There he led the prison baseball team. He returned to his native Iowa upon being paroled.

Art Queisser (1882-?) joined his 1904 battery mate at Guthrie where he appeared in 124 games for the Senators. He played through 1913 in the Western Association, Central League, Kitty, Three-I and one campaign with Galveston in the Texas League.

Tex Jones (1885-1938) was a popular player with the Guthrie fans. Consecutive .300+ seasons in the Western Association earned him an invitation to the White Sox spring training camp in 1911 and he made the trip north. After ten days he was sent back to St. Joseph never to return to the Show. His final season was 1918 with Wichita.

George Dalrymple was another newcomer to Guthrie. Between 1895 and 1909, he played across the Midwest and in the Pacific Northwest. He managed the 1907 Webb City and 1909 Muskogee teams in the Western Association.

Guthrie resident Ben "Dad" Bennett played for Chickasha and Shawnee in addition to Guthrie in the 1904 South-western League. After breaking his leg in 1905, Bennett relieved Argus Hamilton as manager until fired for playing while injured. He then suited up with Oklahoma City who gave him his re-lease when Guthrie invited him back to the helm. He was back with the Senators in 1906 in the South Central League. His last professional action was in 1911 as third sacker for the Lawton Medicine Men of the Texas-Oklahoma League.

Thins game to assist with his convalescence. He recovered, managing the Senators twice with an interlude playing for Oklahoma City.

The Senators fell into a slump. Eddie Hickey, a 1903 Chicago Cub, was brought in as captain to turn around the team. Guthrie quickly fell to seventh with seven wins against eleven defeats. A new grandstand at Electric Park didn't break the jinx. *The Guthrie Daily Leader* of July 11 supplies this narrative.

> The Senators were up against it good and hard in the early part of the season. The management was of the weakest kind. This had much to do with their style of play.

> * * * *

T. A. Neal secured the franchise and started the Guthrie Senators. They played a few games fairly well but things took a turn. Neal got too liberal with the boys. Neal employed an expert baseball manager in the person of A. J. Hamilton. Hamilton turned out to be a boozer and a poor stick for a manager. Matters grew worse. Neal and Hamilton tried hard but failed every particular to manage the Senators. Finally, the things got to the point where the boys would not pay ball unless they got their salaries.

* * * *

. . . . The Leader frequently alluded to the financial condition of the team and plainly that the boys were flunking because they were not getting even so much as their board paid.

However, things did not continue in this light long. The business men, the men who wanted to see Guthrie have a good, first class ball club, and who were enthusiastic over its success held a meeting at the request of President D. M. Shively. Shively went to the parade and then that things had to be changed. Then the Guthrie baseball association was formed. Hamilton was ousted. The books of the team were found in a bad condition. Neal was bought out and the entire management cleaned up.

In the early part of June the change was made effective. Dad Bennett was made manager of the team and Jones, Dalrymple and Downs captain, at various times. On June 10 Guthrie played Oklahoma City and won a two to nothing game. The boys took on fresh courage. They played ball because they knew that when payday came they would get their money and they also knew that their board bills and other expenses were being paid.

The new Guthrie Base Ball Association elected officers. P. T. Walton became president, C.M. Sarchet secretary, and Doc Brown treasurer. New directors included Judge Frank Dale, C. G. Horner, bank president V. C. Goss, real estate developer L. N. Beadles, and junior banker Havinghorst. A week later after losses to Springfield and Sedalia, the Senators dropped to last place with only ten victories in thirty tries.

Bennett released and signed players nearly daily. Muggsy Monroe was given his walking papers while 1904 star pitcher Leo Hite came aboard. Dallas Alderman was inked to complete the pitching staff along with Henderson and Womack. Walter

Rookie Dallas Alderman was signed in early June and cut in early August when Topeka picked him up. He had been wild all season. For 1905 between his two clubs he posted a twelve and sixteen record in 232 innings. He remained in the game through 1912 with Sioux City and Wichita in the Class A Western League.

Queisser was released to make room. For the first time in 1905, the Senators achieved a winning percentage above .400 on June 17. To celebrate, the Senators went on a home run binge that earned the sluggers $65 from the fans over the weekend. Dalrymple was the tops with a purse of $23.30. Tex Jones received $16.56 from the stands after a game winning blast against Leavenworth. Ed Hickey was rewarded with $11.50. Art Queisser got $13.90 for batting in Dad Bennett with his over-the-fence hit. A pair of winning streaks moved the Senators into fifth place at twenty-nine and thirty-three on July 3.

Bennett resigned the helm because the management would not let him play. Benny Henderson was selected to succeed him. Frank McKelvey,

Ben Henderson (1883-?) was Guthrie's top pitcher in 1905 with a record eighteen wins against eight defeats in thirty games and hit .267 in the pinch in another twenty-eight. He jumped the team in early August causing Bennett to be recalled to the helm. He reappeared with Portland in the Pacific Coast League where, after a two season interlude in the independent California League, he finished his playing days in 1912. He won thirty-five games for Stockton in 1907 and twenty-six for Oakland in 1908. He won over twenty games for Portland in 1906 and 1911.

recently cut by Topeka, was signed to bolster the mound staff. By July 11, having won twenty-one of the last twenty-nine games, the Senators climbed to fourth place The largest crowd to that date, 2,500, watched the home team best Joplin six to five. After copping a double header from Springfield, Guthrie went above .500 on July 20.

The Senators reached as high as third, tying Oklahoma City which had signed Dad Bennett to play third base. While winning, the attendance slumped with the Sunday July 30 game drawing

Paul Companion was touted in the Guthrie Daily Leader as having been sent by the Washington Senators when in fact he had been released after winning two of three for Omaha. His tenure with Guthrie was brief. The Senators sold him to Joplin. He pitched in the minors through 1911.

only 450. The clubhouse was an infirmary with Henderson, Hickey and Downs disabled. Paul Companion joined the depleted pitching staff. Wild all season, Alderman was cut. Henderson abandoned the team. Dad Bennett was re-signed to complete the season.

Ownership shook up things again on August 22 after Enid interests made a strong run at the franchise. Walton continued as president and Judge Dale remained on the board. E. F. Shinn, John H. Cotterall, C. D. White, and Paul Newman completed the board. Melvin Carter assumed the treasurer's duties while Shinn became secretary.

Popular Tex Jones was released as Bennett signed Paul Nagle from Joplin for his bat and a pair of pitchers, Baxter Knox and Ora Mize.

Signed at the end of the 1905 season, Ora Mize, a local player, was back with the South Central League Senators in 1906. He split twelve decisions in 1909 with Great Bend and McPherson in the Kansas State League.

Bennett was again released and director D. F. Smith finished the season at the helm. The Senators as reconfigured saw their hopes for a first division finish dashed when they dropped the last three games to Oklahoma City.

President Shively had predicted on September 1 that Oklahoma City and Guthrie would not be in the Western Association in 1906. Two weeks later Mets' manager Gene Barnes expressed guarded confidence of league baseball in 1906 despite an apparent attempt by the eastern teams to freeze out the two territorial clubs. As things turned out, Shively was half right. Guthrie's franchise was awarded to St. Joseph, Missouri but the Senators would join the new South Central League. Okla-

homa City's Mets would remain in the Association until moving up to the Texas League in 1909.

The concluding lines of the Guthrie *Daily Leader's* editorial "Finis Season of 1905" encapsulate the sentiment.

> And so ends the story of a disastrous season and if the local fans are sore they probably have no apologies to offer.

1906

The *Sporting Life* magazine called the South Central League a continuation of the 1905 Missouri Valley League. It was largely correct. The Territorial towns from that league plus two of the State Capital aspirants, Guthrie and Shawnee, with Ft. Smith-Van Buren as sixth formed the loop. The Arkansas entry was the default choice after neither Enid nor El Reno attended the March 17 organizational meeting in South McAlester.

Dad Bennett returned again, this time at age fifty-four as owner, manager, and player. He had a veteran roster under contract and in camp. His infield consisted of

• Billy Hughes first base: Hughes had been in the game since 1884 and played for or managed the 1904 and 1905 Guthrie clubs.

• Howard Speck second base: His rookie season was with Vinita in 1905.

• Ben "Dad" Bennett third base: Age fifty-four. 1905 manager twice; recovered from his broken leg.

• Jesse Weissinger shortstop: Guthrie's shortstop in 1904 and 1905.

Jesse Weissinger was Guthrie's shortstop for the city's first three seasons. He was with Argenta in the Arkansas State League in 1908. The following season he played semi-pro ball with Minco. He was Lawton's shortfielder during its brief 1911 foray into league ball.

- L. R. Kaup outfield: He previously played semi-pro in California.
- "Wee" Willie Weller outfield: He played for Chickasha and Shawnee in 1904 and Little Rock in 1905.
- John Dunham outfield: Fast, he played for Oklahoma City in 1903 and the semi-pro Ardmore Territorians in 1904.
- Ed Davidson outfield: He played with Pittsburg in the Missouri Valley League.
- Tommy Kearns catcher: From Walters, he played for Chickasha in 1904 and the strong Lawton independent club in 1905.
- L. O. Parker catcher: Rookie from Anadarko had played for its semi-pros.
- E. O. Nichols catcher: Reputedly spent 1904 in Missouri Valley and 1905 in Kansas State League.
- Tommy Ross pitcher: He threw for Webb City in the Missouri Valley in 1905.
- Tom Nicholson pitcher: At six feet, four inches, tallest player. Came from "eastern leagues."
- Ora Mize pitcher: From Logan County, he won one and lost one for Guthrie late in 1905.
- Jim Beadles pitcher: From the Three-I League, the highest paid player on the ball club.

The only change to the pre-season line up was that an outfielder named Dutch Selkmeyer seized the right field slot. The season opened with eight consecutive losses. The Guthrie *Daily Leader* remarking about the May 8 home loss wrote "[t]he game was as tiresome as a ten mile walk on a July afternoon and slower than an old fashioned hearse." The paper was convinced the Senators were "hoo dooed." Even Mayor Duke's pitching couldn't break the spell. Bennett's homerun and a fight between Selkmeyer and a Muskogee baseman that had to be broken up by police were counted as the white magic that allowed

the Guthrie nine to record their first 1906 win by a score of three to one with only four hits.

With the Senators having won only four games on the season in late May, and after most of the team showed up too hung over to play, Bennett shook up the staff and then found himself replaced. He released Davidson and signed veteran Loren Brown to replace Kearns. Tom Charles replaced old Billy Hughes. Beadles, who hadn't performed, was released to save money. Pitchers Jim Geer from Webb City and 1905 Senator Harry Womack, cut from Oklahoma City, as well as J. W. Faulkner, seconded from his position as superintendent of the Guthrie trolley system, joined the club. Charles Barry, 1905 keystoner, came back from Waco along with a hurler named Ohme. Outfielder Seeley came down from St. Joseph. Rumor was that Beadles would be re-signed once he had been sober several weeks. Geer became captain and Faulkner manager.

A commentary in the June 7 *Daily Oklahoman* analogized Guthrie to the home of the city whose ball clubs had the worst records in both the American and National Leagues

> Guthrie is proving the Boston of the South Central League, much to the dissatisfaction of the Guthrie fans. Out of the thirty-five games played the hoo doo has been working overtime in twenty-eight of them. The team has changed hands two or three times and various other methods have been resorted to break the spell but all were unavailing.

The owners met on June 25. To help out Guthrie that had won only ten of forty-eight games, it was decided to split the season. The second half would begin on July 8. Subsequently, it was decided that the second half would become a new season with everyone beginning even in the championship race.

During the break between halves, Guthrie players visited Oklahoma City. One, Harry Womack, related that the Guthrie franchise was moving to Enid. That turned out to be untrue. After a dozen games in the new season, Guthrie remained in last place with only three wins. Unpaid, the players walked on July 21. The Guthrie failure had fatal consequences for the Shawnee Blues. Because the league could not continue with five teams, the Blues were dropped. Within three weeks, the South Central League dissolved and Guthrie would not enjoy Organized Baseball during its last season as territorial capital and the first season as a State Capital.

1909

After two seasons playing as an independent, with the intervention of Enid owner J. H. Shaw Guthrie returned to the ranks of Organized Baseball in 1909. The Western Association —that had abandoned Guthrie in 1906— had to fill gaps left when Topeka and Wichita moved up to the Western League and archrival Oklahoma City joined the Texas League. As there was no franchise to move, manager Howard Price, one of the four Price broth-

The baseball grandstand at Electric Park in 1909.

THE PRICES OF ENID

Howard Price was a career Western Association outfielder breaking in with Nevada Lunatics in 1902 and finishing as Guthrie's manager in 1909 and 1910. He was Tulsa's bench manager in 1912 and 1914. Norman Price was the youngest, joining older brother Howard at Guthrie in 1909-1910. He played first base between 1911 and 1916 for Junction City, Tulsa and Oklahoma City. He managed Tulsa in 1915-1916 and Pawhuska in 1920. Norman branched out in 1911 and 1912 to play at Bay City, Michigan and York, Nebraska. Brother Gene Price saw action with the Enid semi-pros in 1903 and the 1904 Evangelists before turning to something more lucrative. Ted opened with Cedar Rapids in the Three-I League in 1901 and 1902 and labored the 1903-1904 and 1906-1908 seasons with Wheeling, West Virginia in the Central League, serving as manager during three of those. He returned to manage Enid in 1909 and 1910. He finished managing Kewanee in 1911.

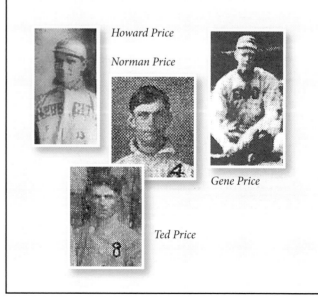

Howard Price

Norman Price

Gene Price

Ted Price

Oklahoma's first Governor, Charles Haskell of Muskogee (1907-1911). He was a regular at Electric Park cheering on his Muskogee team so vigorously that they came to be called, at least in Guthrie, the "Governors."

ers who would be in Oklahoma baseball for two decades, had to create a team from scratch. When the season opened he was ready; or so it appeared. As the *Daily Leader* announced on the front page of the May 1 edition "W-A Season Opens With Due Eclat." Before a crowd of 5,000 at Electric Park, the incumbent State Governor, Charles Haskell of Muskogee, and popular former U.S. Marshal and Territorial Governor, Cassius Barnes, formed the battery for the first pitch with District Judge A. H. Huston at the plate connecting for a solid line drive.

Price and captain Tony Anderson named a mix of rookies and veterans to play between the lines that day. Jesse Clifton was behind the plate

where he remained all season. The manager's brother Norman took first base. A rookie named Wagoner started at second base; he was released after fewer than five games. Two rookies, Adkins and Burkett, started at third and shortstop. Adkins would last three weeks until replaced by swift Milton Pokorney and Burkett was out of the line up within the week with Anderson taking his slot. Rookie Clare Patterson, who would finish the season with Cincinnati, versatile Ted Waring at the beginning of his long career, and Frank Gowan formed the outfield. Freshman Clyde Geist, who would win 112 games in a nine season minor league career, opened on the mound. The new Senators jelled for an eight to six victory over Muskogee.

After an embarrassing nineteen to ten loss on May 2, Guthrie took the rubber game from the Navigators and found themselves in first place. That was the only time in 1909. Things went badly downhill. Thirty-eight errors were committed in the first ten games. The Senators lost all but six games between May 4 and May 31.

New players replaced the ones who took the field in May. Floyd "Slats" Willis joined the staff and added twenty-two victories to the win column. Chick Leuttke came aboard to play a solid season at second base. Veteran Tom Reed added a big bat as well as a strong glove at first base. Howard Price took the field after he traded his brother to Webb

Milton Pokorney (1891-?) was the youngest of the three brothers from Lawton. He was the 1909 and 1910 Guthrie shortstop. He then moved on to Michigan where he played 1911-1914.

Clare Patterson (1887-1913) was as close to a Renaissance Man as ever appeared in Oklahoma minor league baseball. Having played college and semi-pro ball in Kansas as well as penning a newspaper column and writing popular music, Howard Price signed him for his 1909 team after Springfield cut him. Patterson led the Western Association with a .354 average and spent September with Cincinnati. He found himself on the west coast with Oakland in 1911 and 1912. He survived appendicitis but in the damp air of the Bay Area contracted tuberculosis. Relocation to the desert didn't help. He died at age twenty-five on March 28, 1913.

Nicknamed the "Parson," Bill McGill (1880-1959) made his debut with Minneapolis of the Kansas State League in 1905. Thirty-two wins for Austin in 1906 and 1907 earned him a cup of coffee with the St. Louis Browns at the end of 1907, winning his only decision; he was zero for nine in the batting department. He was back at Austin in 1908 but following a 0-3 start was released. He won eight and lost thirteen for Enid's 1908 Western Association runner ups. Howard Price brought him along when he moved south to Guthrie for 1909. The State Capital, where he won twelve of twenty-one decisions, was his last stop in professional baseball. He returned to his home in Alva where he remained the next forty years.

City for big Red Davis. Mel Cooley settled the third base position. Milton Pokorney from the semi-pro ranks became the top shortstop in the Association. Will "Parson" McGill, a future major leaguer from Alva, filled out the twirlers. Rookie Clyde Geist won twenty games.

On June 1, with new players the Senators had found the right chemistry taking a ten to six win in an "uninteresting" game at Joplin. Having won only eight of thirty at that point, the Senators were on top in sixty-two of the next ninety-four outings to climb from the cellar to third place in the final

1909 Guthrie Senators. Upper L-R: Herman Leuttke, Clare Patterson, Bill McGill, Norman Price, Clyde Geist, Tom Reed. Middle L-R: Red Davis, Tony Anderson, Howard Price, Ted Waring, Milton Pokorney. Seated L-R: Floyd Willis, Jesse Clifton, Clarence Nelson.

standings, battling Muskogee for second. Two of those losses were forfeits to the Navigators. Guthrie was the only team to sweep a series from champion Enid. With the Senators' patron J. H. Shaw in line to become president of the Western Association and a solid core of reserved players, the outlook for 1910 was bright.

Clyde Geist won twenty games in his rookie season with the 1909 Senators. In nine minor league seasons he produced a very respectable ERA of 1.42. He won fifty-four games in three seasons, 1912-1914, with Hartford of the Eastern Association. He returned to the South Plains winning twenty games for Tulsa in 1916. He finished the next year at Ft. Worth.

1910

Howard Price along with Bartlesville's Frank Barber were the only two managers returning from 1909. With twelve Western Association players having moved to the big leagues and a couple of dozen promoted to Class A, across the league there would be a number of new faces. Guthrie was an exception with its catcher, Clifton, and most of the infield, Reed, Leuttke, and Pokorney, returning. Floyd Willis was the only pitcher back from the 1909 staff. Newcomer William Harmuth at third base quickly became a fan favorite. Guthrie Baseball Association president Leo Meyer and secretary Thomas Orr were not predicting the Senators' finish but they promised a respectable nine.

Just like in 1909, the headline was "1910 Season Starts Off With Eclat." With most businesses closed and government offices in the State Capital empty, a parade led by the players, the Guthrie Automobile Club, and dignitaries in carriages, the grandstand began filling at noon on April 15 for the 3:00 p.m. call. After Mayor Farquharson

tossed the first pitch, Joe Locke from Texas took the mound against El Reno. A crowd of 5,000 saw the Packers clip the Senators one run to nil. The Senators got swept with Walt Alexander and Henry Edlick earning their first defeats of the season. That became a pattern. Veteran, R. J. Blackburn, joined the Senators on April 27. Price announced that his

Henry Hotchkiss was a product of the Oklahoma-Kansas border leagues. Howard Price named him one of his 1910 starters. He won nine of the club's forty-seven victories. He returned to semi-pro ball and was a member of the league champion 1914 Ponca City team.

Oscar Vickery had posted a winning record for Enid in 1909 and was given a spot on Guthrie's 1910 roster. It was not long before there was a parting of the ways. Vickery finished the season and, as it turned out, his pro career later that season with Spartanburg, South Carolina.

mound staff on May 5 was Henry Hotchkiss, Alex Dupree, L. V. Langfitt, and Joe Chevalier, an acquisition from San Antonio. When Henry Edlick was released to make room for Dupree, Guthrie owned five wins against fourteen loses. Veterans Oscar Vickery and Frank Taylor were signed to augment the club's pitching. With ten seasons under his belt Native American infielder Johnnie Ogee and college star Louis Listen, owner of a June 7 no-hitter against his former team, on the bounce from El Reno came aboard in June. Norman Price returned from Webb City and Frank Bridges rounded out the pitching following Langfitt's exit.

Unlike 1909, there was no rally. The Senators reached their highest winning percentage on June 19 with nineteen wins against twenty-five defeats. Back-to-back road sweeps of Bartlesville and Tulsa made the longest winning streak, six games, of the season. That was followed by El Reno's Rube Robinson's no-hitting the Senators twelve to zero on July 9. Guthrie settled into sixth place.

There were problems around the league. On June 24, N. W. Schantz acting for president Shaw seized the Muskogee franchise and took it over as a league operation. Instead of becoming orphans, the newly named "Governors" (after Governor Haskell) remained in Muskogee. That franchise was moved to Okmulgee on July 19. The beginning there was inauspicious as the scheduled opponent, Bartlesville, failed to appear. Instead the first game in the new home was played against the local independents. Five days later, the Senators became the Tulsa Oilers. The original Tulsa club disbanded and its players scattered; the original Guthrie franchise under the ownership of Louis Scott became the substitute. The Western Association was now a six-club circuit of Joplin, Enid, Sapulpa, Bartlesville, El Reno, and Tulsa *neé* Guthrie until July 27.

It took only three days for a series between Price's Guthrie-Tulsa nine against El Reno to be rescheduled for Guthrie. With the return of popular Clare Patterson, cut by the Reds, Louis Scott realized that his ballclub belonged back in the recently vacated Capital. He loudly protested that he was not involved with the move to Tulsa and had planned all along for the now ex-Senators — because Guthrie had lost the election for the permanent Capital to Oklahoma City— to remain. That, of course, with the admonition that the fans of the team needed

to support it. There was a thinly-veiled threat that baseball could disappear overnight.

The Western Association shrank to four on July 31 when Bartlesville went broke and El Reno was sacrificed to reduce the league to an even number of members. As the *Daily Leader* wrote accurately "[t]he season finishes rather poorly . . . ." The quartet of survivors played a round robin for two weeks. The season for the Senators ended with a whimper, a pair of two to one losses to second-place Enid in the August 15 finale double header. The only remaining team with a winning percentage under .500, the Senators finished with forty-seven victories and seventy-three defeats.

1912

The Oklahoma State League arose because the holder of the territorial rights to Oklahoma City, Abner Davis, wanted to control a league and was unwilling to collaborate with J. B. Bartlett, his Tulsa rival. With the demise of the Western Association and Davis' sale of Oklahoma City's Texas League team, the only Organized Baseball in Oklahoma was on the Red River at Ardmore and Durant in the Texas-Oklahoma League.

When Davis had vanquished the nascent Mid-Continent League, he solicited members. Corb Sarchet, who had been closely associated with baseball in Guthrie since his servings as secretary of the 1904 Southwestern League, was contacted and received a franchise. He secured the services of the 1909 and 1910 second sacker Herman "Chick" Leuttke and late in the spring moved into high gear with assembling a baseball team. The club had a playing field at Electric Park and enthusiasm from the community. The one thing it lacked was a name. Called the Senators from 1905 through 1910, after Oklahoma

Herman "Chick" Leuttke (or Luettke) was Guthrie's popular second baseman in 1909 and 1910. He spent 1911 with Clarinda in the MINK League. When Guthrie won a franchise in the new Oklahoma State League he jumped at the opportunity to return. The season was difficult and the "no-names" —Oklahoma City had stolen the named "Senators" just as it had prematurely seized the seat of government— had won only a third of their games when the season was called on June 21. He played another two seasons in the Kansas State League.

City was voted the new Capital in the summer of 1910, "Oklahoma town" began calling Guthrie's nine the "ex-Senators." Using a different name perhaps would seem to be acquiescence in the premature move of the seat of government.

Leuttke was able to recruit a number of locals and semi-pros for the batteries. The position players all had some league baseball experience. Beside Leuttke, Lon Ury, who played first base and pitched, shortstop Anson Cole, catcher and outfielder Charles Moneymaker, Pearl Bluejacket, another

Following the demise of the Oklahoma State League, Anson Cole was given a look-see by Dallas then sent down. He last played professionally for Waxahachie in the 1914 Central Texas League.

outfielder, third basemen Ginger Lyons and A. C. Gilbert, pitchers Archie Reed and Harry Womack had worn professional flannels. Catchers Dooley and Moore as well as pitchers Clift, Erishman, Rice, and a young hurler just out of Blackwell Baptist College, Elmer Ponder, were rookies.

The season did not progress well after thump-

ing Tulsa eleven to three in the season opener. Two six-game and one twelve-game losing streak doomed the No-Names to the cellar. Before playing the last regular season game, Guthrie managed only one string of three consecutive wins. They did act as a spoiler of Tulsa's winning streak on June 1. Reed got a win on June 6 when he held Muskogee scoreless and Leuttke stole home in the first inning. The day before, Guthrie's nine hammered Muskogee ace Ben Tincup for eight first inning runs and a win to go to ten wins against twenty-five reverses. Frustration boiled over on June 12 when Moneymaker slugged umpire Bill Setly, earning a fine and indefinite suspension; six days later he was on his way to Dallas in exchange for $500. After twice clipping Anadarko in Guthrie, the No-Names whipped rival Oklahoma City in a game played at Shawnee on June 19. This turned out to be the last game of the season.

After president Leo Meyer declared the Oklahoma State League dead on June 21, *The Daily Oklahoman* had a generous comment for the former Capital

> Guthrie was going well in spite of a losing team and desires to remain in organized baseball. To this end an effort is being made to place a good club at Enid, and with two cities on the west side it would not be impracticable for the east side to incorporate these cities in a new league

Ironically, Guthrie caught fire after the league folded. Before the new season began for the revived league on June 28, Guthrie swept three games from the former Anadarko team now representing Enid. Then the No-Names took four of five from Enid including a last game on July 2 that was protested. While officially finishing the short 1912 season with

Elmer Ponder (1883-1974) was a student at Blackwell Baptist College when he appeared for Guthrie in 1912. The next several seasons found him in the Texas League and Southern Association before sticking with the Pittsburgh Pirates in 1917 where, less a year in the military, he remained until 1921 when he was traded to the Cubs. He played in the Pacific Coast League through 1928.

fifteen wins and thirty-three losses, before the bitter end Guthrie improved to twenty-two and thirty-four, a losing percentage but a full third improvement. Like the other players of the Oklahoma State League, Guthrie's scattered with one headed for the Show. Five years after Elmer Ponder made his debut in a three to one loss to Okmulgee on June 7, he would find himself in Forbes Field throwing for the Pirates beginning a career that would run through 1921 in the National League and then another seven seasons in the Pacific Coast League.

1914

For a dozen days in July, Guthrie gave shelter to a Western Association club but never embraced it. The league took over the Joplin franchise on June 26. Tulsa's

Cajun first sacker Ben Blanchette was hired to manage the Missouri Orphans.

Following thirteen years on the field mainly in the Texas League, Jerry Kane was awarded one of the franchises in the new Western Association. He located it in McAlester and shortly after the start of the 1914 season sold it to local interests headed by druggist E. A. McDaniel. Unemployed, Kane attended the July 9 owners meeting and, after posting the $500 guarantee money to acquire the orphan franchise, relocated it to Guthrie. The former State Capital did not adopt the Orphans or put any skin in the figurative game but simply provided a ball park at the Cimarron Valley fairgrounds. After being swept in the first series played there, local support vanished. Recognizing that the Orphans' situation was untenable, the league office again intervened and disbanded the Orphans on July 21.

Eight years and a World War would pass before Organized Baseball returned to Guthrie.

HENRYETTA

HENRYETTA BOOSTERS · WESTERN ASSOCIATION 1914

SEASON	TEAM NAME	MANAGERS	WON	LOST	PERCENTAGE	FINISH
1914	Boosters	Ben Diamond	11	36	.234	8 of 8
		H. R. Thompson				
		Al Nickell				

The rough and tumble mining center of Joplin and adjacent Webb City had enjoyed professional baseball in the Missouri Valley League and Western Association from 1902 through 1911. After a two year absence, with the revival of the Western Association as a

Class D loop baseball was back in 1914. Thin capitalization and inability to sustain operations led to the league pulling the Joplin-Webb City franchise on June 26, four days before the end of the first half of the season. The league ran the former Joplin-Webb City club as "Orphans" to a fifth place finish ahead of McAlester. It was generally assumed that the club would settle in Okmulgee.

Following thirteen years on the field mainly in the Texas League, Jerry Kane was awarded one of the franchises in the new Western Association. He located it in McAlester and shortly after the start of the 1914 season sold it to local interests. Kane attended the July 9 owners meeting and, after posting the guarantee money to acquire the Joplin franchise, relocated it to Guthrie. The former State Capital did not embrace the Orphans nor give them a name. Local support never was raised. Unable to pay the players, Kane gave up. The Western Association disbanded the Orphans and on July 21 awarded the franchise to another mining town, Henryetta, Oklahoma.

Well on its way to nearly 6,000 residents from 1,051 at Statehood, this town in the Creek Nation, named for Henry Beard and his wife, Etta, has always been based on coal mining, natural gas production, and ranching. In the summer of 1914, fourteen coal mines were operating. The town was served by the Frisco railroad and two local lines. The moving force behind Henryetta's first professional entry was W. C. Sanderson who backed the baseball operation financially.

The town had a solid and successful semi-pro club under the management of catcher Ben Diamond (sometimes spelled "Dimond"), whose professional career spanned from 1909 to 1930. The plan was

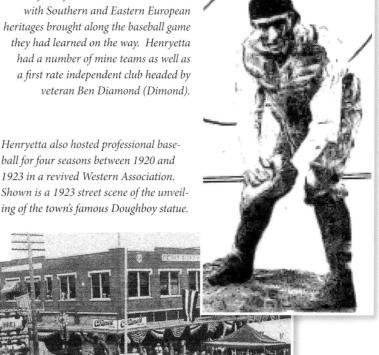

The influx of miners, both coal and zinc, with Southern and Eastern European heritages brought along the baseball game they had learned on the way. Henryetta had a number of mine teams as well as a first rate independent club headed by veteran Ben Diamond (Dimond).

Henryetta also hosted professional baseball for four seasons between 1920 and 1923 in a revived Western Association. Shown is a 1923 street scene of the unveiling of the town's famous Doughboy statue.

The Morgan Opera house was built around 1910 and operated into the 1930s as a motion picture theatre.

for the Guthrie players who had not been sold or released to consolidate with the Independents. With a second half record of four wins and eighteen losses, the club needed an injection of new talent.

Before seven hundred onlookers, on July 23 the amalgamated Boosters *neé* Orphans fell to the first-place Tulsa Oilers by a score of ten to three. The opening line up was principally a semi-pro cast. The catcher Eck, first sacker Basham, keystone Rerzes, third base Walker, shortstop Hadley, right field Hodges and pitching sensation Tony Wilson had not previously been in Organized Baseball. Only Ted Lipps and Ed Burch from the Guthrie Orphans broke the lineup.

Soon the professionals would arrive. The league had kept the contracts of the Guthrie players and called many of them back. In addition to Lipps and Burch, returnees were catchers H. R. Thompson and Ray Smiser, first sackers Floyd Hall and Quinton Gabriel, second base Ralph Heatley, third base Frank Thompson and Sam Lawrence, J. J. "Chief" Robinson shortstop, outfielders Chris Wren, Louis Pelkey, A. L. "Red" Reynolds, and pitchers Earl Sanders, Mack Osborn, Henry Tate, and Frank Taylor. H. R. Thompson continued as field manager, replacing Diamond.

By July 29, the Boosters had added three to the win column but seven more losses. That day the

The first line up that the new Henryetta Boosters fielded was simply the independent club with a couple of refugees from Guthrie. Ted Lipps' was one of those. A rookie in 1914, his career straddled World War I. He played principally in the Western Association and finished with a champion, the 1923 Ardmore Snappers.

Catcher Ray Smiser had been a captain of the University of Oklahoma baseball team. He had several tryouts with Oklahoma City and may have appeared in a few games with the Abner Davis' 1912 Oklahoma City/ Eufaula nine. Officially his only season of Organized Baseball was with the 1914 Boosters. He played in the Oklahoma City sandlot leagues into the late 1920s.

Pitcher and first baseman Quinton Gabriel played for the Tulsa Terriers in 1912 and joined the Henryetta club for most of the remainder of the 1914 season. After being released in early September, he sued the Boosters claiming back pay and had the receipts of a game at Tulsa seized to cover his claim.

Sam Lawrence began with the 1911 Lawton Medicine Men then was traded to Wichita Falls before his team disbanded. He was a member of the 1912 Texas-Oklahoma League champions under Frank Morris' management. He next appears with Henryetta, sharing the hot corner with future major leaguer Frank Thompson.

Clyde (Chris) Wren (?-1955) first played pay-for-play baseball with the Holdenville Hitters in the 1912 Oklahoma State League. He went on to play in the low minors around Oklahoma and Texas through 1925. Along the way he managed Shawnee, Pawhuska and, after retiring from play, the 1926 McAlester Miners in the Western Association.

Texan A. W. "Red" Reynolds played across Oklahoma and Texas both in professional and independent ball over a dozen seasons including 1911, 1912, and 1921 with Ardmore, 1920 with Chickasha, 1922 with Okmulgee, and 1924 with San Angelo. Henryetta was but one of his many stops.

in the fifth, Green went to the press box, got into a shouting match with the Tulsa club president, and only because police were present did they not come to blows. Twice the constables had to separate him from his former field manager, Billy Kelsey. On the hitting side, future Pittsburgh Pirate Don "Swat-em" Flinn came over on the bounce from Muskogee. Ed Bauer did double duty in the outfield and on the mound. Oscar Palmer took over catching duties. The *Henryetta Standard* diagnosed the team's main problems: poor base running and absence of teamwork.

Minor league umpiring had always been spotty. In the first week of August, the owners overruled the league president and fired Umpire "Happy Jack" Ryan. The Henryetta fans by September 1 had seen all of Umpire Taylor they cared for. With the crowd heckling him unmercifully, he charged into the

Journeyman outfielder Al Nickell had been in the game since 1903. After securing his release from Tulsa, he took over the Boosters for the final three weeks of the season. Unemployed after the Henryetta club disbanded, he signed on for his last campaign with the 1915 McAlester club.

headline was "Slaughter at Henryetta." The massacre was against the pitchers. Between the Ft. Smith and Henryetta benches, there were ninety appearances at the plate. There were thirty-two hits in the game with the Boosters finally ending on top by a score of fourteen to thirteen.

Through August 15, the pitchers were ironmen. The battery was Sanders, Osborn, Taylor, or Wilson and H. R. Thompson behind the plate. Veteran outfielder Al Nickell succeeded Thompson for the Boosters after securing his release from Tulsa. Hurler L. M. Gierhart joined the club as did spitballer Hetty Green just in time to throw against Tulsa, his team mates the day before. Things got hot in the second inning when the batsman threw a bat at Green after the hurler intentionally threw at him. After giving up seven runs and being relieved

From the Oklahoma City sandlots, Larry Giehart got a tryout with the Texas League Indians in 1911 then was sent down to Lawton. The next season he signed first with Holdenville then joined Durant where he pitched until 1914. He began that season with his hometown team, was sold to McAlester then, after being released, he found his way to Henryetta. He played for Oklahoma City in 1915 and finished at Paris in 1916.

stands with an uplifted bat threatening to "brain" every man in the bleachers. In what was described as a burlesque, Tulsa took the Boosters by the football score of twenty to thirteen. The Tulsa crowd saw five doubles, two triples, and nine homeruns. It could have been much worse on the field as Tulsa stranded twelve base runners. But the worst part was not on the field. Recently released first sacker Quinton Gabriel sued Henryetta for back pay and obtained a writ of attachment of the gate receipts for the day. The Sheriff sequestered the Boosters' share.

The season ended on September 8 in Tulsa with a pair of seven inning games. Wilson walked in Tulsa's winning run in the first game. The finale was taken lightly. Veteran infielder Louis Pelkey was pressed into service to catch for "Crazy Snake" Flinn. In addition to twelve hits and four free passes, he hit a batter, uncorked a wild pitch and

committed the only two balks seen in Tulsa that season. Still, Tulsa just squeaked by ten to nine.

The Boosters lost sixteen of the last seventeen games to finish with a record while in Henryetta of eleven victories and thirty-six losses, sixth in a six-team league. If the team had a star it was Tony Wilson, a full-blooded Native American from Lamar. Curiously, there is no further record of him in Organized Baseball.

The *Henryetta Standard* was realistic about prospects for the 1915 season:

The Boosters came through the season in first class shape and are in position to either place another team in the race next year or else sell the franchise to some other city. The promoters probably did well to break even this season but next year they should do much better.

Mr. Sanderson returned the franchise to the league and released all the players. On the demise of the Texas-Oklahoma League, the Western Association expanded to the city that had won the 1914 Texas-Oklahoma pennant and would walk away with the 1915 and 1916 Association crowns, Denison, Texas.

Henryetta had proven it would support league baseball. When the Western Association was again revived in 1920, Henryetta would once again be on the Organized Baseball map.

Erratic Don Flinn (Flynn) appears to have broken in with Muskogee then landed at Henryetta for the end of the 1914 season. A good season at San Antonio in 1917 earned him a September with Pittsburgh. He played through 1926 including a season with Wilson in the Oklahoma State League and five years in the Texas League. Ruggles described him as "[a] dangerous hitter and able player, an undisciplined disposition kept him from the peak." "Crazy Snake" was the name given to Creek allotment resister Chitto Harjo who was arrested near Henryetta.

HOLDENVILLE

HOLDENVILLE HITTERS · OKLAHOMA STATE LEAGUE   1912

SEASON	TEAM NAME	MANAGERS	WON	LOST	PERCENTAGE	FINISH
1912	Hitters	James Bouldin	11	36	.234	8 of 8
		John Hendley				

Holdenville got on the map when the Choctaw, Oklahoma & Gulf line running from South McAlester to Oklahoma City, built in 1895-1896, was intersected by the Frisco running south from Sapulpa to the Red River in 1901. Theretofore it has been a small trade center that arose out of a CO&G construction camp at Fentress, I.T. Incorporated as a town at the end of 1898, by Statehood its population stood at 1,868, growing to 2,296 in the next regular Census. It continued to serve as an agricultural center and, after defeating Wetumka for the honor, became the County seat for the new Hughes County. The oilfield over which the city sits was not discovered until after 1912. Boasting five banks and three newspapers, the one thing Holdenville did not have was league baseball. A professional team would really put the city on the map.

The smallest town to have Organized Baseball in 1912, Holdenville sought the prestige of a league team to put it on the map. As things turned out, Holdenville's franchise was the most stable and only profitable one in the ill-stared Oklahoma State League.

Two residents of the new county seat had backgrounds in semi-pro baseball, Al Vorhees and Attie Roberts. Having gotten wind that a new professional league was being formed, Roberts applied for a franchise. Being the smallest town in

the oversubscribed competition, to avoid a fight for the eighth spot Roberts' application was withdrawn with the understanding that if a slot opened in the Oklahoma State League, it would receive it.

The new league owners and president, State Auditor Leo Meyer, met on March 27. All were there except Ft. Smith. State Senator Homer Hurst attended the meeting, lobbied those present, and persuaded them that Holdenville should replace Ft. Smith to make the new league all Oklahoman. He had a $500 check for the guarantee and upon delivery, Holdenville had a franchise. The following day the Holdenville Base Ball Association was organized on a temporary basis to appoint Vorhees as general manager and solicit investors in a corporation that would hold the franchise and operate the club. A lease of the site where the old ballpark had stood was secured and Roberts was directed to get the playing field in shape and begin construction of a new grandstand, bleachers and fence. He also was to send contracts to all applicants and begin tryouts as soon as possible. G. L. Benson, Horace Bernard, John Jacobs, Lloyd Thomas, W. B. Key, C. C. Stan-

The Keystone was the best hotel in Holdenville.

ford, N. B. Fagan, and Dr. W. B. Atkins formed the first board of directors. They reported that there were only a few sticks in the mud who disapproved of baseball coming to town. They issued a statement published in the March 29 *Holdenville*

Democrat

Anyone knocking this proposition is knocking the chances of progressing in the very way that every member of the commercial club and similar organizations are striving for.

Vorhees was elected president and Benson secretary and treasurer. Roberts was appointed field manager and captain. The Dixon Theater held a three night vaudeville benefit for the new Base Ball Association, giving it ten percent of the gate.

The preceding season had been a rough one for minor league baseball. A number of leagues as well as teams had failed and disbanded. As the 1912 season began, there were a good number of unemployed players with experience in Classes C and D. There was no shortage of heads in the try-out camp.

Mayor Singleton issued a proclamation that April 30 would be a half holiday with all local businesses closing so that the town could fill new Athletic Park and cheer on the Hitters against the McAlester club. Admission would be 25¢ plus an additional fee for a seat in the grandstand. Following a good exhibition performance, there was reason to believe Holdenville would be a contender.

Senator Hurst could not resist a chance to speak to a crowd of about one thousand, congratulating the residents on becoming the smallest city in the United States to host a professional baseball club. Vorhees, in the absence of the Mayor, threw the first pitch beginning Holdenville's short season in Organized Baseball. With veteran Chris Wren and rookie H. W. Saunders from Dallas each going three for four, despite Larry Fucich yielding eleven hits and the Miners scoring all their runs on two errors, the Hitters won their home opener by a score of six to five.

Typically in the low minors, prospects were put into a game or two to see whether they possessed enough potential to sign. The Hitters were no exception. A number of players appeared for a game or two yet the Holdenville line-up remained stable. Webb caught the first eight games then Tom Robinson succeeded him for the rest of the season. Veteran Jim Bouldin held down first base and acted as field manager until relieved in the latter capacity by John Hendley. Saunders spent most games

Thomas Robinson cut his professional teeth with Holdenville. After the league folded, he went to Beaumont then signed with Durant for 1913 and 1914. He played the rest of his career in the pre-War and post-War Western Association with Denison, Muskogee, Pawhuska, and, finally, the 1921 Henryetta Hens.

Jim Bouldin came to Oklahoma City in 1900 to play semi-pro ball with Frank Quigg's independents, followed him to Enid, then was he first sacker for the 1903 Mets. After a few professional games at Iola and Leavenworth in the Missouri Valley League, he was a member of both of South McAlester's league teams in 1905 and 1906 before heading east to the Arkansas State League. A member of the 1911 Durant Educators, in 1912 Bouldin managed the Hitters until he was replaced on May 18.

John Hendley played in southwest Kansas and the Indian Territory before he turned to umpiring. After Bouldin proved again that he couldn't manage, Hendley was called in to preside over Holdenville's last month in league baseball.on May 18.

The name "DeLongy" (also Deloungy) appears on the rosters of Altus in 1911 and Tulsa and Holdenville in 1912. This player seems to be Harry D. Longley who rambled around the Southern Association and Texas League from 1900-1910.

at second base. Leo Nevitt —good field, no hit— presided over the hot corner while at shortstop Harry Burge of Red Oak was continuing a baseball career that would span a decade. After recovering from a gunshot wound suffered in the off-season in his native Hartshorne and having been cut by the Ardmore club in the Texas-Oklahoma League, Pat Patterson joined the Hitters as an infielder. DeLongey, who had been unemployed since the Altus Chiefs failed in 1911, pitched, caught and played outfield once he was signed. John Kaiser of Durant, Pearl Bluejacket of the Cherokee Nation, Manager Hendley, and from the local semi-pros Powell and Manley covered the outfield. Fourteen appeared on the mound but the core of the staff was Larry Fucich, Clifford Hill, E. H. Lancaster, and Roy Grady. Collectively they started thirty-two of the

forty-four contests officially played. Fred Fisher, Vance McDonald, and Thompson accounted for nine more.

On June 15, Secretary Farrell, the arbiter of all minor league disputes, ordered the Hitters to no longer play pitchers Grady and Harrison and out-fielder C. H. Clarkson. Central Kansas League had a prior claim to them.

C. H. "Tom" Clarkson was picked up on the bounce from Okmulgee. Another contract jumper, the Hitters couldn't play him the last week of the abbreviated season.

Clifford "Red" Hill (1893-1938) first played professionally for Holdenville. A twenty-win season for Baltimore in 1917 earned him a one-game, two-inning appearance for the Athletics in September 1917. He was a seven year Texas Leaguer. "A left hander with exceptional control and key figure in three Waco flags. Began as a fastball pitcher, ended as a slow ball southpaw with extremely deceptive delivery. . . . " according to Ruggles. His last season was with Mt. Pleasant, Texas in 1924.

E. H. Lancaster played for Arkansas City in 1909 and 1910 with an intermediate stop with Guthrie's 1909 Senators. He was the Hitters' fourth starter. The National Association deemed him a contract jumper and barred playing him after June 15.

Another alumnus of the 1911 Durant Educators, Roy "Irish" Grady was picked up by Dallas after the Oklahoma State League dissolved and threw for the Texas League Giants through 1914.

The section on the 1912 Oklahoma State League (*see* page 49) explains the circuit's demise when president Leo Meyer dissolved it on June 22 and the managers revived it on June 29. A new Hitters' battery in the new OSL was formed when Burge was traded to Tulsa for veteran catcher Loren Brown. Brown was behind the plate for four of the last five games. Old Attie Roberts who built the ball park was pressed into service in the fifth. Lancaster and Patterson each threw two while DeLongey one of the five contests in the post-dissolution afterlife of the Oklahoma State League.

Loren Brown spent his first three professional seasons with Guthrie's first three league teams. He divided 1909 between Bartlesville and El Reno and was the Packers regular catcher in 1910. He was with Durant some time in 1911. He began 1912 with Tulsa then finished what turned out to be a short season at Holdenville.

127

BASE BALL JULY 4

Holdenville vs. Eufaula

A double header will be played between these clubs of the State League on the above Date. Fast games are assured, with plenty of exciting situations and sensational climaxes, and a "sane" Fourth will be impossible when the spectators "come alive."

Indian Ball Game

A game of Indian ball will take place between two teams whose long rivalry will exact all the exciting thrills of this popular Indian sport of former years and which is now seldom witnessed by a white audience.

Games Called as Follows:

10:00	Base Ball
1:00	Indian Ball
4:00	Base Ball

Nowhere can you find better attractions on the Fourth than these games Don't miss them.

A big Independence Day celebration was planned in Holdenville with a doubleheader against new McIntosh County rival Eufaula. It never happened.

Holdenville was the best run and financially successful franchise. The Hitters were ready, willing, and able to complete the season as the advertisement for a July 4 game with Eufaula —new home of the Oklahoma City Senators— shows.

They won the July 2 game over Muskogee twelve runs to eight, a slugfest with twenty-seven hits; the contest was the last professional one played in Holdenville. The next day, the Okmulgee Glassblowers disbanded over a missed payroll. Tulsa's Terriers were also on the ropes. In the series with Tulsa June 29-July 1, the largest crowd was seventy-six. They couldn't even pay the guarantee. Bill Reukauff, the Oklahoma City manager who was fired when the league took over the franchise, sued the league and asked for appointment of a receiver. That was the final nail. The Oklahoma State League's life was over but would resurrect a decade later with Guthrie the only survivor from the 1912 experiment.

HUGO

HUGO HUGOITES · TEXAS-OKLAHOMA LEAGUE · JULY 7, 1913
HUGO SCOUTS · TEXAS-OKLAHOMA LEAGUE
DISBANDED JUNE 18, 1914

SEASON	TEAM NAME	MANAGERS	WON	LOST	PERCENTAGE	FINISH
1913	Hugoites	Fred Morris	21	24	.467	6 of 8
1914	Scouts	Lon Ury	19	32	.373	disbanded June 18

The east-west Frisco line from Hope, Arkansas to Ardmore gave rise to a settlement in late 1901 named after the French author, Victor Hugo. By the time the Wichita Falls ball club moved to town, Hugo had a population of over 5,000.

1913

Since the Texas-Oklahoma League was founded in 1911, Hugo had been trying to gain a place. It looked as though the Altus franchise would relocate there in July, 1911 but George Partain, the Altus manager, could not make a deal and the Chiefs went further down the line to become Honey Grove, Texas' semi-pros.

In late May of 1913 the league office had told Hugo interests that the Wichita Falls club was theirs provided the money to put the club on a solid financial footing was raised. Hugo did that but was thwarted when the Texans rallied to save their Drillers. A group from Hugo had negotiated a purchase of the Ardmore franchise— then with three wins against twenty losses— in early June, 1913. John Owens, head of the Ardmore Baseball Association, rallied the town, returned the Giants to solvency and, just to be safe, on June 8 filed suit for an injunction to prevent the Hugo sale from closing.

When Wichita Falls became too weak to the complete the season and lacked even the funds for

SIX BIG LEAGUERS, ONE HALL OF FAMER

For a city of 5,000 that had league baseball for fifteen weeks in 1913 and 1914, it had a remarkable number of major leaguers pass through for the Hugoites then the Scouts. The most famous was all time batting champion, Rogers Hornsby (1896-1963) who joined Denison when the Scouts disbanded. Fred Nicholson (1894-1972) was a sixteen year-old when he appeared for the 1911 Ardmore Blues. Traded to Wichita Falls, he followed the team to Hugo. As a first baseman and outfielder, he had a career Major League batting average of .311 with the 1917 Detroit Tigers, 1919-1920 Pittsburgh Pirates, and 1921-1923 Boston Braves. He later served as president of the Lone Star League in 1947 and 1948. Bill Brown (1893-1965) began at the top with the 1912 St. Louis Browns then found his was down to Hugo the following season. Hugo was the last stop for Harry Kane (1883-1932). Between 1902 and 1906 he had thrown for the Phillies, Browns, and Tigers. Lon Ury (1877-1918) was a five-season star for Dallas of the Texas League. "[O]ne of the famous loop players of the first decade of the century" per Ruggles. He appeared in two games for the St. Louis Cardinals at the end of 1903. He managed Muskogee in 1907, 1908, and 1911 before taking over Hugo in 1914. Jim Scoggins (1891-1923) had one appearance with the Chicago White Sox on August 26, 1913 following a strong rookie season for Hugo. He amassed a 71-54 minor league record playing in the Western, Pacific Coast, and Texas Leagues. His last season was with Columbia in the Sally League following Wartime service.

Hornsby

Nicholson

Brown

Kane

Ury

Scoggins

train fare from Denison to the next series at Bonham, on July 5 President C. O. Johnson of Durant took over the club for the benefit of the league. Hugo then pounced with cash in hand. Johnson quickly secured the consents of the other league members and on July 7, the Hugo Hugoites were born as Hugo's first and only foray in Organized Baseball. David A. Stovall traveled to Denison to take over the club and get the players to their next stop.

Hugo Baseball Association was capitalized with $3,000, $900 of which was paid-in following a meeting on July 9 in the First National Bank's board room. George Chandler, J. W. Dawley, Lon Wright, Will Baird, B. D. Jordan and T. R. Allen joined president Stovall on the board of directors. G. Earl Shaffer acted as secretary.

Following eighty-one games as the Wichita Falls Drillers, the Hugo club occupied sixth place with a thirty-three to forty-six record, comfortably ahead of Ardmore and Durant. The team that represented Hugo for the first week of its life on the road had an infield of Fred Nicholson at first,

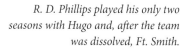

Leo Nevitt divided 1912 between Holden-ville and Galveston before his new owner, Dallas, assigned him to Wichita Falls for the 1913 season. A nifty fielder, but too weak at the plate. The 1914 Hugo Scouts were his last team.

R. D. Phillips played his only two seasons with Hugo and, after the team was dissolved, Ft. Smith.

R.D. Phillips on second, and Leo Nevitt then Babe Green, and Dailey dividing the chores of third and short field. Ed Workman, Bill Brown, Ed Kizziar, and Callahan roamed the outfield. Dick Naylor and C. M. Lawson were behind the plate. Jim

Babe Greene had caught for the 1912 Oklahoma City Senators before finishing his playing at Hugo.

Ed "Red" Kizziar played between 1911 and 1925. His first ball club was the Chiefs of his native Altus. When they disbanded, Waco signed him. 1913 and 1914 were with Hugo. He spent some time in semi-pro and near semi-pro ball in the Central Texas League. He re-emerged after the War with Ardmore and Green-ville in a revived Texas-Oklahoma League. After a 1923 season with McAlester, he played his last two seasons with Greenville in the East Texas League.

Scoggins, Harry Kane, Nelson Jones, W. O. Brady, and manager Fred Morris toed the slab. Morris' charges dropped two of three at Bonham and then defeated the Sherman Cubs two to zero in first of a three-game Tuesday-Thursday set there.

The premier of professional baseball in Hugo would be on July 11 against Sherman. A grand-stand was assembled at the foot of Crockett Street, within two blocks of paved streets, and readied for the first home stand. Most businesses agreed to close for the opener. Hugo won it three to two. As the Hugoites, the team split the next ten games, including taking three of four from Sherman, to re-main in sixth place. Higher classifications had in-terest in the Hugoites. Nevitt was sold to Ft. Worth on July 31 and Scoggins went to Lincoln then to the White Sox.

The season continued with little change in standings but a bitter dislike for Denison's fans de-veloped. After 125 games, Hugo still was securely in sixth place. Denison had run away with the pen-nant. It was fairly apparent that the Blue Sox were ignoring the $1,200 per month salary cap as well as the fourteen player limit. When Hugo contingents traveled to the Katy hub to cheer on their nine the locals called them "outlaws, rough necks, thieves and other epithets that could not" be put in print.

1914

Briefly a member of the league in 1912, McKinney, Texas, made an unsuccessful bid for the Hugo franchise at the November, 1913 owners' meeting. Hugo had reserved Brown, Green, Kizziar, Lawson, Nevitt, Nicholson, Phillips, and Workman for 1914. Management released Morris after three seasons with the club —he soon found

Youngest of the Covington brothers, Robert signed with Hugo then joined his home-town team in Denison for three straight pennants. He migrated east after the Western Association cracked down on the salary cap, throwing for Evansville in 1917, in the Virginia League in 1918 and 1919, and finally with Oklahoma City in the Western League in 1920.

a position with Durant—and hired veteran minor league manager and former St. Louis Cardinal Lon Ury in February, 1914. A scout for the St. Louis Browns and Dallas Texas Leaguers when hired, he was respected as a particularly keen judge of talent. He signed a new shortstop, a skinny rookie from Texas named Rogers Hornsby who had seen his offer to play for Ft. Smith for $75 per month turned down the season before. Another rookie who would win sixteen games for Denison in each of 1914, 1915, and 1916, Robert Covington, joined the mound staff. Ury had led Muskogee in 1910, 1911, and 1912 and never finished below third. He also brought a few of his 1913 stars from his Salina club of the Kansas State League including pitcher Vance McDonald. The name of the club was changed to a more conventional one, the Scouts.

The 1914 season opened at Ardmore. Ury's opening day batting order was Nevitt at third, Green shortstop, Brown center field, Nicholson right field, Kizziar first base, Workman left field, Phillips second base, rookie John Jordon behind the plate and Brady on the mound. Businesses closed for the game that Ardmore won by a tally of six to three. Ten Hugo errors including four by shortstop Green and three by catcher Jordon were responsible for that loss. Rain during the first home stand combined with the poor following of a club that played under .400 ball placed the Hugo Baseball Association in the red.

A syndicate of six substantial residents agreed to see the Scouts through the end of the season if the franchise could be delivered debt-free. A $700 operating loss and another $550 due the league made the stipulation impossible. The franchise was turned back to the league and the board members set about the task of settling the outstanding debts. The players scattered. Hugo's loss was Denison's gain, scooping up Hornsby, Covington, Nicholson and Naylor. Egan went to Sherman, Workman to Paris and Wright to Durant. Hugo's loss was also Ardmore's loss. To reduce the league to six teams and cut down on travel, Ardmore playing .500 ball and supported by the community, was dropped. The Texas-Oklahoma League finished its last season before 1921 with three Texas and one Oklahoma members.

Little Hugo would never again host a professional team. Yet, for a town that had hosted league ball for eleven months, it turned out a remarkable number of Major Leaguers. In addition to Hall of Famer Hornsby, Bill Brown, Harry Kane, Rollie Naylor, Fred Nicholson, and Jim Scoggins all appeared in the Show.

LAWTON

LAWTON MEDICINE MEN · TEXAS-OKLAHOMA LEAGUE · 1911

SEASON	TEAM NAME	MANAGERS	WON	LOST	PERCENTAGE	FINISH
1911	Medicine Men	C. O. Clark	17	31	.354	disbanded June 17
		William B. Metcalfe				
		Ed Pinkerton				

Less than a decade old at the time, the city of Lawton, Oklahoma was the last to receive a franchise awarded by the Texas-Oklahoma League when it organized in 1911. The key people in landing a professional baseball club were banker and Chamber of Commerce leader N. A. "Rol" Robertson who served as president of the baseball association, attorney C. O. Clark who gave up his practice to wear both business and field manager hats, young William Buehler "Cap" Metcalfe, a 1908 University of Nebraska graduate whose father was associate editor of William Jennings Bryan's *The Commoner*, both as an infielder and captain, and Matt Koehler, prominent dry goods merchant, who donated the land and built the ball park named, appropriately, Koehler's Park.

Before the April 4 tryouts began, Metcalfe ordered a dozen uniforms of white flannel with maroon trim bearing the word "LAWTON" across the front of the jersey; it would be another month before those arrived so hand-me-downs from Texas League Oklahoma City were used in the interim. A contest was held to name the new club. Over 225 entries were offered. Comanches, Apaches, Coyotes, Chiefs, Mountaineers, and Billikens

were among the favorites. The three editors of the Lawton newspapers chose "Medicine Men" because it spoke of an Indian leader but better than that, it was alliterative with Metcalfe. Miss Anna Noble, a stenographer, won the season pass for the moniker "Medicine Men."

Thirty-two aspirants were in camp before the first cut on April 15. After dropping series of exhibitions to the Anadarko semi-pros and the Cheyenne tribe's nine, on April 25 the Medicine Men boarded the 6:30 a.m. Frisco bound for Altus for their premier that afternoon. In raw weather, 549 spectators made the trip out to the new ball park in Altus to see their Chiefs behind their ace Alex Malloy vanquish the Medicine Men six to five. Lawton dropped the second game played in a cold drizzle before only 250 and then the third before some two hundred visitors from Lawton who had travelled to be the first to root for their home town team.

The Lawton line up for the home opener on April 28 had P. M. "Squeak" Lawrence at third base, temperamental Claremore rookie C. E. Alberta at shortstop, in left field local boys Otto Pokorney and Huff, Lindsey Mathis in center field, past OU standout E. Pierce from Hinton in right field, Metcalfe at

P. M. "Squeak" Lawrence played third base for Lawton. Dallas picked him up briefly the following season. He was with Sherman in 1913 and 1914.

C. E. Alberta came from the semi-pro ranks after failing his try out with Oklahoma City. A strong hitter but amateurish fielder, he was traded to Altus for the Chiefs' Ted Sherwood, a move that cost manager Muggsy Monroe his job. His temper as well as his glove kept him out of professional baseball. He was a member of the 1911 Anadarko independents after the Chiefs' folded.

second base, Bill Reynolds, who would have a cup of coffee with the Yankees in 1913, behind the plate, and outlaw George "Bugs" Stone who under the name Hillcock had jumped contract with Larned in the Kansas State League. Cotton Ellison and veteran Hugh McCullum joined the outfielders on May 1. McCullum was released to Ardmore on May 17. Ellison and Huff jumped to the Anadarko semi-pros on May 21.

The Medicine Men had a busy revolving door. Jensen, the Cheyenne tribe's top hurler, was signed the first day of the season and cut after dropping the May 5 contest in twelve innings to Gainesville. Old Bill Kemmer, who had appeared with Louisville

Otto Pokorney (1885-?) was the middle Pokorney brother from Lawton. He made his debut in 1907 with Portland of the Pacific Coast League then played independent ball in 1908. He patrolled the outfield for Sapulpa in 1909 and 1910 before signing with his hometown team. He finished the season with the Anadarko independents. After 1913 and 1914 with Sherman, he moved to the east coast where he played for Charlotte and Columbia in 1915.

in the then-major league American Association, signed on for first base but he didn't move well nor did he deliver at the plate. Roy McDonald replaced Huff in the outfield. Hultz had a short career after making two errors in his first appearance. Josh Billings, Oklahoma A & M spitballer, began a thirty year career at Lawton that included eleven seasons in the American League. Aggie team mate Lurent Wells played shortstop for twelve days until veteran Rabbit Garrity replaced him on June 2. University of Missouri star pitcher Ralph Hamilton, sent down

E. Pierce was a standout player for the University of Oklahoma. After June 17, he played for Laredo and Beeville in the Southwest Texas League. He appeared for Okmulgee's 1912 Oklahoma State League club.

Bill Reynolds (1884-1924) was the Medicine Men's catcher in his rookie season. After two campaigns with Houston, the Yankees called him up for five games at the end of 1913 and looked at him for five more in early 1914. He spent 1914-1917 on the top rung of minor league ball in the International League.

George "Bugs" Stone threw for Lawton, Durant, Anadarko and Oklahoma City during the early part of the second decade. Chick Leuttke, Guthrie manager in 1912, called Stone out as a contract jumper who had played in the Kansas State League under the name Hillcock.

Rabbit Garrity (1888-?) was a well-traveled, light hitting third baseman and shortstop from Kansas who played between 1910 and 1920. His first league season was in the Kansas State League with three teams. 1911 found him first at Gainesville and then Lawton in the new Texas-Oklahoma League then at Ardmore after his first two teams failed. He next appeared in 1920 with four different ball clubs in the Western Association.

Ralph Hamilton was a star twirler for the 1904 and 1905 University of Missouri nine. He went pro with Guthrie in 1905 and remained in 1906. He spent 1910 with Enid. He appeared briefly for Oklahoma City before snagging a job with Lawton. The Texas League Indians recalled him before the Lawton club failed.

Henry Tate was new manager Ed Pinkerton's battery mate at Wellington, Kansas in 1910. After his stint at Lawton, he saw action in ten games for the 1912 Galveston club in the Texas League.

from Oklahoma City, toiled for a couple of games before being called back up on May 8. Pitcher Henry Tate was sent down from Oklahoma City. Kansas State Leaguer C. Hayes, another of Pinkerton's hurlers, joined the mound staff a week before his battery mate from Wellington, Kansas took over as the Lawton manager. Third baseman F. B. Taylor and outfielder F. F. Gowan joined the club in time be part of the disbanding. Pitcher William Beeker, whose recent experience had been in the Southern Association, made Lawton his final career stop. Chesher joined Hinton rookie John Daugherty and Stone, who persuaded Metcalfe to give Daugherty a tryout, as the three pitchers who were with the Medicine Men for their entire existence. Baron Ozee, late captain of the Gainesville Blue Ribbons, went from the frying pan to the fire when he signed with Lawton.

Sunday baseball was an issue for most towns in the Texas-Oklahoma League and Lawton was no exception. On April 17, the Oklahoma Criminal Court of Appeals ruled that Sunday baseball was legal when no admission is charged. In *obiter dictum* the author of the opinion, Judge Henry M.

Foreman, observed "[T]he truth about the business is that our Sunday laws are a farce anyway. A man can gamble on Sunday and only be fined. . . . .The law should either be amended or repealed. I don't like to criticize the legislature but here is where they made a great mistake." The Medicine Men were scheduled to play Gainesville on Sunday May 8. The Lawton ministerial alliance to a man conspired to have the game raided and the teams arrested for breaking the Sabbath; a complaint had been drafted and was in the hands of a pliable county attorney. To come within the letter of the court's opinion, no admission was charged but cushions and hand fans were sold for the same prices as admission. The grandstand passed the hat and raised another $100. The *Lawton Daily News* reported that the bleacher bums contributed nothing and the "tight-wads" who watched games from the side of a hill west of Koehler's Park missed out on free admission. In any event, the Sabbatarians were thwarted.

The Medicine Men experienced the sublime and the ridiculous in their short season. It was the mound staff that earned the accolades. John Daugherty threw a one-hitter against Ardmore at home. He had a gem going until the ninth inning with two out when a pinch hitter tapped the ball to shortstop who couldn't handle it because of a

John Daugherty was a semi-pro player from Hinton whom George Stone persuaded manager Metcalfe to give a tryout. But for an obstinate scorekeeper, he would have had a nine-inning no-hitter against Ardmore. After the Medicine Men disbanded, he returned to the semi-pro ranks with the Anadarko independents.

bad bounce on a rough infield. Both teams asked the official scorer to call it an error but he wouldn't change his mind. The day after Ed Pinkerton took over leading the team and with Rabbit Garrity replacing Wells at shortstop and Gowan taking E. Mathis' place in the outfield, Lawton played errorless ball, bunched hits for three runs and combined with "Ole Reliable" Chesher's two-hitter to shutout Durant. On the second day of the second half of the season, C. Hayes of Wellington, Kansas twirled the Texas-Oklahoma League's first no-hitter on June 10, blanking Altus six to zero at Lawton; Hayes supported his cause with two singles and the biggest homerun seen at Lawton. Tagging Gainesville pitchers for twenty-four hits and seventeen runs, the Medicine Men took "a six inning burlesque" in which the Blue Ribbons' "pitchers [were] slaughtered in a farcical contest."

There were plenty of goats. While team hitting at .277 was third a month into the season, fielding was sixth at .906. Alberta easily was the Medicine Men's worst gloveman with seventeen errors and a .700 percentage but also first among the regulars with a .365 batting average. In the "the rottenest baseball ever seen in Southwest Oklahoma," Lawton committed fourteen errors; Lawrence, soon traded to Wichita Falls, had five, Captain Metcalfe playing first base dropped three, and Hultz in his first and last game bobbled two. Pitcher Beeker, after striking out nine, was so disgusted with the play behind him that he left the park after the seventh inning. The *Daily News* summarized "[t]he Medicine Men played grammar school ball and made the game such a joke toward to the last that McDonald was brought in from the outfield to pitch." In a game on May 27 where "[c]louds of dust and a shrieking wind made it almost impossible for men to hold the ball and bothered the pitchers," Lawton and Ardmore traded seven errors each but Giants' spitballer Rube Towers and captain Pete Trammel allowed only five hits for five runs while their backups scored nine on twelve safeties. In losing to Bonham ten to five on May 31, both sides played "miserable ball" but Lawton's work was "much the poorest" with eight errors.

A showdown between the owners and manager Clark occurred on May 20. Robertson did not like the way Clark was directing on the field and, when Clark was away for a few days, announced that he was taking over management and Metcalfe's days as field captain were over. Metcalfe resigned. Returning the following day, Clark had Robertson ejected from the park after he came on to the field. After the game, Clark made it plain to Robertson that he was the manager. Robertson, a forty year old banker from Iowa, threw a punch that hit a bystander; the players intervened to halt the fisticuffs. The following day, peace was restored across a table in front of the Lawton Baseball Association directors. Clark stayed in the dugout, and Metcalfe remained on the field. All involved, however, realized the franchise needed to be reorganized.

A veteran of the Kansas State League and independent baseball, Ed Pinkerton was hired on June 2, replacing Clark, who returned to his law practice, and Metcalfe, who remained as second baseman. The Medicine Men responded the next game with a

Ed Pinkerton look over the Medicine Men on June 2 after his Wellington, Kansas team disbanded. He began with Parsons in 1906 before joining Wellington in 1909. He was that club's manager in 1910. When his Lawton players dispersed, he landed at Nebraska City.

pair of homeruns to go along with Henry Tate's three-hitter taking Bonham to salvage one game in the last home series before a road engagement. After the June 4 game at Durant, sheriff's deputies arrested both teams for breaking the Sabbath. Metcalfe remained behind as a "hostage" while the team caught the train to Bonham. Lawton dropped two of three games at both Durant and Bonham to end the first half in last place with fifteen wins to twenty-seven losses.

The franchise was $1,000 in debt. A plan to catch up and get ahead was hatched. A new top of the line Buick worth $1,500 was to be raffled off at the June 26 game against Gainesville. As fate would have it, neither team would be playing that date.

Ironically, on June 15 Lawton unknowingly ended the season the same as it began with a one-run loss at Altus. The *Daily News* called it "one of the prettiest and snappiest games of the season." The Medicine Men caught the Frisco back to Lawton to begin a four-game series with Gainesville. On arrival,

they learned that the Blue Ribbons had disbanded. Chickasha interests had declined to pick up the pieces. On June 17, the Medicine Men disbanded. Players scattered. Pokorney and Gowan headed north to Kansas. Wichita bought Reynolds. Sherwood was sold back to Altus. Taylor and Mathis joined the Taylor, Texas semi-pros. Stone went to Durant. Ardmore picked up Garrity. Daugherty joined the champion Anadarko Independents. Banker Robertson saw to it that all the players were paid.

Matt Koehler was left holding the bag. After sinking thousands into the project, he was left with an empty ball park and a dozen soiled uniforms. The playerless organization had a post-game raffle ten days later for which enough ducats had been sold to pay off the team's debt but no team to play. It would be thirty-eight years before Organized Ball returned to Lawton with the 1947 Giants of the Sooner State League.

OKMULGEE

OKMULGEE GLASSBLOWERS · OKLAHOMA STATE LEAGUE · 1912

SEASON	TEAM NAME	MANAGERS	WON	LOST	PERCENTAGE	FINISH
1912	Glassblowers	Frank Gardner	39	9	.812	1 of 8

It is not entirely accurate to say that the 1912 Glassblowers were Okmulgee's first professional ball club. For nearly one week in July, 1910 Okmulgee was a member of the Western Association. Arriving there took a twisted route.

The Muskogee franchise failed on June 22. W. L. Tull, who became the sole owner on June 21, walked away from his investment after the June 22 game finished $100 in the red because of poor attendance; it was time to cut his loss. Tull released the players. N. W. Schantz at the behest of president Shaw paid the players what was due and took over operation of the Navigators. Groups from Shawnee and Okmulgee were seeking that franchise. President Shaw, however, wanted to keep Muskogee in the league. On June 29, Tull was given back the operation with the stipulation that ties with the Texas League in the form of players on option or subject to buy-back would be cut. For operating capital, Tull put up $1,000 which the Western Association matched. Players who were not the property of another club were recalled.

Two weeks later, Tull was in Okmulgee trying to interest the manager of its strong Red River League semi-pro operation, Frank West, in taking over a professional operation. Tull offered a choice. For $500, Okmulgee could simply give shelter to the Navigators for the eighteen remaining home dates with Tull retaining ownership. A group from Okmulgee could purchase the operation for double that amount.

On July 18, West announced that the franchise would be relocated to Okmulgee with an option to purchase it at season end. That afternoon a game was to have been played against Bartlesville but the Boosters failed to appear. Instead, the newly purchased team and the Okmulgee semi-pros squared off. The amateurs tattooed the professional

hurlers for nine hits and a three to two victory. The following day at the new home, the Okmulgee pros whipped Bartlesville by a score of five to two to break a nineteen-game losing streak. A road trip began the following day that started with a nine to nil loss to the Boosters at their home field. Two days later, the Okmulgee franchise was dropped to reduce the Western Association to six after the Tulsa Oilers disbanded. The franchise finished with thirty-six wins in 101 outings.

Okmulgee's glory days in Organized Baseball came between 1920 and 1927 in the re-born Western Association when Troy Agnew led the Drillers during four seasons and produced in 1924 one of the top one hundred minor league teams of all time with a record of 110 wins against only forty-eight losses. The Okmulgee clubs of the 1920s produced seventeen future major leaguers. During the oil boom, Okmulgee's population approached eighteen thousand.

What is generally not known even in baseball circles is that Okmulgee had an earlier foray into league ball when a good team was fielded in the short-lived Oklahoma State League. The local movers and shakers were determined to put their young city on the map by landing a professional baseball team. From 2,322 at Statehood, Okmulgee in the Creek Nation had nearly doubled by 1910 and was

1924 Okmulgee Drillers. Tony Agnew's Western Association club has been ranked as one of the 100 best minor league teams. Earl "Red" Snapp brought to Okmulgee the core of his 1923 championship Ardmore team. The Drillers won 110 games in 1924.

Okmulgee was a boom town, one of the fastest growing in the new State. The view shown is from the 1920s.

Like every prospering city, Okmulgee had a streetcar line.

Frank Gardner took the initiative of landing a franchise. He had led Okmulgee's strong independents.

adding an average of over 1,300 every year so that in 1920 there would be 17,430 Oklahomans who would claim the city as home. The Commercial Club there had attracted Southern Indiana Glass Co. and Baker Bros., both major employers, in 1911. Discoveries of oil and gas were beginning to be made. The municipal trajectory was upward.

A mass meeting was held on January 31 to examine how professional baseball could be brought to town. The most promising opportunity was the Mid-Continent League, a loop Tulsa's J. B. Bartlett was forming. Okmulgee had been awarded a space but due to the conflict between Bartlett and Abner Davis, whom the National Association, minor league baseball's governing body determined owned the rights to the Oklahoma City territory, the Mid-Continent league was never more than an idea on paper. Davis, on the other hand, proposed a Class D circuit comprised of Oklahoma cities to be called the Oklahoma State League. On March 16, Frank Gardnerwas awarded a franchise. The Okmulgee Athletic Association was organized on

March 21 at the Parkinson Hotel where $3,000 of the $5,000 capitalization was subscribed. Mayor George W. Mitchell, was elected president, J. L. Fuqua vice-president, E. J. Rogers secretary, and R.E. Butler treasurer. Directors were, in addition to Mitchell and Fuqua, Dr. L. S. Shelton, W. Thornburg, A. W. Fierstine, A. M. Milam editor of the *Okmulgee Daily Herald* and weekly *Okmulgee Republican*, W. P. Morton, A. P. Seider, and C. S. Dawes.

Committees canvassed the local businesses and raised most of the remaining $2,000 needed in a matter of days. Frank Gardner was elected manager and began recruiting a team. He sent telegrams to thirty prospects asking them to come to Okmulgee for tryouts and spring training beginning April 1 for the season commencing April 30.

The field and grandstand on West 6th Street, called West End Park, were put into shape. During three weeks of exhibitions against the Kansas City Blues, Topeka's Western League Club, and the Colorado Springs team among others, attendance averaged eight hundred. Of the more than forty hopefuls who came through spring camp, manager Gardner put together a line-up that remained largely intact through the season. Jefferies and Webber shared catching duties. Roberts handled first base. Pierce and manager Gardner held down the keystone while Bennett and Bairer played the hot corner. Baxter and Mattick were at shortstop. Clayton, Henley, Clarkson, Williams, Farrell, and several other players and pitchers roamed the outfield. Burnett, who threw an opening game no-hitter, veteran Everdon, Patterson, Taylor, Gallia, Upton, and Harrison were the mound staff.

1912 Okmulgee Glassblowers. Upper L-R: Wally Mattick, Dan Upton, E. Pierce, Roberts, Jim Jefferies, Bernie Everdon, Frank Gardner. Middle L-R: Powell Burnett, Bill Clayton, Frank Taylor. Seated L-R: C. M. Clarkson, Harris, Horace Ash, Roy Baxter.

The Glassblowers were the class of the Oklahoma State League. They jumped to the top of the heap winning the first eight contests and never looking back at the rest of the pack. Later, they enjoyed a twelve game winning streak. Only twice all season did Okmulgee loses back to back games, in both cases at the hands of the Tulsa Terriers. The first highlight of the season was Powell Burnett shutting out Muskogee five to zero with a no-hit, no-run performance in the first game of the season. Even with Jefferies, Gardner, Clayton, and Mattick sidelined with ankle injuries, Okmulgee managed to defeat Guthrie on May 21. The town supported a winner. Over 2,500 watched the first loss at home despite Clarkson's two home runs. Everdon struck out twelve Anadarko Indians and added a grand slam to chalk up the first game of the last home stand.

Losses were taken seriously. The June 4 game that snapped the twelve-game streak was dropped at Tulsa in ten innings two to one. Following the game, manager Gardner assaulted Umpire McKee outside the ballpark for which he was suspended indefinitely. The following day, McKee appeared in a belligerent mood. Tulsa manager Howard Price

accused him of being drunk and a fist fight ensued. Gardner came out of the stands and mixed it up with McKee. Then McKee pursued two Okmulgee players under the stands before finishing in a near riot with punches thrown at Price again. League president Meyer fired McKee.

Bernie Everdon and Powell Burnett were the mainstays of the pitching staff. In addition to his opening no-hitter, Burnett threw and won both ends of a Decoration Day double header to begin a sweep of a series at Muskogee. Horace Ash joined the club on June 13 and made his debut with a home run to top Oklahoma City and the next day stole home to pin another loss on the Senators.

The last regular season game Okmulgee played was on June 16 at McAlester where the Miners handed Burnett his first loss of the season. The next two games there were rained out and followed by open dates after the end of the first half. Okmulgee was five games ahead of Tulsa. Anadarko disbanded on June 21. On June 22, league president Leo Meyer declared the Oklahoma State League dissolved. Following a day of limbo, Bartlett of Tulsa, who was behind the Mid-Continent League, summoned the franchise owners including Ted Price who succeeded to Anadarko's slot and had moved the remnants to Enid. They decided to proceed with a second half. The Oklahoma City franchise which the league had been operating was sold to H. B. Ernest who moved its games to Eufaula. Meanwhile, Okmulgee swept the best-of-three first-half playoff with Tulsa and then proceeded to open the second half on June 29 against Eufaula *neé* Oklahoma City at home. Burnett scattered six hits while the position players played errorless ball and feasted on the visitor's pitching for sixteen hits and twelve runs. The two teams traveled to Eufaula for the June 30 game with Okmulgee losing to the hosts by a score of six to five.

Owed $500, the Okmulgee played refused to suit up on July 1. As there was no one from the Okmulgee Athletic Association to bring the players current, they walked away. The telegraph lines from Okmulgee were buzzing. The result is that management sold the team to the Kansas City Blues with Clayton, Burnett, Chase, Gallia, Roberts, Everdon, Farrell, Baxter, and Mattick becoming that club's

Bert Gallia (1891-1976) was one of the Okmulgee players sold to Kansas City. The next season he was playing with the Washington Senators. Optioned to Kansas City for 1914, he was back in Griffith Stadium in 1915 winning seventeen games that year and the next. He was traded to the Browns in 1917 and sold to the Phillies in 1920. He never returned to the minors.

Wally Mattick played in Iowa 1906-1911 before moving south to Okmulgee in 1912. Like Gallia, he was sold to Kansas City when the Glassblowers disbanded. He was quickly sold upstream to the White Sox where he appeared in seventy-nine games. He began 1913 with the White Sox then was sent back to Kansas City at mid-season. He labored for the Blues through 1915. In 1916 he jumped to Vernon of the Pacific Coast League playing in 200 games that season. 1917 began in California but ended in Dallas where, with an eight game trip to the St. Louis Cardinals, he would remain through 1921.

property and the rest of the team assigned to Kewanee, Illinois. From the proceeds, the players were finally paid. Dissolution of the Glassblowers sounded the death knell of the first iteration of the Oklahoma State League. Okmulgee would not enjoy league ball until 1920.

SAPULPA

SAPULPA OILERS · WESTERN ASSOCIATION · JULY 18, 1909-1911

SEASON	TEAM NAME	MANAGERS	WON	LOST	PERCENTAGE	FINISH
1909	Oilers	Frank Everhart	29	20	.592	5 of 8
1910	Oilers	Larry Milton	65	61	.516	3 of 8
1911	Oilers	George McAvoy	23	21	.523	W.A. disbanded June 19

The great contest of 1909 in Sapulpa was with her slightly younger sister city, both of whom were beneficiaries of the Glenpool Field opened in 1905, over which would be the terminus of the Santa Fe's forty-mile cut off connecting with the oil transfer point at Cushing. The new line would shorten the distance from Kansas City to Galveston by one hundred miles. While served by the Frisco since 1886 when Sapulpa Station was established, intersection with the Santa Fe would make Sapulpa a major oil center eclipsing what would later call itself "Oil Capital of the World." As 1909 opened, the one thing neither Tulsa nor Sapulpa had was a professional baseball team.

Sapulpa vied with Tulsa to become the Oil Capital. A view of a bustling Dewey Avenue looking east from Main Street.

Discovery of the Glenpool Field made Sapulpa a boomtown.

Today Webb City is a suburb of Joplin, Missouri. A century ago it was a mining center for lead and zinc, a major locus in the Tri-State mining district that left, among other things, the Picher, Oklahoma Superfund site. The mining business

then was cyclical. In July of 1909, that cycle turned down and with it the two Missouri teams of the Western Association departed for greener pastures. Joplin was the first to fail; it moved to El Reno on July 4. Her sister city moved southwest to Sapulpa two weeks later. When the move occurred, sixty percent of the season had passed with the "Webbfeet" or Triplets in the first division pushing Bartlesville for third and with first place not out of reach.

League baseball was then the one thing rival Tulsa lacked after the Oklahoma-Kansas League dissolved following the 1908 season. As has been said a number of times earlier, having a professional baseball club was a badge that a city had arrived with a prosperous future. Sapulpan Lou Fisher took the initiative and raised the cash to effect the move.

Manager Frank Everhart was a product of the Texas League. He arrived in Webb City courtesy of his release by Oklahoma City the previous season.

A. J. "Jim" Jefferies was with Webb City when that club relocated to Sapulpa in 1909 and was the regular catcher in 1910. After that season, he moved north, finishing in the Central League in 1914.

Gus Kellerman also spent two seasons at Sapulpa. He then moved to Dallas in the Texas League for five seasons. Ruggle wrote of him "[a] very good fielding second baseman but only average at short." After the War, he played two seasons in the Three-I League and a third in Virginia.

Frank Lofton played for the 1905 Vinita Cherokees before joining Oklahoma City in 1906. He was traded to Webb City in 1907 and played there until the 1909 move to Sapulpa. He led the league in 1909 with 108 runs. He ended his career with five seasons for Springfield in the Three-I League.

He had a set roster, many of whom would appear for the 1910 Oilers. Arthur Jefferies shared catching duties with Perry Reniker. The infield was Otto Pokorney of Lawton at first, Gus Kellerman at second, Everhart at third, with Al Meander and, later, Will Reed at shortstop. Seventeen year old Yancy Davis, Frank Lofton, who also caught, Henry Goodrich, Jimmy Long, and George Watson rotated

Pitcher "Smick" Myers (Meyers) came with Webb City and played two seasons with the Oilers. He was a member of the McAlester club in the 1912 Oklahoma State League.

Dick Crutcher (1889-1952) toiled for eight seasons in the minors including a stint with Enid and four seasons at St. Joseph before he made the 1914 "Miracle" Boston Braves that later won the World Series in four games over the favored Athletics. The Braves sent him down to Jersey City at the end of June. Through 1919 he split his time between Kansas City and Joplin.

in the outfield. The trio of twirlers were Davis, Charles "Buz" Taylor, and "Smick" Myers. Half of rookie Davis' appearances for Webb City-Sapulpa were on the mound where he amassed a record of thirteen wins against a dozen losses. Taylor triumphed in seventeen of thirty outings. Myers won thirteen and lost eleven. Future major leaguer Dick Crutcher appeared in seventeen games, winning five. James McClintock contributed five victories in nine decisions.

Immediately upon changing homes, the newly christened Oilers stoked enthusiasm in Sapulpa by sweeping three games from Bartlesville at the Boosters' home grounds. After dropping three to Muskogee, the first home stand at Athletic Park

began on July 24 against Bartlesville. Everhart's charges dropped the opener six to nil and lost the second. William "Jake" Wolverton, picked up after receiving his release from Bartlesville, blanked his former team mates over the protest of his former captain, Frank Barber, that Goodrich's walk off homerun was foul.

William "Jake" Wolverton joined the Oilers on the bounce at the end of 1909 and lifted the team. He spent four more seasons in the Central Association and Western League.

The Oilers vacillated between third and fifth the remainder of the season. The campaign ended in Sapulpa with Bartlesville again as the guest. The Boosters grabbed the first two to assure that Sapulpa would finish one-half game behind Bartlesville. On the last day the Oilers won a morale booster as they clobbered the visitors eleven to two behind Wolverton's three-hitter.

1910

Frank Everhart hung up his cleats after leading the Oilers to twenty-nine victories of forty-nine contests. Sapulpa management turned to Larry Milton who won his only appearance for the St. Louis Cardinals at the end of the1903 season. He began pitching professionally in 1900. He spent the next eight seasons in the Three-I League and Western Association. After managing Webb City in 1908, he reached his highest minor league playing level in 1909 with Little Rock of the Southern Association.

After Texas League veteran Frank Everhart gave up management following the 1909 season, pitcher Larry Milton (1879-1942) was called on to lead the 1910 edition of the Sapulpa Oilers. He had been in the game since 1900, all in the minors except for four innings with the 1903 St. Louis Cardinals. In his final season as a player, he won eighteen of twenty-eight decisions.

Frank Coe (1889-1940) joined the 1910 club from St. Joseph after batting a disappointing .146. He was the regular Oilers' backstop for the rest of the season. His glove was good enough to keep him in the Nebraska State League and Western Association with Sherman, Muskogee, and Ft. Smith through 1916.

Alex "Goat" Dupree threw for the semi-pro 1903 Oklahoma City Mets, then the 1904 Shawnee club. Between 1906 and 1908, he won sixty-seven games in the Texas League. In 1906 he twice threw no-hitters against Greenville. Sapulpa was one of three teams he played for in 1910, the others being Guthrie and Macon in the Sally League. According to Ruggles, Dupree was " [o]ne of the greatest of Texas League hurlers."

Milton inherited a solid nucleus. Pokorney, Kellerman, Reed, and Goodrich returned. Jefferies was back behind the plate assisted by newcomer Frank Coe who also won seven of eleven pitching decisions. Meander was joined in the outfield by Yancy Davis whose bat was too valuable to keep in the bullpen. Myers was back. Milton, Frank Taylor, and Guiton Scott joined them to form the pitching corps. Milton experimented during the first six weeks of the season trying to find the right combination, particularly in the infield. He played catch and release giving amateurs Erdlick, Coverdale, Gleason, Williams, Schwales, and Swaley look-sees. Pitchers Knowlton and Boggs were tried and returned. Edmond Normal student Louis Listen was cut before he signed with El Reno then threw a no-hitter for Guthrie. Ray "Chief" Halley played briefly before moving on to the Nebraska State League. Alex Dupree was on the mound staff for a couple of weeks. Reuben Isaacs briefly held second base. With Pokorney's and Kellerman's versatility, what the Oilers needed was a first sacker and second baseman. The former was filled by former Guthrie standout Clyde Geist. The latter came in George McAvoy who would manage both Sapulpa and Ardmore in the Texas-Oklahoma in 1911. The season ended with Coe behind the plate, Geist at first, McAvoy at second, Kellerman at third, Reed at short field, and Davis, Meander and Goodrich in the outfield. The four pitchers, Scott, Taylor, Myers, and Milton all posted double digits in the win column. Goodrich led the league in hits and home runs.

Will Reed got his start at Dallas in 1909. With a good Ellsworth, Kansas club, he attracted Milton's attention and played shortstop for Sapulpa the rest of 1910. When Sapulpa disbanded in June of 1911, he joined Altus in the Texas-Oklahoma League.

Despite winning ways, attendance was not commensurate with performance. On July 12 a ticket-selling contest was launched with prizes including a diamond ring and gold watch. It was designed to increase interest and guarantee a certain revenue stream. Over the remainder of the season it was successful.

Joplin ran away with the pennant race finishing twenty-two and one half games ahead of runner-up Enid and twenty-six in front of Sapulpa. Along the way, Muskogee-Okmulgee, Tulsa,

Bartlesville, and El Reno had fallen by the wayside. A number of the 1910 Oilers would be promoted up. Milton went on to other endeavors. He would next appear as a promoter of the stillborn Mid-Continent League in 1912.

1911

Management turned to a young veteran whose minor league career would run through 1922 and include a stint with the Phillies, George McAvoy. While he was putting together a ball club, a committee of fans was endeavoring to underwrite the season by selling 330 ticket books at $15 each. The financial underpinnings were uncertain and McAvoy warned the public that the Oilers could find a new home.

Kellerman, Reed and Smick Myers were the only returning players from 1910. McAvoy raided the Okmulgee semi-pros to take their pitcher and outfielder Lake and third baseman, Patterson. Lester Claybrook assumed first base duties and George Ives appeared in the outfield. Tom Goldwaithe was signed as the first string catcher. A semi-pro named Leroy would serve as relief catcher and outfielder. Another named Heckathorpe played in the outfield.

Tom Hayden, from Webb City, took the league president's chair in a coup when Enid lost its team and the Association was demoted to Class D. He resigned in April then withdrew his resignation and announced that he had the Tulsa franchise. There was disorder. There was no schedule until one week before the May 5 openers. There was a feud between Hayden and Ft. Smith owner and manager Art Riggs. The latter accused the former, with some justification, of trying to steal his team. The season was not well begun.

The Oilers dropped two of three games at Independence then lost the home opener in fourteen innings by a seven to six score. Five games into the campaign, Joplin and Springfield dropped out.

Meanwhile, the Oilers with a supportive city—the doings of the Oilers had been front page news in the *Sapulpa Evening Light* since 1909— were having perhaps the best season of the three seasons they called Sapulpa home. A win over Tulsa at home pulled the Oilers to even. By June 13, Sapulpa upped its record to twenty wins against eighteen losses following taking all three at Muskogee. On June 14, Coffeyville failed to appear in Sapulpa. The White Sox and Howard Price's Independence team disbanded. That left Tulsa, Muskogee, Ft. Smith and Sapulpa in the league. President Hayden on June 19 sent a telegram to the remaining teams that he had split the season with the team in first place on June 14, Ft. Smith, the first half winner. That evening Sapulpa played at Tulsa. The Railroaders disbanded after the game. While Muskogee and Sapulpa wanted to continue, the Tulsa franchise could not be moved quickly enough to save the Western Association.

The *Evening Light's* post-mortem attributed the demise as being caused by four large cities—Muskogee, Ft. Smith, Springfield and Joplin—being captured in a small town league. Whatever the cause, Sapulpa would not see a profession team at Athletic Park for another decade.

Sapulpa was ready to play ball even as the Western Association collapsed around it. The two Kansas clubs disbanded on June 14 and Ft. Smith and Tulsa fell on the 19th. With only Muskogee and Sapulpa left standing, both disbanded.

SHAWNEE

SHAWNEE INDIANS, ORIOLES, BROWNS · SOUTHWESTERN LEAGUE · 1904
SHAWNEE BLUES · SOUTH CENTRAL LEAGUE · 1906

SEASON	TEAM NAME	MANAGERS	WON	LOST	PERCENTAGE	FINISH
1904	Indians	W. M. Hazlett	2	2	.500	*
1904	Orioles	W. M.Hazett	6	14	.333	†
1904	Browns	L. A. Lackey	3	3	.385	††
		Deacon White				
1906	Blues	Joe B. Roe	29	42	.408	disbanded July 21
		J.B. McAlester				
		Norman Nelson				

* Played four games at Enid before moving to Chickasha until June 22. Record in Chickasha was 13-24

† Hazlett club moved to Shawnee July 1. Hazlett left July 17. Suspended July 23-31. Charles Palmer of El Reno took over the franchise on August 1 and disbanded August 5. Played as semi-pros through August 12.

†† L. A. Lackey formed team at Shawnee in a re-organized league on August 11. The 4-2 official record apparently does not consider the final Oklahoma City series. The club disbanded September 5.

Shawnee was a horse and buggy town when professional baseball came in 1904.

Railroads made Shawnee. Its population exploded from 250 to 2,500 after the Choctaw, Oklahoma & Gulf extended there in 1895 and later moved its main repair yard there. The facility expanded when the Rock Island acquired the C O & G and a terminal was built. As an agriculture and cotton center —there were seven cotton gins— in 1903 and 1904 the Katy and Santa Fe railroads arrived and built terminals. Shawnee was surrounded on three sides by tracks of different carriers. By Statehood, forty-two passenger and sixty-five freight trains passed through Shawnee each week. A streetcar system was begun in 1903.

In 1907 Shawnee began its campaign to become the new Oklahoma Capital, challenging the incumbent Guthrie and the growing giant Oklahoma City.

The Statehoods in 1902 and Blues in 1903 under the leadership of Roy Congdon had represented Shawnee in Territorial semi-pro leagues with some success, especially against the Oklahoma City Metropolitans. Professional baseball came to Shawnee with the arrival of the first Santa Fe train on June 29, 1904. W. M. Hazlett, Chickasha promoter and avid first baseman, advised the Southwestern League on June 24 that he would re-locate his franchise to Shawnee. Re-locate because the first series of the season at Enid's Waverly Park was played as the Shawnee Indians. When it came time for the home opener, the Indians were diverted to Chickasha where the ball club remained until it went broke on June 22. The first game in Shawnee would be called on July 1.

Ed Pokorney and Pete Hauser, a Jim Thorpe team mate at Carlisle, came over to Shawnee and Shorty Allen, O. C. Wilhite, recent St. Louis Cardinal Lon Ury, and Harley "Cy the Third" Young, recently released from Oklahoma City, signed on. The standings on July 4 showed the Chicka-

Pete Hauser followed Hazlett from Chickasha.

Harley "Cy the Third" Young (1883-1975) broke in with Shawnee. He played through 1920 amassing a minor league record of 153-112 that included a 40-45 performance for Oklahoma City in three Texas League seasons. He worked in the National League between April 21 and July 4, 1908 with Pittsburgh and Boston.

sha team to now be Shawnee with one win against three losses. At some point the aggregation took the name the "Orioles." Hazlett abandoned the team on July 18 pleading the excuse of an ill wife; second baseman Cousins went with him. Since July 1,

the Orioles had won five and lost twelve when *The Daily Oklahoman* reported

[t]he Shawnee team is on the ragged edge and its survival as a member of the league is questionable. Hazlett, the manager, gave up the ghost several days ago.

When this ball club played its last game on July 24, the Orioles defeated Oklahoma City to finish this stage of existence with a record of six wins and fourteen defeats. The team went temporarily dormant. Some players such as Bennett, Allen, and Barnes joined the Ada semi-pros.

The semi-pro group from El Reno represented that they could take over the Shawnee franchise and several of the Orioles including Ury, Bennett, and Cousins signed with the new team. It debuted on July 31 with a four to two loss to Enid. On August 4, the league owners formally awarded Charles Palmer of El Reno a franchise, revised the standings so that El Reno stood at five wins and only nine losses then drew a new schedule that erased prior games in the standings. On August 6, those three former Orioles were the only ones who departed the train from El Reno for the anticipated game at Guthrie. They told the people and press that the El Reno club had disbanded. The Southwestern League was down to three members. It looked as though it was every team for itself and that the Mets, Blues, and Backsliders (formerly Evangelists) would finish 1904 as semi-pros. There were no league games played between August 6 and 12.

Meanwhile L. A. Lackey organized a team that included "Dad" Ahorn, Chick Brandom, Clarence Nelson, Alex Dupree, Al Ritter, future umpire Dit Spencer, and once again Harley Young. Named the "Browns," Lackey's club was admitted to the Southwestern League on August 11, as the standings were

Dad Ahorn came to Shawnee from the Texas League where he pitched in 1902 and 1903. The next season, 1905, found him with the South McAlester Giants.

Chick Brandom (1887-1958), the University of Oklahoma's first major leaguer, first played for the Shawnee Browns. He moved up to Muskogee in 1905 and spent 1907 and 1908 as well as 1910 and 1911 with Kansas City. 1913 and 1914 were in the International League. The end of 1908 and all of 1909 were spent with Pittsburgh. He jumped from Organized Baseball to Newark of the Federal League in 1915. He was blackballed after that.

Clarence "Peaches" Nelson (1883-?) was one of the early star pitchers in Oklahoma. He was the top hurlers for the 1903 Mets and threw for Guthrie as well as Shawnee in 1904 before jumping to the Mets at season end. He was 54-31 in the Texas League including a twenty-three win season at Houston in 1905. Through 1922 he played a total of fifteen professional seasons including 1906 and 1908 at Oklahoma City and 1909 at Guthrie. His career record was 194-153.

A. L. "Dad" Ritter played for the Shawnee Browns and then for Galveston, Muskogee, and teams in Arkansas. His best success was as a manager. In 1911 and 1912 he led Cleburne to championships in two different leagues. He copped a second Texas-Oklahoma League flag in 1914. His last job in baseball was at the head of Sherman in 1915.

re-set to zero, and once more a new schedule was drawn, this one ending on October 1. *The Daily Oklahoman* for August 26 reported

> [a] rumor reached the city last night to the effect that the Shawnee team of the Southwestern league is again out of business, its manager having decamped between days with the funds of the association.

The rumor was true. The players elected sexagenarian first baseman James "Deacon" White to be captain and voted to continue the seasons as an orphan franchise playing the remainder of the season at the home of whomsoever was scheduled.

The first appearance for the Orphans would be

a weekend series at Guthrie. There is no report of those contests being played. Next they began a six-game series at Oklahoma City on August 30. The first game, called a "comedy of errors," was a nine to eight win for the Mets. The Browns exacted a measure of revenge the next day, taking advantage of eleven Mets' errors for a seventeen to seven victory. The next two games were split with the home team embarrassing Shawnee twenty to one on the first. Behind Ahorn's pitching, the Orphans won the next day four to two. Young baffled the Mets on the third for a three to one win. Oklahoma City ace Clarence Nelson, having jumped from the Browns, scattered six Shawnee hits for a six to zero Labor Day victory to gain a split of the series. The extant records do not reflect these two series.

The next stop was Enid. At this juncture, the

team decided to quit their gypsy existence and end their season early. The Browns disbanded on September 5. Some appeared on September 6 as a "Holdenville-Shawnee" club. It would be back to a semi-pro Blues season for 1905.

1906

Joseph B. Roe of Sedalia, Missouri was credited with being the father in 1902 of the version of the Missouri Valley League that became the Western Association three seasons later. Indeed, he wrote that league's first schedule. He served as manager of the 1905 South McAlester Giants in the residual, small town Missouri Valley League that season. He spurned J. B. Galbraith's attempt to organize a circuit to be called the Indiahoma Base Ball League and instead became one of the founders of the South Central League, successor to the Missouri Valley League.

Roe assembled a ball club featuring Clyde Milan at bat and Leo Hite on the mound. Harry Welch, Charles Nichols, Frank Browning, D. P. Sparks, J. O. Simpson, Clyde Cobb, James Haney, F. B. Cooper, and R. E. Grace completed the roster. There was much potential but the talent and resources were mismanaged.

Clyde Milan (1887-1953) played sixteen seasons for the Washington Senators, 1907-1922. 1905 was his rookie season divided between Clarksville, Texas and South McAlester. The next season, he followed his manager, J. B. Roe, to Shawnee. He left the team when it disbanded and signed with Wichita.

Shawnee Blues owner and manager Joe B. Roe, having exhausted all his cash on the trip, had to borrow to purchase train tickets home for the team on May 9 at the conclusion of a series at South McAlester. The new grandstand announced on April 10 had not been built so home revenues were far less than predicted. On May 23, management called the team home from Muskogee because the club had run out of cash. *The Daily Oklahoman reported*

> Owing to the fact that the team is not making sufficient money to pay expenses, the management of the Shawnee Blues, of the South Central league, called the team home from Muskogee [on May 23], and a benefit game will be played tomorrow with the Rock Island team at League park. No grandstand has yet been erected in the park, and consequently the attendance at the games here was light. It is probable that a new management may take charge of the situation if the old feels itself unable to cope with the situation.

On May 26, league president J. B. McAlester resigned to take over management of the Blues, ousting Roe in the interim. He also temporarily assumed field duties as the club couldn't afford another mouth to feed.

McAlester temporarily saved the Shawnee

Big "Bun" McAlester resigned the South Central League presidency to intervene to save the Shawnee club. After the dust settled, he played nine games for Dallas.

franchise with much local support in the form of a new owner led by C. F. Barrett as president and Roy Congdon, who played at St. Joseph as "Condon" in 1896, as manager on and off the field. On June 7, the new Shawnee Baseball Association directed Congdon to cancel the series with Ft. Smith that was to begin the following day due to the imminent insolvency of the club. As the Association did not assume Roe's debts, it was problematic whether it would continue with the franchise. Somehow Shawnee remained on the field. Local entrepreneurs, the Carey brothers, seemingly acquired control of the franchise. Norman Nelson, hired as manager to replace volunteer Congdon, turned around the ball club and added seven new players including Lefty Holmes and hard-hitting University of Kansas star Ernie Quigley. The Blues began playing above .500 ball. The fans were placated. Shawnee was sailing on an even keel but a sister club was headed for the rocks and would take down the one in tow.

Traveling from Guthrie though Oklahoma City on the way to a series at South McAlester on July 22, the Ft. Smith players gave a waiting room interview that included word that the Guthrie team had disbanded the day before. They added that the game plan was to drop Shawnee leaving a new four-member league. That was exactly what happened. On Saturday next, a mob of fans "hunted up the Carey brothers" and extracted $1,600 from them to pay the players and run the club. The next day, president Harper telephoned the Shawnee manager to break

the news. The fans were livid and threatened litigation as well as a protest to the National Association.

A reversal by J. H. Farrell of the decision South Central president made would have been a Pyrrhic victory. On August 7, president Harper announced that he had transferred the failed Tulsa franchise to former Shawnee owner J. B. Roe who began moving the club to Shawnee. The effect would be to break up the tight little circuit of short hops between South McAlester and Ft. Smith (110 miles), Ft. Smith to Muskogee (73 miles) Muskogee to Tulsa (55 miles), and Tulsa to South McAlester (91 miles) that allowed day trips reducing rail time, hotels, and meal money. Shawnee would be an outlier adding nearly 155 miles from Muskogee and an overnight stay. Muskogee, wrapping up in Ft. Smith, had been scheduled to arrive in Tulsa on August 8 for a day trip. Now the Indians were looking at three nights in Shawnee. They simply couldn't afford it. The Ft. Smith and Muskogee managers disbanded their clubs and played an exhibition to raise train fare.

So ended baseball in Shawnee until 1923.

SOUTH McALESTER

SOUTH McALESTER GIANTS · MISSOURI VALLEY LEAGUE · 1905
SOUTH McALESTER MINERS · SOUTH CENTRAL LEAGUE · 1906

SEASON	TEAM NAME	MANAGERS	WON	LOST	PERCENTAGE	FINISH
1905	Giants	Joe B. Roe	33	63	.344	8 of 8
1906	Miners	Deacon White	59	32	.648	1 of 6

1905

South McAlester I.T. was the last city to join the castaways of the new Western Association in a circuit of four Kansas and Missouri towns and four southern, Indian Territory,

South McAlester in the Choctaw Nation was a bustling community at the intersection of two railroad lines to the south of J. J. McAlester's general store in what commonly was called "North Town" or simply "McAlester." Because the two towns were under federal jurisdiction, in preparation for Statehood on November 16, 1907, Congress merged the municipalities with North Town providing the name and South McAlester the city government. The South McAlester post office was closed on July 1, 1907. Before then, "South Town" was the home to a ball club that turned around from a doormat to league champion.

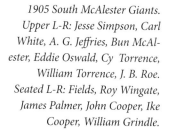

J. J. McAlester came to the Indian Territory following the Civil War and established a trading post. He was the second Lieutenant Governor of Oklahoma.

Roe assembled a motley aggregation under the name "Giants" with a monthly payroll of $400.

The pitching Torrence brothers, captain William and Cy, the White brothers, catcher Foley, outfielder Carl, and first sacker Harry, joined the Coopers, Ike and F. B., to form the Giant's core.

1905 South McAlester Giants. Upper L-R: Jesse Simpson, Carl White, A. G. Jeffries, Bun McAlester, Eddie Oswald, Cy Torrence, William Torrence, J. B. Roe. Seated L-R: Fields, Roy Wingate, James Palmer, John Cooper, Ike Cooper, William Grindle.

towns. The town's namesake, J. J. McAlester, was figurehead president of the ballclub but the owner and field manager was Joseph B. Roe of Sedalia, Missouri who was instrumental in forming the predecessor of the new Western Association with whom he remained associated. In fact, he drew that league's schedule for 1905.

Harry Lally from the local mines, J. W. Anderson, Jesse Simpson, Art Jeffries, William Grindle, A. "Dad" Ahorn, Aubrey Pickens, Hugh McCullum, Barney Hanratta, old timer Jim Bouldin, Roy Wingate, and another dozen or so who made brief appearances rounded out the roster. Many had bounced around the low minors particularly the Texas League.

The season opened on May 15 at the Giants' Sunday home field, Krebs park, a town of Roman Catholic coal miners who subscribed to the Scripture that the Sabbath was made for man. The visiting Muskogee crowd, some 300, experienced the trip to the ball park as related by the *Muskogee Democrat*

The ball park is reached by the Traction line and is only a short ride from the city. The traction company was long and earnestly cussed by all who failed to buy tickets before getting on the cars, as the fare charged was fifteen cents each way. Adding the usual admissions price charged to the ball game, it makes the fans down there pay out too much money to see a game. Baseball won't be a success there under that arrangement.

When the dust settled, the Redskins (or "land grafters" as the "coal barons" called them) were on top with three runs. South McAlester's ninth inning rally fell one run short. The following day was the grand opener in town. The contest was preceded by a street parade headed by the Kali-Inla band, a carriage containing Mayor Dr. T. S. Chapman, Joe Roe, umpire Steve Collins, and Muskogee leader G. A. Sabin. The uniformed teams followed. On the field, the home team was less hospitable and walked away with a big win and a measure of revenge. The next day, the Giants took the third game in the series by eleven runs to three.

The Giants were also the opponent for Muskogee's home opener at Benson Park on May 19. Wild and allowing six walks in four innings, Ike Cooper handed Muskogee a thirteen to six win. This was to be the story of the season.

The most exciting contest of the 1905 season was between the Missouri Valley League and the South McAlester baseball club. On the morning of July 9, manager Roe received a telegram from league president, Richard Robertson, Jr. that read:

South McAlester franchise transferred under constitutional provisions on grounds advanced by club owners that for business reasons this club's membership is no longer desirable.

Apparently the other owners had handed over the ball club to one Charles E. Shaftt of Tulsa who was planning to immediately move it to Ft. Smith. Roe conceded that the other managers had complained about the grounds —which had been remediated since the first round of visits by the other teams— but they were better than the grounds at Pittsburg or Ft. Scott. South McAlester had its forfeit money posted, was current on dues, and was in good standing with the league. A subsequent telegram said that Shaftt was in route, had full authority to take over the franchise, and that Roe had no further rights.

Robertson, at headquarters in Kansas City, was inundated with telegrams and letters from the people of South McAlester and, it seems, a summons to defend the league in federal court in the Southern District of the Indian Territory. Robertson showed that he had one of the best reverse gears of his time or as the *South McAlester Capital* wrote "back pedaling as fast as human energy can command." On July 13 he telephoned Roe —long distance telephone calls were an exotic in 1905— to advise that there was no transfer and that the Giants should carry on as though nothing had happened. Despite what some of the best reference books write, South McAlester's franchise never was moved to Ft. Smith.

The Giants continued the season in South McAlester finishing last with thirty-three wins in 109 games forty games behind champion Pittsburg. The rift between the league members in the States and the Territorials was too great to bridge. The

Joseph B. Roe came from Sedalia, Missouri. He was deeply involved in formation in 1902 of the original Missouri Valley League of mining towns in the Tri-State district. When the larger cities split off in 1905 to form the Western Association, Roe joined the small towns that formed a new Missouri Valley League and took a franchise in South McAlester. He showed up with the Shawnee club in the successor circuit, the South Central League. While the 1905 attempt to oust him from league membership may have been motivated as much by geography as management, Roe's ouster from the Shawnee operation was based strictly on ineptitude. When news came late in the 1906 season that he was in control of the Tulsa club and was moving it to Shawnee, the other teams disbanded. His attempt to form a new league for 1907 was stillborn. There is no record of him having played in Organized Baseball and no further word of him after 1907.

BROTHER ACTS

South McAlester had two fraternal duos in 1905 and one trio in 1906. Older brother Oscar "Cy" Torrence (1874-?) pitched for Evansville in the Three-I League in 1901 and gradually migrated south to the Indian Territory. William, the 1905 Giants' captain, was also a hurler. He spent 1903 and 1904 with Pittsburg in the Missouri Valley League before signing with South McAlester. F. B. "Ike" Cooper went from South McAlester to four good seasons in the Texas League where his record was 43-36. Third sacker John H. Cooper went to the Texas League in 1906 and 1907 then finished in 1910 in the East Carolina League. In 1906, the Whites led the club. Carl, Harry and Foley White were all Texas Leaguers. Outfielder Carl debuted with Paris-Ardmore in the 1904 Texas League and played league ball through 1910. First baseman Harry was with Dallas in 1896 and Paris in 1902 and 1903. Foley (?-1955), a catcher, played in eight different Texas League seasons with five different teams. He finished the final two years of his playing days with Ardmore in the Texas-Oklahoma League.

"Cy" Torrence

William Torrence

"Ike" Cooper

John H. Cooper

Carl White

Foley White

Harry White

two sides would go their own ways in separate leagues the following season.

1906

South McAlester had a new owner in a new league, the South Central. McAlester Amusement Co. headed by baseball buff W. F. Harper, president of the local electric and street car company, with M. B. Brewer as secretary, held the franchise. Some familiar names were back with the new league. J. B. Roe owned the Shawnee club and 1905 interloper Charles Shaftt had the Tulsa franchise until he returned to a day job as an outfielder for St. Joseph. The owners hired James "Deacon" White, who had

James "Deacon" White (1847-1939) was the only player or manager in Oklahoma professional baseball to have lived through the Civil War. He played first base for twenty major league seasons (1871-1890). He was a playing manager for Shawnee in 1904, South McAlester in 1906, McAlester in 1907, and Tulsa in 1908.

briefly led the Shawnee Browns in 1904, to lead the renamed Miners on the field. J. B. "Bun" McAlester was league president.

Clad in navy flannels with an elaborate "McA" logo, white belts and white caps the Miners were all veterans of the 1905 Missouri Valley campaign. The same line-up of position players appeared in nearly every game: Foley White catcher; first base James Bouldin; Aubrey Pickens second base; Hugh McCullum shortstop; J. W. Anderson third base; Bill Lattimore, Carl White, Harry Lally, and Harry White roamed the outfield. C. M. Porter was the pitching ace along with Cooper who won over a third of the 1905 Giants' games.

In a 180° reversal from the previous year, the Miners took the lead on the first day and never relinquished it. While Muskogee gave South McAlester a contest, the Miners had the best record winning fifty nine of ninety-one among the four finishing clubs, each of whom had a winning percentage above .500. The pennant these Miners won was only the first of many.

1906 South McAlester Miners. Upper L-R: Carl White, Ike Cooper, C. M. Porter, James Bouldin, Foley White. Lower: Hugh McCullum, Harry White, Bill Lattimore, Harry Lally. Seated L-R Aubrey Pickens, mascot, J. W. Anderson.

VINITA

VINITA CHEROKEES · MISSOURI VALLEY LEAGUE · 1905
VINITA CHAMPS · KANSAS STATE LEAGUE · JUNE 6-JULY 5, 1906

SEASON	TEAM NAME	MANAGERS	WON	LOST	PERCENTAGE	FINISH
1905	Cherokees	Ed Finney	41	63	.394	7 of 8
1906	Champs	Bill Burns	14	10	.583	disbanded July 5

1905

The first representative from the Cherokee Nation in Organized Baseball, Vinita of the Missouri Valley League was a town of some 3,000 in 1905.

City Marshal and entrepreneur H. E. Ridenhour was the impetus behind the local Players Association that operated the club. He owned the ball field, Sportsmen's Park, and even bought adjacent lots to the west so that the grandstand and bleachers could be moved and the playing surface leveled.

The only town in the Cherokee Nation to have a professional baseball team, Vinita is the second oldest town in Oklahoma and was the first to have electricity. The second Civil War Battle of Cabin Creek was fought there before a Katy survey crew came through in 1871 and set up a station at a township site that Col. Elias Boudinot, II had laid out. He named the town after sculptress Lavinia "Vinnie" Ream. It was the seat of the federal court for the Northern District of Indian Territory.

After dropping all but one of the exhibitions, the Vinita Cherokees made their league debut at home on May 14. The series was scheduled for Tulsa but the Creek Nation's District Attorney had banned baseball on Sundays. When the team left for the first trip outside Indian Territory, the club was playing .500 ball. Coming into Muskogee for a series June 1 – 4, the local fans were so disgusted with their Reds after a three-game sweep by Tulsa that they stayed away with the result that Vinita received only the $20 guarantee. For the Sunday game, a third of the 600 in attendance were from the Vinita area. The Cherokees came out on top six to three but Muskogee protested the game claiming pitcher Henry Daye was under contract to Dallas (in fact he soon appeared there). Overall, Vinita was supporting its ball club better than Muskogee, Tulsa, or Ft. Scott.

The Cherokees went into a tailspin dropping from second to sixth by June 28. At that juncture, the Players Association was incorporated and placed under the control of a board of shareholders: Ewing Halsell, president, J. H. Butler, secretary-treasurer, H. E. Ridenhour, W. P. Phillips, Adolph

1905 Vinita Cherokees. Clockwise from 1: Argus Hamilton, Goad, Lawrence Bonfoy, Ed Finney, Frank Lofton, Shannon, Fred Finney, Adair Bushyhead "Paddy" Mayes, Higley Raleigh Aitchison, Henry Daye, Cude Harland .

Schoenherr and pitcher Argus Hamilton, recently relieved of managerial duties at Guthrie. The players were not playing up to their potential and had been "soldiering." Operations were taken from a troika of Ridenhour as business manager, John Meade as field manager and Ed Finney as captain and centralized in Finney's hands so that the players would have a single authority to obey.

Vaughan and Hamilton, the "Pitching Parson," were ironmen for the Cherokees several times hurling both ends of double headers. Toward the middle of August, the club, with additions, was playing first division baseball. When, however, the season was truncated by three week because Pittsburg's lead was so great, the on-field enthusiasm waned. The final two games against Ft. Scott were characterized as "disgusting." The final contest of the season against Ft. Scott at Vinita featured fifteen errors, twenty-eight hits and fifteen runs.

1906

When the Missouri Valley League split, Vinita was left without a club in either the Kansas State League or the new South Central League. The 1905 Missouri Valley winner, Pittsburg named its team the Champs for 1906 and joined the Kansas State League. Not making expenses by the end of May, the Champs became orphaned. *Vinita Chieftain* publisher A. Garland Marrs bought the Pittsburg nine for $500 on June 6 and set them up in Sportsmen's Park with the hope that he would at least break even. Harry Lally came down from Pittsburg as did 1905 star Paddy Mayes. Two three-game series quickly followed against Chanute and Independence. The Champs were one game above .500 when they came to Vinita. They had fourteen wins in twenty-four contests during their month in the Indian Territory.

A double header against Ft. Scott was played at Sportsmen's Park on the Fourth of July. The *Vinita Chieftain* reported on July 5, 1906 that the players had not been paid for a month. Marrs had not come close to breaking even. The former Pittsburg orphans disbanded. The same article also related that several teams were "on the verge of dissolution" and "Chanute and Ft. Scott were both in a hard way." In fact, Ft. Scott's Giants disbanded that same day. The Kansas State League began a new season on July 10 without Vinita or Ft. Scott. With that news, the story of Organized Baseball in Vinita came to an end.

Harry Lally has a peripatetic season in 1906. In the Kansas State League, he played for Pittsburg, Kansas, then in Vinita, and Bartlesville before returning to South McAlester. He last appears in baseball records with Poplar Bluff in the 1908 Arkansas State League.

Paddy Mayes (1885-1963) appeared in two games for the Phillies during a six day stay with the club in June of 1911. He divided the rest of the season among Galveston, Oklahoma City, and Mobile. He last played for Beaumont in 1912.

BIBLIOGRAPHY

The starting point for this book was *Glory Days of Summer* issued by our shared publisher, Oklahoma Heritage Association. It contained the first ever survey of minor league baseball in Oklahoma. The section on Ardmore is a truncated version of the first two chapters of my 2011 book *Territorians to Boomers*. The largest part of the research for this book was done through microfilm and digital media of newspapers and periodicals published before 1920 including *The Sporting News, Sporting Life,* and *The Daily Oklahoman*. The two former are subscription-based The latter is in the microfilm collection of the Oklahoma Historical Society, Oklahoma City, Oklahoma. Local newspapers of the period from each city were also accessed through the microfilm collection of the Oklahoma Historical Society. Oklahoma City attorney Doug Loudenback has written a detailed history of early baseball in Oklahoma City that has been most helpful. His blog may be found at http://dougdawgz.blogspot.com/2010/08/oklahoma-city-baseball.html. David Davis is the creator of the website www.picsaweb.google.com/WrightWingOOTP/ that contains public domain photos of players who have appeared in the major leagues (National, American, and Federal) organized by year and is the source for many of the photos on the www.baseball-reference.com site. For players who appeared in ten or fewer major league games, SABR's *2000 Cups of Coffee* is a valuable supplement to Davis' work. Materials published on or before December 31, 1922 are in the public domain because until 1998 the longest life of a copyright was seventy-five years.

Ardmore Public Library, Ardmore, Oklahoma McGalliard Collection

Burke, Bob, Franks, Kenny, Parr, Royse, *Glory Days of Summer: The History of Baseball in Oklahoma,* Oklahoma City: Oklahoma Heritage Association 1999

Chadwick, Henry, ed., *Spalding's Official Base Ball Guide 1894* (New York: American Sports Publishing Co. 1894)

----*Spalding's Official Base Ball Guide 1903* (New York: American Sports Publishing Co. 1903)

----*Spalding's Official Base Ball Guide 1904* (New York: American Sports Publishing Co. 1904)

----*Spalding's Official Base Ball Guide 1905* (New York: American Sports Publishing Co. 1905)

---*Spalding's Official Base Ball Guide 1906* (New York: American Sports Publishing Co. 1906)

---*Spalding's Official Base Ball Guide 1907* (New York: American Sports Publishing Co. 1907)

--- *Spalding's Official Base Ball Guide 1908* (New York: American Sports Publishing Co. 1908)

----*Spalding's Official Base Ball Guide 1909* (New York: American Sports Publishing Co. 1909)

Chickasaw Regional Library System, Microfilm Collection, *The Daily Ardmoreite*

Corden, Seth K. and Richards, W. B. compilers, *The Oklahoma Red Book* (2 vol.), Oklahoma City: State of Oklahoma 1912

Foster, John H., ed., *Spalding's Official Base Ball Guide 1910* (New York: American Sports Publishing Co. 1910)

----*Spalding's Official Base Ball Guide 1911* (New York: American Sports Publishing Co. 1911)

----*Spalding's Official Base Ball Guide 1912* (New York: American Sports Publishing Co. 1912)

----*Spalding's Official Base Ball Guide 1913* (New York: American Sports Publishing Co. 1913)

----*Spalding's Official Base Ball Guide 1915* (New York: American Sports Publishing Co. 1915)

----*Spalding's Official Base Ball Guide 1916* (New York: American Sports Publishing Co. 1916)

---*Spalding's Official Base Ball Guide 1917* (New York: American Sports Publishing Co. 1917)

----*Spalding's Official Base Ball Guide 1918* (New York: American Sports Publishing Co. 1918)

--- *Spalding's Official Base Ball Guide 1919* (New York: American Sports Publishing Co. 1919)

----*Spalding's Official Base Ball Guide 1921* (New York: American Sports Publishing Co. 1921)

----*Spalding's Official Base Ball Guide 1922* (New York: American Sports Publishing Co. 1922)

----*Spalding's Official Base Ball Guide 1923* (New York: American Sports Publishing Co. 1923)

----*Spalding's Official Base Ball Guide 1924* (New York: American Sports Publishing Co. 1924)

----*Spalding's Official Base Ball Guide 1925* (New York: American Sports Publishing Co. 1925)

Hackley, Lucille Thompson, *Bonham-The Era has Gone-But Memories Linger On* (Fannin County Historical Commission 1980)

Johnson, Lloyd and Miles Wolff ed., *The Encyclopedia of Minor League Baseball* 3d ed. Durham, NC: Baseball America, Inc., 2007 (Durham, NC: Baseball America, Inc. 2007)

Murname, T. H., ed., *Official Guide of the National Association of Professional Baseball Leagues 1902* (New York: A. G. Spalding & Bros. 1902)

---- *Official Guide of the National Association of Professional Baseball Leagues 1903* (New York: A. G. Spalding & Bros. 1903)

---- *Official Guide of the National Association of Professional Baseball Leagues 1904* (New York: American Sports Publishing Co. 1904)

----*Official Guide of the National Association of Professional Baseball Leagues 1908* (New York: American Sports Publishing Co. 1908)

---- *Official Guide of the National Association of Professional Baseball Leagues 1910* (New York: American Sports Publishing Co. 1910)

---- *Official Guide of the National Association of Professional Baseball Leagues 1911* (New York: American Sports Publishing Co. 1911)

----*Official Guide of the National Association of Professional Baseball Leagues 1912* (New York: American Sports Publishing Co. 1912)

----*Official Guide of the National Association of Professional Baseball Leagues 1913* (New York: American Sports Publishing Co. 1913)

----*Official Guide of the National Association of Professional Baseball Leagues 1915* (New York: American Sports Publishing Co. 1915)

---- *Official Guide of the National Association of Professional Baseball Leagues 1916* (New York: American Sports Publishing Co. 1916)

---- *Official Guide of the National Association of Professional Baseball Leagues 1917* (New York: American Sports Publishing Co. 1917)

Okkonen, Marc, ed. *2000 Cups of Coffee* (SABR 2009)

Petree, Patrick K. and Hampton, Bing, *Oldtimes to the Goodtimes* (privately printed: no date) [promotional booklet]

Pierce, Peter G., *Baseball in the Cross Timbers: The Story of the Sooner State League*, (Oklahoma City: Oklahoma Heritage Association 2009)

---- *Territorians to Boomers: Professional Baseball in Ardmore 1904-1926* (Oklahoma City: Oklahoma Heritage Association 2011).

Reach Official American League Baseball Guide (Philadelphia: A. J. Reach & Co. 1905)

Ruggles, William B., *The History of the Texas League of Professional Baseball Clubs*, (Dallas, Texas: privately published 1951)

Society for American Baseball Research, SABR Minor Leagues Database, http://www.baseball-reference.com/minors

---The Baseball Biography Project, http://bioproj.sabr.org

Sports Reference LLC, http://www.baseball-reference.com [also houses the SABR Minor League Database]

PHOTO CREDITS

Introduction

Page 6 Author's Collection

7. Poster www.americaslibrary.gov; Sheet music www.library.jhu.edu

8. *The Daily Ardmoreite* and Laurie Anne Williams

9. Author's collection

10. Map Author's collection; Interurban. www.snu.edu

11. Spalding Official Baseball Guide 1907 (hereafter "Spalding Guide [year])

13. www.en.wikipedia.org

15. Saloon Oklahoma City Chamber of Commerce Collection; Imbibers www.anotherwineblog.com; Nation www.en.wikipedia.org

Southwestern League 1904

17. Spalding Guide 1906

18. Rogers www.baseball-reference.com/players/r/rogerem01.shtml; Flaherty www.baseball-reference.com/players/f/flahepa01.shtml; Sullivan www.picsaweb.google.com/WrightWing-OOTP/1884 (hereafter WW/[year])

19. Spalding Guide 1905

20. Track Oklahoma City Chamber of Commerce collection; Delmar Garden Oklahoma County Assessor collection

21. Spalding Guide 1908

22. Spalding Guide 1905

23. Spalding Guide 1905

Texas League 1904

24. Spalding Guide 1905

Western Association 1905-1911

25. Shively Spalding Guide 1907; Iola Spalding Guide 1905

26. Hurlbert *The Daily Oklahoman* 1905; Halla www.baseball-reference.com/players/h/hallajo01.shtml; Genin www.baseball-reference.com/players/g/geninfr01.shtml

27. OC 1906 Spalding Guide 1907; Bloomer Girls Advertisement *The Daily Oklahoman* 1906; OC 1907 Spalding Guide 1908; McFarland WW 1902; Gill WW 1908; Hoffer WW 1892

28. Spalding Guide 1908

29. Enid Spalding Guide 1910; Shaw Spalding Guide 1910

30. Spalding Guide 1907

Missouri Valley League 1905

31. Spalding Guide 1911

32. Spalding Guide 1907

33. Adams WW 1906; Aitchison Spalding Guide 1906; Rhodes and Crisp Okkonen, Marc ed., 2000 Cups of Coffee (SABR 2009) (hereafter "2000 Cups")

South Central League 1906

34. Frantz Spalding Guide 1905; McAlester www.mcalesterphotos.com; Callahan WW 1894

Kansas State League 1906

36. Bartlesville Team Spalding Guide 1907; Alberts WW 1884; Cheney WW 1911

Oklahoma-Arkansas-Kansas League 1907
Oklahoma-Kansas League 1908

37. McDaniel Spalding Guide 1908; Bartlesville 1907 (2) Spalding Guide 1908

38. St. John Spalding Guide 1905; Thomason WW 1910; Powell WW 1913; Kelly WW 1914

Texas-Oklahoma League 1911-1914

39. Spalding Guide 1905

40. Donahue Spalding Guide 1912; Ritter Spalding Guide 1912; Morris Spalding Guide 1912

42. Spalding Guide 1907

44. Humphries Author's collection; Bonham Fannin County Historical Commission; Leslie 1923 Salt Lake City zeenuts www.starsofthediamond.com/zeenuts.html; Anderson Spalding Guide 1907

45. Reed Spalding Guide 1912; Napier Spalding Guide 1921; Russell WW 1913

46. Poindexter Spalding Guide 1911; Peebles Spalding Guide 1911; Appleton Author's collection

47. Tincup WW 1914; Torrey Spalding Guide 1911; Covington WW 1913; Haislip WW 1913

48. W. Covington WW 1911; R. Covington Spalding Guide 1915

49. Spalding Guide 1915

Oklahoma State League 1912

50. Advertisement *The Daily Oklahoman* 1911

51. Kelsey WW 1907; Meyer Oklahoma Red Book 1912

52. Beckley Oklahoma Heritage Association; Leuttke Spalding Guide 1906; Gardner Spalding Guide 1917; Kane Spalding Guide 1913

53. Schedule *Okmulgee Daily Herald* 1912; Advertisement *The Daily Oklahoman* 1912

54. Linda McGill Wagner

55. *The Daily Oklahoman* 1912

Western Association 1914-1917

56. Holliday www.newsevents.tcu.edu; Milton Spalding Guide 1911; Baker Spalding Guide 1910

57. Map Sanborn Insurance Map 1922, Metropolitan Library System, Oklahoma City, from www.dougdawg.blogspot.com/2010/08; Maag Spalding Guide 1911

58. Spalding Guide 1916

59. Spalding Guide 1916

60. Sinclair www.justonebadcentury.com; Covington team www.nkyviews.com; Newark www.bdecsports.com; Hill Spalding Guide 1916

61. Spalding Guide 1916

63. *The Paris News* 1958

65. Spalding Guide 1917

66. Tearney www.memory.loc.gov; Youngs WW 1917

67. Crittenden Spalding Guide 1913; Everdon Spalding Guide 1913; Brill *The Daily Oklahoman* 1918

68. Thompson Spalding Guide 1917; Faircloth Spalding Guide 1917; Johnson WW 1918; McAlester Spalding Guide 1918

69. Spalding Guide 1918 (2)

70. Duncan *The Daily Oklahoman* 1917

Altus

71. www.epodunk.com

72. Monroe *Old Times to the Goodtimes*; Adams, Malloy, Latham Spalding Guide 1911; Frierson Spalding Guide 1913

73. Ray Spalding Guide 1917; McMahan Spalding Guide 1913

Anadarko

74. www.epodunk.com

75. Team, Ellison, Ellison, Dayton *The Daily Oklahoman* 1911; Kahl Spalding Guide 1909; Isom Spalding Guide 1906; Tanner Ruggles, *History of the Texas League of Professional Baseball Clubs*; White Spalding Guide 1915; Liese 2000 Cups; Jasper WW 1914; Orem Spalding Guide 1910; Billings WW 1913

77. Grandstand *The Daily Oklahoman* 1922; Reed *The Daily Oklahoman* 1910; Plum *Anadarko Tribune* 1912

Ardmore

78. Author's collection

79. McCullum Spalding Guide 1915; Hamilton Spalding Guide 1906; Zook Spalding Guide 1911; Blair Library of Congress, Benjamin K. Edwards baseball card collection LC-DIG-bbc-0649f (1909); Team Ardmore Public Library, McGalliard Collection

80. Rogers Spalding Guide 1894; Williams Library of Congress, Prints and Photographs Division, Bain Collection, LC-DIG-ggbain-13898

81. Gordon Spalding Guide 1915; Wilson Spalding Guide 1913; McAvoy 2000 Cups

82. Gray Spalding Guide 1910; Allen *Old Times to the Goodtimes*; Pelkey Spalding Guide 1911

83. Palmer www.baseball-reference.com/players/p/palmeed01.shtml; Gordon Spalding Guide 1910; Leslie 1926 Hollywood www.starsofthediamond.com/zeenuts.html

84. Tierney 1927 Hollywood www.starsofthediamond.com/zeenuts.html; Fenner Spalding Guide 1917; White Library of Congress, American Memories Collection, baseball card collection; Tyer Spalding Guide 1924

85. Streetcar Ardmore Public Library, McGalliard Collection; Speer Library of Congress, Panorama Photographs Collection, LG-DIG-pan.6a29516; Allison, Hall Spalding Guide 1916; Kauffman Spalding Guide 1911; Hayes *Chickasha Star* 1920

Chickasha

86. Street Scene Advertising insert, *The Daily Oklahoman* 1905; Hauser www.americanindianathletichalloffame.com

87. Weller *The Daily Oklahoman* 1909; Andrews Spalding Guide 1910; Pokorney Spalding Guide 1905; Johnson www.verdun2.worldpress.com

88. Minco Team *The Daily Oklahoman* 1909; Streetcar Grady County Historical Society Museum

Durant

89. www.civilwaralbum.com

90. Morrison Hall www.campusexplorer.com; Conner WW 1895; McKee Spalding Guide 1910; Hiett Spalding Guide 1913

91. Brownlow Spalding Guide 1913; Corzine Spalding Guide 1911; Armstrong Spalding Guide 1906

92. Spalding Guide 1913

93. Kaiser *Ada Weekly News* 1923; Eppling Spalding Guide 1911; Deardorff Spalding Guide 1913; Harper WW 1911; Palmer Spalding Guide 1918

94. Kerlin WW 1915; Knaupp Spalding Guide 1917

95. Durant Team Author's collection; Jewell *The Daily Oklahoman* 1909; Naylor Spalding Guide 1916; Long and Johns Spalding Guide 1910; Taylor and Herman Spalding Guide 1913; Robinson Spalding Guide 1917

96. Morris Spalding Guide 1913; Heatley *The Daily Oklahoman* 1921

97. Carey Spalding Guide 1911; Francis WW 1922; Humphries www.baseball-reference.com/players/h/humphbe01.shtml

El Reno

98. www.legendsofamerica.com

99. Peaches Park El Reno Carnegie Library; Southern Hotel www.virtualtourist.com; South Bickford Linda McGill Wagner

100. Fisher *Spalding Guide* 1905; Balenti *Spalding Guide* 1911; Burns *Spalding Guide* 1908; Landes and Levine *Spalding Guide* 1911; Willingham *The Daily Oklahoman* 1911; Beltz *Spalding Guide* 1915; Pollard *Spalding Guide* 1908; Crowson *Spalding Guide* 1910

102. Robinson WW 1911; Luhrsen *Spalding Guide* 1911; James *Spalding Guide* 1917; Riggs *Spalding Guide* 1905; Perritt *Spalding Guide* 1917; Listen *The Daily Oklahoman* 1911

Eufaula

104. Team *The Daily Oklahoman* 1912; Langley *Spalding Guide* 1911

Guthrie

106. Dale, Tammie Chada on www.rootsweb. ancestry.com/ logan county; Guthrie 1889 www. legendsofamerica.com; Claimants www.dgranna. blogspot.com

107. Guthrie Team *Spalding Guide* 1905; Island Park Oklahoma Heritage Association

108. Pettigrew *Spalding Guide* 1922; Beeker *The Daily Oklahoman* 1911

109. Hamilton *Spalding Guide* 1911; W. Queisser *Spalding Guide* 1906; A. Queisser *Guthrie Daily Leader* 1905; Downs www.baseball-reference.com/ players/d/downsre01.shtml

110. Jones *Spalding Guide* 1911; Dalrymple *Spalding Guide* 1907; Bennett *Spalding Guide* 1905

111. Aldreman *Spalding Guide* 1910; Henderson *Spalding Guide* 1913; Companion *Guthrie Daily Leader* 1905

112. Mize *Spalding Guide* 1910; Weissinger *The Daily Oklahoman* 1909

114. Electric Park Linda McGill Wagner; H. Price *Spalding Guide* 1908; N. Price *Spalding Guide* 1910; G. Price *Oldtimes to the Goodtimes*; T. Price *Spalding Guide* 1905

115. Haskell www.ok.gov; Pokorney *The Daily Oklahoman* 1911; Patterson *Spalding Guide* 1910

116. Guthrie Team and McGill Linda McGill Wagner www.tabloid.okielegacy.org

117. Geist *Spalding Guide* 1916; Hotchkiss *The Daily Oklahoman* 1914; Vickery *Spalding Guide* 1910

119. Leuttke *Spalding Guide* 1910; Cole *Spalding Guide* 1915

120. WW 1917

Henryetta

121. Morgan Theater www.cincematour.com; Street Scene www.doughboysearcher.weekly.com/ henryetta-oklahoma.html; Dimond *The Daily Oklahoman* 1922

122. Lipps *The Daily Oklahoman* 1916; Smiser *The Daily Oklahoman* 1920; Gabriel *Spalding Guide* 1913; Lawrence *Spalding Guide* 1913

123. Wren *Spalding Guide* 1913; Reynolds *Spalding Guide* 1923; Nickell *Spalding Guide* 1905; Gierhart *Spalding Guide* 1916

124. *Spalding Guide* 1918

Holdenville

125. both www.epodunk.com

126. Robinson *Spalding Guide* 1917; Bouldin *Spalding Guide* 1907; Hendley *Spalding Guide* 1906; DeLongy *Spalding Guide* 1911

127. Hill *Spalding Guide* 1915; Lancaster *Spalding Guide* 1911; Grady *Spalding Guide* 1910; Clarkson *Spalding Guide* 1915; Brown *Spalding Guide* 1905

128. Advertisement *Holdenville Democrat* 1912

Hugo

128. Street Scene www.ancientfaces.com

129. Hornsby Spalding Guide 1916; Nicholson Chicago Daily News negatives collection SDN-0622830, Chicago History Museum; Brown 2000 Cups; Kane WW 1902; Ury Spalding Guide 1907; Scoggins 2000 Cups

130. Kizziar Spalding Guide 1917; Greene *The Daily Oklahoman* 1912; Phillips Spalding Guide 1917; Nevitt Spalding Guide 1912

131. Spalding Guide 1917

Lawton

133. Lawrence Spalding Guide 1913; Alberta and Pokorney *The Daily Oklahoman* 1911; Pierce Spalding Guide 1911; Reynolds 2000 Cups; Stone *The Daily Oklahoman* 1911; Garrity Spalding Guide 1911

134. Hamilton Spalding Guide 1910; Tate Spalding Guide 1913; Daugherty *The Daily Oklahoman* 1911

135. Pinkerton Spalding Guide 1911

Okmulgee

137. Spalding Guide 1925

138. Okmulgee Scenes 24.2-24.3 http://urbane-chaos.hubpages.com/hub/Historical-Okmulgee-Oklahoma1920-1929 ; Gardner Spalding Guide 1917

139. Spalding Guide 1913

140. Gallia ww 1913; Mattick WW 1912

Sapulpa

141. Street Scene www.rootsweb.com/~okcreek; Tanks www.epodunk.com; Jefferies Spalding Guide 1913; Kellerman Spalding Guide 1911; Lofton Spalding Guide 1906

142. Myers Spalding Guide 1913; Crutcher WW 1914; Wolverton Spalding Guide 1913

143. Everhart Spalding Guide 1906; Coe Spalding Guide 1911; Dupree *Old Times to Goodtimes*; Reed Spalding Guide 1911

144. *Sapulpa Evening Light* 1911

Shawnee

145. www.epodunk.com

146. Hauser *The Daily Oklahoman* 1909; Young *The Daily Oklahoman* 1911

147. Ahorn Spalding Guide 1904; Brandom WW 1908; Nelson *The Daily Oklahoman* 1903; Ritter Spalding Guide 1915

148. Milam WW 1907; McAlester Spalding Guide 1906

South McAlester

150. Street Scene www.epodunk.com; McAlester Oklahoma Red Book 1912; Team Spalding Guide 1906

152. Roe Spalding Guide 1906; Torrences, Coopers Spalding Guide 1906; Whites Spalding Guide 1907

153. D. White http://digitalgallery.nypl.org; Team Spalding Guide 1907

Vinita

154. www.familyoldphotos.com

155. Team Spalding Guide 1906; Lally Spalding Guide 1907; Mayes 2000 Cups